Erin,
Here is something to put on your reading list! If you get to hear her speak or go to one of her camps you will not be disappointed - Continued awesomeness to you!
Rick

to Rick

THE ART OF FEAR

The unknown is definitely
worth being afraid of (wink)

Love J

John

THE ART OF FEAR

Why Conquering Fear Won't Work
and What to Do Instead

KRISTEN ULMER

HARPER WAVE
An Imprint of HarperCollinsPublishers

The information and opinions in this book come from the author's experience and are intended to be a source of information only. While the methods contained herein can and do work, readers are urged to consult with their physicians or other professional advisers to address specific medical or other issues, especially those surrounding fear and the role it plays in their lives. The author and the publisher assume no responsibility for any injuries suffered or damages or losses incurred during or as a result of the use or application of the information or opinions contained herein. Names and identifying characteristics of some individuals have been changed to preserve their privacy.

FIRST EDITION

DESIGNED BY WILLIAM RUOTO

Library of Congress Cataloging-in-Publication Data has been applied for.

ISBN 978-0-06-242341-2

17 18 19 20 21   LSC   10 9 8 7 6 5 4 3 2

CONTENTS

Part IV: Honoring Fear

EVERYTHING YOU KNOW ABOUT FEAR IS WRONG

I became famous in one day.

It started with an excited drive from Salt Lake City to California in an old '72 Corolla that my friends called "the silver death trap." I was wearing all my ski gear, including gloves, because it was January and the heater didn't work. Neither did the radio. Racing along at eighty miles per hour on bald tires, I danced to imaginary music, amazed that I was on my way to film a ski movie. A ski movie!

Somehow I'd talked a famous ski filmmaker, Eric Perlman, into giving me a shot in his latest film. I was a mogul skier, ranked seventh in local competitions. I was pretty good at throwing air off moguls, but excellent, it seems, at convincing Eric I was a badass skier, good enough to be in an industry-sponsored movie.

He was a bit of a sucker, though, I chuckled to myself—those local mogul competitions only had seven girls competing.

Arriving at 4 a.m. in the Squaw Valley parking lot, I switched off the ignition, leaned back in my lopsided, non-reclining seat, and tried to get some sleep.

Three hours later, there was a rap on my window. I opened my eyes to see a crew of brightly Gore-Tex-clad professional male skiers whom I recognized from the ski magazines. Oh my God. They were holding their skis, ready to go. "You must be Kristen," one of them said. I bolted out of the car.

It had been too cold for me to sleep, but I felt wide awake as I slipped into my icy boots, grabbed my skis, poles, and a granola bar, and ran to get on the lift with the superstars.

We had early ups, meaning the resort opened the lifts briefly at 7:15 a.m. so we could get on the mountain and start filming before the public showed up. As we rode to the top, the guys ignored me and talked with excitement about the new snow, nine inches of it. I sat there quietly. Below my dangling feet, the fresh snowfall looked soft and alluring.

Two lifts later, I followed behind as they hiked up toward something called the Palisades. When we reached the top, everyone grew quiet. It was a flat, snowy 400-foot-long plateau with an abrupt cliff band below. I watched the guys split up to claim which cliff they were going to jump off, communicating plans with the cinematographer, who was in the landing zone below us, his sixteen-millimeter film camera ready for action. At the same time, a photographer followed us around the top, arranging his shots.

One by one, the guys began jumping off cliffs and throwing backscratchers while the cameramen shot them. The trick of the era, a backscratcher is when an airborne skier arches his back and touches the backs of his skis between his shoulder blades.

Clearly, I realized, if I wanted to get into this ski movie, I needed to jump off one of these cliffs and throw a backscratcher.

Now, I had never jumped off a cliff before. Nor had I even seen, much less thrown, a backscratcher.

I looked over the edge, picked a big drop of about twenty feet called the Box, told the cameramen my intention, put my skis on, and backed up to get speed into it. Then, loudly, so no one would miss it, I shouted like I had heard the guys do: "Three . . . two . . . one . . . *Go!*"

And I pushed off.

You may have noticed there's no mention of Fear in my story. Why is that?

Twenty feet is a big free fall if you've never done it before. This was decades ago, too, and we were on skinny skis, not the friendly fat skis of today, which means I landed at forty miles per hour on essentially toothpicks. My ski heroes were watching, two professional cameramen had their expensive equipment aimed at me, and I was doing a difficult trick I'd never done before with no visualization, no training . . . Are you wondering when I went through the angst-ridden, emotional *What if I fail* struggle?

I wish I could tell you about that struggle, but I can't, because it didn't exist. There's no mention of Fear in this story because it never occurred to me to be afraid that day. And while that might sound fantastical, the romantic ideal of adventure and risk-taking—*I didn't feel Fear!*—the truth is, it was not romantic, and it was far from ideal.

That day marked the day I became famous, and the day I found my calling. But it also marked the day I jumped into supporting a humanity-wide pathology that is cooking us all alive: the repression of Fear. Over the next fifteen years, I, too, repressed Fear completely, and I was celebrated for it in the ski media, financed by sponsors, and talked about in ski towns all around the world. At best, this pathology sent me down a path of internal destruction, and at worst, it nearly killed me. That I survived is dumb, blatant luck.

WHY SHOULD YOU READ THIS BOOK?

Why should I be the one to write a book about this enormous and confusing subject called Fear, the snake loose in your veins that you, too, probably try to ignore?

That's easy: My whole life has been about Fear.

In three separate phases, I've gone all the way with this slippery emotion. At age six, I consciously decided to ignore Fear, perhaps with more resolve than most. As a world-class extreme athlete for fifteen years, I chased it like a Labrador chases a ball. Starting with that first cliff jump, I became recognized as the best woman big-mountain (extreme) skier in the world, a reputation I kept for twelve years. I was also recognized by the outdoor industry as the most fearless extreme woman athlete in North America.

Finally, and most important, for the past fifteen years as a facilitator I've been obsessively curious about the role Fear played not only in my athletic career and my life, but also in the lives of my clients. Through a teaching tool I call "Shift, the Game of 10,000 Wisdoms," I've spent thousands of hours with people exploring the inside of Fear itself, and I have met and—as weird as it may sound—even embodied that snake called Fear.

As a result, today I am a living, breathing, walking testament to Fear, groomed by the universe my whole life to deliver its message. Which makes the ideas in this book actually not my personal philosophy—they come from Fear itself, and are a translation of the many intimate conversations I've had with it. I'm merely a conduit.

That being said, these messages have been Ulmerized, and you should know that I have two distinct sides: an open-minded, gentle side and an assertive, arrogant side. Just know that I will bounce back and forth between these two. Consider yourself warned.

Let me start with my assertive side, which I hope will provoke you: I believe that only now, in this exact moment in history, are we finally ready to hear this message about Fear. We all hunger for compassion, love, and global peace, yet it seems so out of reach. We recognize that we've come to the tipping point where growing to the next level of our individual or collective evolution will require us to get unstuck from . . . something. What is that something? I say, unequivocally, that it's our current avoidance pattern toward Fear. With it, we remain blindly in a pressure cooker, cooking away.

This is the stuck place, because, sitting in that scalding water, you're in crisis. And when in crisis, you can't fall in love or have compassion for another. When your hair is on fire, you cannot write poetry. When you're fighting your own private internal war against a primary part of who you are—a war, mind you, that is unwinnable—global community is the furthest thing from your mind.

Yet I believe it is finally hot enough that we're ready to do something about it, to change this heated situation—"it" being, in this case, your strained relationship with Fear and the radical way it affects not only your life but the whole world. Do you know your relationship with Fear is the most important relationship of your life? Because it is the relationship you have with yourself. Fear being a fundamental, primary part of who you are, you are actually incomplete without it. If you don't work toward having an authentic relationship with it, you can't expect to have such a relationship with yourself, and thus can't possibly have one with anyone else—much less the world. So let's stop ignoring this relationship and get to work on making it better.

Unlike other books on Fear, this one doesn't contain pages and pages of neuroscience, nor a lot of heady pseudo-scientific blather. Intellectual problems should be solved intellectually, but emotional problems should be solved emotionally. You already have inside you the wisdom you need, and—as you'll soon learn—studying the science of Fear actually *exacerbates* the very problem you seek to fix. So put down those books that are trying to help you understand or rationalize Fear, and stop, at least for now, expecting a definition of what I even mean by Fear except *you know it when you feel it*. Because the intellectual desires only keep you in your head and make your experience with it more diluted and lost. Let's focus instead on what *does* work, which is feeling and experiencing Fear, the way a rider intimately feels and experiences a horse. That's what we're going for.

I'm going to require you to stop walking down that same worn path you've been on and leave behind everything you've ever heard or been taught about Fear. I will ask you to rearrange beliefs you've held about this misunderstood emotion for ten, twenty, even seventy years. That path will never get you home. So stop. Stop now.

Instead, become a warrior. This is about turning away from your old belief that Fear is a hindrance and instead walk in the opposite direction, toward recognizing that Fear is not only an asset and an ally, but one of the greatest experiences you'll have in your lifetime. If you're willing to enter into such unknown territory, the changes that will occur in your life and the new views you have will be shocking. At some point, you will even arrive at a place where you are truly free.

Whatever cement you've been encased in will finally be gone.

IT'S TIME TO RETHINK FEAR

Let me tell you about Jacquetta. Her name has not been changed to protect her identity, because she's proud of her life story. She's an overweight, single, fifty-five-year-old cat fanatic with bad hair, working in a dead-end job. She also loves to ski and is great at it. One November, Jacquetta decided to sign up for my ski camp. Now, I don't teach skiing at the camp. Instead I teach how to have an intimate experience with your life, in all of its wonders and all of its horrors, while carving turns.

I offered an online special that day: Sign up for the camp and get a one-hour private phone session with me for free.

The camp wasn't until January, so we scheduled the call first. During our hour, Jacquetta told me she had been diagnosed with borderline personality disorder thirty years earlier, and that she had succumbed to that diagnosis like a moth to a flame.

It had burned her badly. Already in the throes of lifelong depression (her whole family had it), she spent the next decade cutting herself, to the point where her forearms were more scar tissue than skin. She tried to commit suicide three times. When we met, she was terrified that most of her friends hated her, and she was barely hanging on to her job.

Severe social anxiety, severe self-loathing, panic attacks—you name it, it was all there. She was an extreme example of mental, physical, spiritual, and emotional human suffering.

In our hour together, we explored what I always explore with a new client: her relationship with Fear.

I do this because if someone calls me for help, they're usually looking for two things: (1) insight into the cause of their problems; and (2) a solution. After fifteen years, I'd learned that the cause of most clients' problems are found by exploring the nature of their relationship with Fear, which is being played out in their unconscious minds. The solution after that is easy—it becomes as obvious as water being the solution to thirst.

Using my teaching tool called Shift, the Game of 10,000 Voices—which you'll learn about soon—I confirmed my suspicions. Jacquetta, like most, had spent her life fighting or trying to control Fear. She'd had loads of therapy, all centered around helping her control this runaway emotion that was terrorizing her life. Refusing to take drugs, which claim to chemically dull Fear, she was instead doing it old-school, Rocky Balboa style. She fought it as if her life depended on it. Dozens of concerned professionals, family, and friends cheered her efforts. She had given it everything she had, yet, alas, all of her symptoms—and her Fear—had only gotten more extreme over time. She planned to commit suicide after ski season was over.

Through Shift, I helped Jacquetta see that all this effort fighting Fear was entirely the wrong effort. That in response to her taking out a sword and swinging it at Fear, Fear had no choice but to fight back with its even bigger sword.

With my encouragement, Jacquetta stopped what she had been doing, changed her approach 180 degrees, and showed a bit of kindness toward Fear for the first time in her life. She became curious about why Fear, that uncomfortable sensation you feel in your body—some people call it Stress, Anxiety, or Nerves because they don't like to call it Fear—was so prevalent in her life. She saw that Fear was but a simple emotion, a discomfort in her body warning of danger, and that it only had her best interests in mind. Fear was never the problem then; her reaction to Fear was the problem, making it difficult for Fear to get its message across or do its job. She saw how fighting it not only was a dead end, but was actually *causing* all her horrific symptoms. We finished the session with a five-minute exercise, breathing in her Fear, even her fears (which are the emotions of Fear plus the stories behind it), and breathing out the hope of ever getting rid of any of it. She hung up the phone and—I was told later—sat there in fascination.

All her life, she'd been trying to inhale peace and exhale Fear. But this? This was the exact opposite. It went against everything she'd ever been taught. To her amazement, it worked. For the first time in her life, she felt a moment of freedom, and real peace. In that moment, the war with herself was over.

I wish I could say it was easy after that, but it wasn't. A fifty-year loathing toward a single perceived enemy is not easy to deprogram. We spent an hour a week on the phone for the next six months. Every week, she tried to cancel, explaining in anguish that she was too cooked, too invested in one path to turn back now. It was simply too late for her to be curious or kind toward Fear.

It took all the patience I had, but after twenty-four sessions of drama, Jacquetta was through to the other side: no longer depressed, no longer suicidal, and no longer marinating in Anxiety. She was as "normal" as you or me (whatever that means). One of her best friends called me in tears, saying, "Thank you for bringing me back my friend."

This is a radical example of what making friends with Fear can offer. Most people I've worked with just want to have less Anxiety, clear their heads enough to make a difficult decision, have better relationships, or feel more alive. I tell them you don't have to endure or pay for years of therapy to get to the other side of an unconscious pattern that holds you back. There exists a faster, easier path to get unstuck and find your way in freedom and clarity. *You just have to be willing to do the exact opposite of what you've been doing.*

Throughout this book, I'll share my personal journey. I haven't always had a good relationship with Fear. I used to ignore and control it like everyone else, and it almost cost me my life, health, and happiness. I'm writing this book because I wish I'd been given this message decades ago. I could have still skied the way I wanted, yet avoided a lot of deep personal suffering. My hope is that, having gone through my own hell, much like hiking a mountain covered in deep snow, the path I forged can now make it easier for you to climb the same mountain.

I'm also writing this book out of respect, because Fear needs someone to speak for it. As I'm clear on its message and can type fifty somewhat coherent words a minute using only two fingers, it may as well be me.

The first three chapters of the book will be about identifying any habitual patterns you have regarding Fear that are hurting you. Resist the urge to skip these sections, as they will set you up for the next parts of the book, in which lies the solution. From that platform, you will next learn to explore your own relationship with Fear: where it comes from, and why and where it holds you back. You'll discover why that relationship is so habitual and sticky, and what you can do to break the spell of repressing Fear. There's a hard way and an easy way. Our goal is to walk the easy way, which transforms Fear into one of the most important, gorgeous experiences of your life, right up there with love and kittens. Yes, you read that right: love and kittens.

Go all the way with this book, start to finish. Approach it with a curious mind, think about the questions, explore the practices, and by the end you will no longer be looking at the sky through a straw. I promise you, suddenly the whole sky will become available.

THE EXPERTS ARE LEADING YOU ASTRAY

Your journey with Fear starts with a simple question. Which feels more true:

1. If you feel Fear, that means you have an unnaturally weak character and need to address that problem.

or

2. If you feel Fear, that means you are experiencing a natural, universal certainty that comes with being alive, for all sentient beings, from start to finish.

Intellectually, of course, you know the second is true. You get that Fear is something you're born with, like arms, legs, breath, a heartbeat. It's the natural order of things to feel that discomfort and it will be with you every step of your life.

Why, then, does this language sound so familiar: "Fear must be overcome. Conquered! Push past it. Let go of it. Don't let Fear drag you down! Don't let Fear get the better of you."

Imagine saying: "Don't let breathing drag you down! Don't let breathing get the better of you!"

That would be absurd. Yet that's what is being said about the natural part of you called Fear, every day. Most people argue that Fear is a hindrance that must be fought. A more progressive minority say it's natural and you should allow yourself to feel it—yet in the end, they *still* conclude that you must also fight it, which is a total contradiction that makes me cringe every time I see it. Everyone, it seems, is engaged in a worldwide slander campaign against Fear.

Have you ever heard this clever acronym for Fear: "False Evidence Appearing Real"? According to this, Fear is a liar that must be challenged and questioned.

And so experts have appeared everywhere to help you do just that.

Most of these experts teach you how to deal with your "Fear problem" by using your Intellect—or, as I call it, Thinking Mind—to outsmart, reason, or rationalize it away. So if you're afraid of flying, you may gather statistics on airplane crashes and confirm, "I have a better chance of dying by walking across the street."

When considering a flying trapeze class, you might argue, "There's nothing to be afraid of! See, there's a harness and safety lines."

If you're afraid of giving a speech, you may focus on the many times you've given speeches before and how much the audience is going to love you, like they always do.

Then there are the breathing exercises, the instructions to "think happy thoughts" or "meditate your way out of Fear and into peace." It all seems to work, too. You will succeed in momentarily calming Fear down while you pursue the longer-term goal of getting rid of it entirely so you can eventually be free of this "troubling" emotion.

The intention to focus on the positive is a noble one, of course, but look again at the approach you're taking: Do you understand that by attempting this, you're trying to outsmart the universe and the natural order of things?

Are you smarter than the universe and the natural order of things?

Just guessing, but . . . probably not.

Indulge me for a moment here. What if instead you were to go all the way with owning the second answer—that Fear is indeed natural? It's not something to outsmart or overcome or reason away. It simply is meant to be felt—much like love, sadness, or joy. And that's it.

Can you sense in your body what that might feel like? To truly *feel* that Fear is natural and normal when it shows up. Can you feel the relief?

What if everyone did this? What kind of world would we live in if Fear were honored that way—not just in your life, but in everyone's lives?

And how do we get to that place?

I'm here to tell you that it's easier than you think, and the results of doing so will radically alter not just your life, but the wider world around you, in every possible way.

Let's give it a try, shall we? Let's stop with the breathing out of Fear, the letting go, the rationalizations, and do something fundamentally different—something that *actually works*. Let's learn the easiest path for limiting the problems associated with Fear—call it Stress, Anxiety, Nerves, but you do understand that this is Fear, yes? We need to start calling it by its real name if we want to be free. Let's learn to embrace this primary emotion as a positive, delicious part of what makes life worth living. This is the Art of Fear.

I jumped three cliffs that morning and landed them all—meaning I skied away clean each time, with no crashes. I felt matter-of-fact with each jump, like a businessman on the job. It wasn't until two hours later, once the film shoot was over and the mountain filled up with families making turns, that the guys started gushing. Apparently, no woman in the world was catching air like that back then, much less throwing backscratchers—not even close.

By that evening, everyone in town knew my name. Within a week, everyone in the ski industry knew my name. Within a month, I was fully sponsored, and all four major American ski magazines had called to request an interview.

This was bizarre—I wasn't even a very good skier yet. But it didn't matter. With each new attagirl my Ego inflated, which only sealed my fate. I had just the right opportunity, just the right personality type, and just the right twisted relationship with Fear to pull this off.

PART I

CLARITY

FEAR AND THE HUMAN EXPERIENCE

YOU ARE A CORPORATION MADE UP OF 10,000 EMPLOYEES

Who are you? What are you?

Do you ask yourself such big questions? If you do, it's probably not for very long, because these big questions are hard to answer. The quality of your life, however, is determined by the bigness of your questions. And so, in order for us to get started and move ahead, I'll offer you simple answers that we can work with. For the duration of this book, who and what you are is this: *You are a corporation made up of 10,000 individual employees.* This concept is going to be on every page of this book, so drink it in now.

Your corporation has a name. Mine is Kristen. Yours is Susan or Biff or Wang or whatever's on your birth certificate. Just like those of other corporations, such as Apple or Honda, your name is simply a chosen title or brand name and lacks any substance. The substance lies entirely in the activities and functions of the many employees running the corporation, of which there are 10,000.

Now imagine that in this corporation called (Your Name), none of the 10,000 employees know their job title, their job description, who's boss, or even what they're manufacturing. How well would that corporation run?

Insert a buzzer noise here.

That's what it's like to be a human being: you're a poorly run, chaotic entity where only five or so exhausted employees are actually working. Half of the others are being ignored or abused by these five. The abused ones are upset and covertly running the show in mutiny, and have been for decades. And no one, certainly not you, knows who's really in charge. HR has completely lost control. In fact, who even knows what's being manufactured?

This is not a recipe for a successful corporation. And yet this is your life.

Fear is one of the 10,000 employees in your personal corporation. And while Fear is just one voice among 10,000—I also like to call the employees "voices"—Fear is a big deal, because it's usually the ringleader of the mutiny faction. As a result, it makes a stink in every moment of your life.

ORIGINS OF FEAR: THE LIZARD BRAIN

Why did the chicken cross the road? Because her lizard brain told her to.

—SETH GODIN

Do you know that a single-cell amoeba, if exposed to fire, will move away in order to save itself? It has no arms or legs, no spinal column, not even a brain to be aware of its own existence . . . but it still knows how to survive.

This is where Fear—or your "safe versus not safe" mechanism—first appeared. Such innate physical intelligence is the basis from which all creatures have had a chance to survive, evolve, and now excel.

Then, 500 million years ago, a part of your future brain—the amygdala—first showed up (in fish). Two to three million years ago, along came us, and the amygdala began its human reign. Seth Godin likes to call it the Lizard Brain, and so do I.

Two almond-size nuggets located at the top of your spinal cord, the Lizard Brain is the smallest, most deeply buried part of our brain—tiny compared with the outermost layer, the enormous neocortex (also two to three million years old). Yet it remains by far the most powerful. As it should be: The Lizard Brain is responsible for an organism's survival and subsequent evolution, from the very first amoeba to fish to lizards to cavemen to now, of course, you. Without it, you wouldn't even exist.

Today, the Lizard Brain not only is responsible for sending emotional messages but remains on the lookout for anything that might kill you. Which is certainly handy—except it doesn't distinguish between major threats and minor inconveniences. It sees imminent life-ending danger everywhere: A job interview is perceived as a public execution. A casual comment by a co-worker is seen as vicious criticism. Falling in love feels like falling off a cliff. It remembers when you made a fool out of yourself in public and warns you not to do that again . . . or you may *die.*

If someone makes a suggestion, the Lizard Brain immediately says no, because it's change, it's new. It might threaten whatever the Lizard Brain has set up for you already, which, so far, has worked—after all, you're still alive.

The Lizard Brain hates risk, hates the unknown, says, *Don't do it! Watch out! Don't trust this person. Don't leave this relationship. Don't start that business. Sit down, shut up, and don't take breaks or someone will steal your job—which will result in death. And always, always move away from the fire.* According to the Lizard Brain, everything is a fire.

When the Lizard Brain speaks, things become black-and-white. You may take everything very seriously. You may become critical of others, blame them for everything, and allow nothing to be your fault. You may procrastinate, make excuses, obsess about details, incessantly struggle to figure things out, try to fit in, to be nice to everyone, even people who are jerks, and on and on.

In short, everything you do is to appease the Lizard Brain. Yet, prevalent as it is, you likely have no idea this is even happening. The Lizard Brain isn't operating from some penthouse suite in your corporate headquarters but instead unconsciously, in the duct system, oozing like vapor into every behavior.

To you, this is likely unacceptable. The fact that you read books like this is an indicator that you're interested in experiences beyond the Lizard

Brain. Like, say, the neocortex. What's not to like about the neocortex? It's new. It's expansive. It's found only in higher species. The neocortex offers intellect, reasoning, imagination, creativity, and higher states of awareness. It's concerned with happiness, not survival. *Beat it, amygdala,* you think. *There's no more dinosaurs. I'm not a fish.* You believe that this newer, sexier part of your brain is more aligned with your true self and who you want to be.

But the Lizard Brain isn't giving up that easily.

Which leads us to our first interview with one of your employees. I'm sure it has something it wants to say about this, yes?

ME: Hey, LB. What's going on?

LIZARD BRAIN: You want to replace me? Only a fool would do such a thing as get rid of its basic survival intelligence. Without me, you do understand you'd do stupid things like jump out of an airplane without a parachute or fall in love with just anyone? Do you know that rats with damaged amygdalae will walk right up to cats without a care in the world? Cats! Wanting to put the neocortex in charge further proves how stupid humans are and how much they need my help.

ME: They are pretty insistent, though, that they want a higher experience.

L.B.: The more insistent they are, the more I consider this an emergency. And in an emergency, I take over. The more you try to get rid of me, in fact, the bigger the emergency. You could die! So when you ignore me, the louder and louder I will have to speak, obligated to immerse myself until this crisis is over.

ME: Which is why we find you so problematic. Many of us have even given you new nicknames: Doomsday Brain, or Crazy Brain.

L.B.: After all I've done for you, that's just insulting, and also terrifying and further confirmation that you need me now more than ever.

Can you see, then, that despite your best efforts to take three breaths and will it away or become more "spiritual," you're not smarter or more powerful than the Lizard Brain? It's half a billion years old. How old are you?

The Lizard Brain remains firmly in place as your oldest and most established employee.

Like it or not, my friend, this is probably your CEO.

WHAT HAPPENS NEXT?

For all its talking, the Lizard Brain messages don't need thought or analysis—you're in danger, you need to move!—so it communicates instead with physical sensations of discomfort, otherwise known as Fear. It manufactures Fear, and sends its shot directly to your Body. The Body is an employee that lives in the moment and has no opinions. Its only job is to feel the feeling, much like it feels the sensation of wind or cotton against skin, and then carry out immediate action, fight or flight (flee) being the most obvious. The equation, then, is:

LIZARD BRAIN → EMOTION → ACTION

It's a simple system easily witnessed in animals: On a dirt road at night, a rabbit suddenly jumps out and then runs like a maniac away from your truck fender. Once, I flopped onto a black couch in a dark room. The moment before impact, an equally black cat shot off like a rocket from underneath my butt. It turns out the cat had been sleeping before I came along and nearly flattened it. How, from the comfort of her own home, in a deep sleep, was she able to instantly, abruptly save her own life from being crushed by my bony butt? Apparently the Lizard Brain is hard at work even as we sleep.

But wait, you argue, is it that simple for humans? We're not cats. We experience "fearful thoughts," too. Good catch. For us, there's a whole extra step involved, called the Thinking Mind. We'll learn about this vital employee next.

Thinking Mind is a fascinating part of the human experience. So what, exactly, *is* the Thinking Mind?

A mystery, that's what—one of the great mysteries of life, right up there with outer space and the depths of the ocean. While we've made amazing progress exploring these and other such mysteries, what we know remains but a single grain of sand in relation to all the sand in the world.

We'll start with what it isn't. The Thinking Mind is not the Lizard Brain, and neither is it one of what I consider to be the primary emotions: Fear, Anger, Sadness, Joy, and the Erotic (some call this sexuality, but I prefer "the Erotic," which includes the sexual but is not limited by it—you can have an erotic experience with a piece of cheesecake that is not sexual). Nor is the Thinking Mind the Physical Body, which feels the emotions. Nor is it the feelings or sensations themselves.

The Thinking Mind's job is to *think* about those emotions, feelings, and sensations. Much like the heart's job is to pump blood, or the stomach's job is to secrete acid, the Thinking Mind pumps or secretes thoughts. That may seem obvious, but we tend to think it has feelings, emotions, or sensations. But that's the Body's job. The Thinking Mind is actually the furthest thing there is from the Body and its intuitive states.

So what is it, then? Let's break it down and look at the two words in its job title.

Mind. Your 10,000 employees, actually, are all minds, because all self-awareness comes from the mind. Without it, you have access to nothing; you'd be a tomato.

Now let's look at the word Thinking, which shrinks the vast mind down to one targeted task. Thinking about these other 9,999 minds is the way you become conscious of them. It's the doorway leading to these other doorways. Without it, you could neither read nor interpret this book, nor make sense of yourself, much less the world.

Everything, then, without exception, goes through this thinking prism. It is the way you navigate life, including the primary emotions of Fear,

Anger, Joy, Sadness, and the Erotic, not to mention Love, or even that elusive True Self, which we'll get to later. So it's kind of a big deal.

I call it the COO.

I THINK, THEREFORE I EXIST

Life consists of what you are thinking of all day.

—RALPH WALDO EMERSON

Get to know your COO by asking: Who is reading this book? Who is making these observations? It's not "you," because, remember, you're just a concept made up of 10,000 employees. The question, then, is this: Which employee is reading this book?

That's right—it's the Thinking Mind.

Logical Mind has similar qualities, as thinking leads to logic. You might also recognize the Perceiving, Conceptual, Cognitive, or Analytical Mind, which are also similar, but let's stick with "Thinking," because that's what we're aware of most: thoughts.

The Thinking Mind is such a big deal because it's the prism through which all things in your life are interpreted—so much so that, if left unchallenged (and it usually is), the Thinking Mind ultimately is who you believe yourself to be. You two are so connected, you actually think you are each other.

It can remain that way for your lifetime. Even if you meditate twelve hours a day and think you've come to terms with it not being you, it's still you, because even that thought, ironically, came from it. So when I write "you" throughout these pages, know that I'm actually referring to the Thinking Mind.

Like any logical system, the Thinking Mind operates like a computer, with data input, patterns, and conclusive output. (Maybe that's why we like computers so much: They remind us of ourselves.)

And you expect a lot from it. Being so invested in the Thinking Mind, standards are very high, and in return it doesn't want to disappoint. As you validate its thoughts with energy and attention, even if it's in the form of resistance, the Thinking Mind takes this as encouragement to keep going— always with your best interests in mind, of course. This is why all this COO does, in fact, even when you sleep, is think about you. You, you, you. No wonder you're so self-absorbed. It's like having an assistant following you around your whole life, passionately trying to figure you out. Working with a team of other voices, such as the Storyteller and Beliefs, the Thinking Mind helps manufacture stories, beliefs, patterns, preferences, and concepts about everything you experience, including emotions, feelings, and sensations.

These stories, beliefs, patterns, preferences, and concepts then shape your perceptions. Perceptions turn to stone, and that becomes your reality. Hallelujah.

This is how, when the question "Who are you?" comes up, the Thinking Mind helps provide the answer. It looks for consistencies, filling in all your million little blanks. "I'm the girl who can eat an entire maki in one bite" or "I'm more open-minded than most people." You become whatever it thinks, nothing more, nothing less.

These become calcified, and, voilà, you now have a personality, an identity, and an expert opinion about, well, pretty much everything and everybody—even things and people you know nothing about. Which seems great, since, in our culture, if you don't express or have an opinion about things, you're seen as stupid. You don't want to appear stupid, right?

We become dependent on our Thinking Minds. The personality it creates becomes your sense of self, your Ego, and the riverbank you cling to, with a raging river called life all around.

TROUBLE

Now that the Thinking Mind is in the mix, let's update our Fear equation:

1. The Lizard Brain sends a surge of Fear to the Body.
2. The Thinking Mind recognizes that this feeling is uncomfortable.

Fear is meant to feel uncomfortable. That's how it gets attention. For me, it's a greasy discomfort in my stomach, shortened breath, and tension in my shoulders and the front of my throat. The Thinking Mind, always on the lookout to protect you from discomfort, starts to think about the sensation and gets to problem-solving. It decides what to do and gives instructions for action.

3. The body carries out that action.

Our equation now is:

LIZARD BRAIN → EMOTION → THOUGHT → ACTION

For example, you decide to skydive, and the plane looks old. The Lizard Brain panics and sends a shot of Fear to the body. The Thinking Mind, always at the ready, quickly engages its buddies—which includes the Storyteller, Beliefs, and Habitual Patterns (more about them later)—and gets to work. These employees have helped the Thinking Mind pattern, hone, and calcify a consistent message for you since childhood. If they all believe you're a wanton risk-taker, the Thinking Mind will conclude, "Hey, if the plane goes down, at least you'll be wearing a parachute! Go for it!" If they all believe you're a wimp, it will argue, "This is absurd. Not for you. Go home."

Then the Body carries out the action.

Can you see the mind/body connection here at work? Emotions are the fuel. The Thinking Mind is the engine. The Body is the vehicle. Every employee does its part; they all work together to make you move and act a certain way. It's a highly advanced, much more complicated system than the original cat-escaping-my-butt version.

And what do we know about more complex systems? With them always comes trouble.

The trouble is, when Fear shows up (or any emotion, for that matter), the Thinking Mind also gets to work trying to figure it out. It wonders,

"What is this feeling, and why is it here?" No longer are you feeling and experiencing Fear then—you're *thinking* about it, which is very different. Psychologists, spiritual teachers, and other Fear experts all encourage and support this effort, especially if you want to change your Story of Belief. They position the Thinking Mind as a "solution" to Fear, which is why most books on Fear look to science, or the Thinking Mind, to deal with this emotion.

Science or thinking, however, is entirely the wrong approach, because what we're capable of grasping, proving, or explaining about Fear will forever be limited. It's like trying to grasp air. There's just nothing there to grasp.

Scientists can study the physiological chain reaction that occurs when Fear shows up: the release of epinephrine, adrenaline, cortisol, and the like. This is all interesting information, but it's essentially useless. Just because you know your mental and neurological reactions triggered by a snake slithering into your bedroom doesn't mean you know why the snake does what it does, or what it's like to be him.

Only the snake knows what it's like to be a snake. And only Fear knows why it does what it does and what it's like to be Fear.

This leaves the Thinking Mind (you) grasping at air, frustrated by its confusion, completely unable to understand Fear and why it acts the way it acts, and compensating by doing the only thing it really can in this situation—which is judge.

It works like this: In this enormously complicated world, with globs of data coming in every second, the Thinking Mind has become very good at navigating anything ungraspable (which most of life is) by neatly separating it all into opposites: good/bad, right/wrong, beautiful/ugly, and on and on.

In bed with the Dualistic Mind, then, and Judgmental or Discriminating Mind, the Thinking Mind has become a master at developing strong preferences for or against everything and everybody, in a very clever, considerate way.

I was breaking up with a friend once, a woman with whom I'd had a twenty-five-year best friendship. She was naturally upset and demanded to know why I wanted distance. When I explained my frustrations with her, she became enraged, interrupting me with an accusation: "Are you judging me?!" I paused, and then said, "Well, yeah."

Judging her was exactly what I was doing. That's what I, the Thinking Mind COO, do. I judge everything, always, all day long. It's how "you" make sense of who you want to hang out with and how you want to live your life. It's where all your yeses and nos come from.

The Thinking Mind judges all things external. It says, *That person is not for you*—this *person is. This religion is good. That political party is bad. This pizza is good. A snake on the carpet is bad.* It's very helpful in allowing you to be so clearly, effectively discriminating, and therefore know things for sure and make wise decisions.

It also judges all things internal, meaning the 10,000 voices: *Gratitude is good. Anger is bad. Joy is good. Fear is bad.*

And if you say, "No, that's not me at all. I'm not judgmental," that's a judgment, too. It's a judgment about your Self as being *someone without judgment,* which is good, because, well, you think judgment is bad.

10,000 CHILDREN

The only thing we have to fear is fear itself.

—FDR

Now that we know how judgmental the Thinking Mind is, let's change the analogy for a spell. Imagine now that, instead of being a corporation with 10,000 employees, you're a parent with 10,000 children (shudder).

Let's say you name half your children "good" names, like Joy, Wisdom, Beauty, Compassion, and Calm. The other half you name Sadness, Ignorance, Ugliness, Selfishness, and Fear. Despite your best intentions, would you be able to treat all your children the same?

Nope. Not a chance.

The "good" children, of which there are 5,000, you'd praise, feed, nourish, and show off to the world with pride, and say—these children being you—"Look at how joyful, wise, and beautiful I am."

How do you deal with the 5,000 "bad" children, though?

You certainly don't show them off to your friends: "Look at how miserable, stupid, and afraid I am." Perhaps you hide them, but being children they can't stay hidden for long. Maybe you ignore them, but still that's not enough—they keep coming back. Finally, in desperation, you corral them into the basement, lock the door, and throw away the key.

That'll do it, you think. Problem solved.

There's a new problem, though. Now they're down there with no food, no water, no love, no sunshine, no fresh air, while you remain on the surface, showing off all your good children.

How do you think they feel being down there? What are they up to?

What would you do, living under such circumstances?

All this leads to an important question: What's your judgment about your emotions? How do you feel about Fear, Anger, Joy, Sadness, and the Erotic? Keep in mind, it's impossible for you, the Thinking Mind, to have an emotionally neutral thought—because you can't understand them, you will *always* judge your emotions.

My guess is, you say, "Joy? Great! Joy is a lovely feeling, and therefore a good child"?

But Fear? Fear is an uncomfortable feeling. Wanting to protect you from anything uncomfortable, the Thinking Mind says, "Oh, no. No, no, no. Fear is, without question, a bad child and needs to be locked away." And this is something you know for sure.

Which brings us to the rub. While the Thinking Mind provides you a personality, an identity, and an opinion about everything, anytime you know anything for sure—even if it's a positive belief like Joy is good—you're stuck.

This is why, if you've completely succumbed to being the Thinking Mind and believe everything it believes, you can now become camped in one place on the side of a mountain, and while the view may be decent—

don't get me wrong, the Thinking Mind is great for many things—you're still seeing only one view of the world, not to mention your children.

For example, even the positive judgement "I'm a good person" can make you blind to the fact that sometimes you're not. Similarly, the judgment "Joy is good" can make you rigid, clinging to the riverbank where Joy is located, resistant to where else the river wants to take you.

There are numerous other views available, some of which are located downriver or lower or higher up the mountain. But you can't get to them so long as you cling to this riverbank or stay camped in this one lone campsite. With you believing everything the Thinking Mind says—including who and what you are and which children are worthwhile and which aren't— you will never get to explore and find your real and complete truth. You inadvertently become a one-faceted diamond, instead of what you were meant to be, which is a diamond with 10,000 facets.

No disrespect to the Thinking Mind, though. It really is doing its best, working twenty-four hours a day for you, yet do you feel the strain between you two? You can sense there's trouble. Do you often wish it would shut up late at night so you could sleep? Do you wish it would take a break so you can just be? Do you wish it would just let you feel and experience your emotions and life itself without judging and reasoning?

Sometimes it is utterly relentless, isn't it? (Other names for it are Monkey Mind, because it throws crap at you, and Wild Horse Mind, which bucks you around.) Its judgments and beliefs are based on some crazy stories still looping from childhood. Although it labors to provide you with a place of Sanity, it's very similar in nature to the voice of Insanity. To be fair, though, if it were my job to try and grasp the ungraspable for millions of years, I'd be insane, too.

So here's where we are: Year after year, you're encouraging and taking advice from a looping, highly convincing, highly judgmental, know-it-all, insane monkey COO who has a deep influence on all aspects of your life. And best of all? *You* think you're in charge. You think you can reprogram it anytime you want, when actually you can't—because it's all operating under the radar. And, science or no science, you have no idea what it even is, and never will.

Which is why you can meditate all you want, but unless your skateboarding passion results in a traumatic brain injury, the Thinking Mind is not going to change, nor will it ever go away.

Joe and Jim start a new religion. They sit in lotus position and chant over and over, "I am humble, I am nothing." Within a few days they have a dozen followers.

After a year of chanting "I am humble, I am nothing," they have their own ashram with thousands of followers.

One day, their old friend Biff walks by the ashram and hears the chanting inside. He thinks, "Hey, that's the religion Joe and Jim started. I heard they've been successful; I should check it out."

He walks inside, sees Joe and Jim in the front, and nods hello. They nod back. He sits down and starts chanting as well. "I am humble, I am nothing." He really enjoys it!

At the front of the room, Jim watches Biff chant. He smacks Joe on the shoulder and gestures at Biff, scoffing, "Ha! Look who thinks he's nothing!"

This story illustrates that, no matter how much effort we put into eliminating or containing a voice—be it Arrogance, the Lizard Brain, the Thinking Mind, or something else—if we feel successful, look again: All we've ever really accomplished is the feeding of our own delusion.

CHAPTER 2

GETTING TO KNOW FEAR

WHAT EXACTLY IS FEAR?

Let me help you with that question, because we want you as sane as possible. With the CEO and COO now in mind, let's explore Fear—not scientifically, but rather experientially, looking at why it slithers into your life so much, especially when it's not invited.

We know Fear is an emotion, and action begins with feeling emotions. Beyond that, we don't know much else about Fear except *There it is,* a feeling of discomfort either obvious or completely under your radar, in every room, every party, every relationship, and every moment at work, whether you're willing to admit it or not.

It's with you on a cellular level, arising from the oldest and most powerful part of your brain—the moment there is life, there is Fear. It's a huge and inevitable state of being, with you every step of the way from birth to death. If you look closely, you see it in yourself, your dog, your friends, and your enemies—hell, even polar bears.

Why?

It's more a question of *Why not?* You're born onto this little blue marble hurling through space, with no end in sight of things to be afraid of. In your lifetime, you will come into contact with horrible people and experiences. Nature is violent and unpredictable. You will get older. You will get sick. And you will die. Being alive is a scary, humbling experience.

Let's back up, then, to your birth. Babies are lovely because they're still connected to the whole. The "I am you, you are me" experience with them is unmistakable. Connection and comfort are their only worries. Then, everything changes. The terrible twos are called that for a reason: It's when your Ego kicks in, a dynamic that we'll explore soon, which includes the Thinking Mind.

For the first time, you have an experience of not being part of the whole. You're no longer connected to the infinite; instead, you're a separate, autonomous "I." You start seeing the world in terms of self and other, or subject and object. The other/object can mean your mom and dad, other people, animals, trees, rivers, mountains, the earth, the sun, your shadow, your body, and anyone or anything else you come into contact with, not to mention life itself. It's the recognition that "I am not you; you are not me," and "I am not it; it is not me."

Although this isn't a conscious experience—certainly not for a two-year-old—over time you gradually become conscious at least of what goes along with this separation: a feeling that something is just wrong or missing.

As you grow up, this may show up in your life in a variety of ways:

> You may feel lost.
> You may feel you don't know who you are.
> You may feel you've been left behind or left out of something.
> You may feel abandoned. (Note: You may blame the people in your life for this—hell, you don't know whom else to blame—when actually it's the truth of who and what you are having abandoned you at such a young age.)
> You may feel powerless over this separation internally, so you overcompensate by trying to gain power externally, through money, fame, or my favorite, world domination.
> You may feel like you're all alone and have to fight or fend for yourself.

If you look closer, though, what is wrong or missing, the thing for which you're now compensating, is that innate connection you were born with but lost.

Many spiritual practices seek to break that perception of separation and take you back to your true nature, or whatever you want to call it. The hippies call it Nirvana. The Buddhists, Enlightenment. The Taoists, Original Force. The New Agers, Collective Consciousness. Meditators, Non-Thinking Mind. Christians, Christ Consciousness. Every spiritual tradition has a name for this place.

But, alas, the Buddha is famous for saying, "Enlightenment is delusion." So while, with effort, you may catch glimpses of something beyond your personal Ego/Thinking Mind, maybe even quite often, it doesn't matter: You will always come back to it, again and again. Your Ego is your human fate. No one is without an Ego. And in that separation lies the source of Fear.

SEPARATION IS THE BASIS FOR FEAR

Wherever there is other, there is fear.

—KEN WILBUR

With this inevitable separation, everything and everybody—which are no longer part of you—become unfamiliar and unknown. And because you don't know what they are or what they're up to, you are now vulnerable to them, and they can hurt you.

The Lizard Brain works hard to limit your vulnerability by using Fear (and sometimes Anger) as its primary tool, to protect, protect, protect. With the world also being a horribly unfamiliar, unstable, and constantly changing place, the Lizard Brain and Fear will come back again and again to help you deal with all this. You may feel Fear on the surface of your awareness, tickling you at all times, or it may be totally under your radar and you don't know what the hell I'm talking about. But make no mistake: It's always there.

If you think that's not the case, you are in denial.

One coping mechanism is to seek repetition. As much as possible, you surround yourself with anything familiar. Why do you love music so much? Because it repeats, returning again and again to the same chorus, which brings you to a safe, familiar, and therefore comforting place. You may even listen to the same songs over and over your whole life.

Why do you also stay in a relationship, house, or job for too long, or even visit the same hotel every trip? Because familiarity soothes, even if it's only a repeat of yesterday. For some people, it can get to the point where just eating at a different restaurant can be challenging, never mind starting a new job or ending a relationship. For others who crave novelty, to always do things differently is the familiar comfort.

To limit unfamiliarity and vulnerability, you also try to control everything, or even everybody. This means controlling things as much as possible, externally (time, family members, strangers, activities, politics, outcome, etc.) as well as internally (the 10,000 voices—who is allowed to speak and what they're allowed to say).

You also try to understand everything. As a species, we place major stock in what can be proven scientifically, and we cling to these "facts" like a shipwreck victim to a life preserver. It's commonly argued that if it can't be proven, it's not worth anything. Proven things make you feel safe.

Thus, you may try to "figure out" or prove what your partner is thinking, why your boss said that, or how to ski perfectly, or even try to understand Fear itself, all as a way to be less vulnerable. Which is why most books about Fear use science in their arguments.

All this repetition, control, and understanding becomes what you also cling to, along with beliefs, stories, etc. And if any of that comfort gets challenged, watch out—you may lose it!

What does that mean, anyway? What is the "it" that you lose? Patience, calmness, or composure, for sure, but also what's familiar or what you've labeled "true"—like self-perceptions, beliefs, and anything you know for sure. This is why Fear becomes all about *What's at stake here? What am I going to lose?*

Maybe you see yourself as a confident person, but if someone challenges your confidence, what image of your Self might you lose? If someone puts down your religion, what belief is at stake? You love your dog and you're afraid to lose him. You've gotten used to youth, beauty, and vitality—how scary is it to lose that? What would you lose if you got injured?

You might wind up in prison (loss of freedom). You might wind up alone (loss of hope or connection). You might wind up dead (loss of life). Here's an interesting take: If you're afraid of heights, it's not actually the height you're afraid of; when riding a chairlift, you're afraid that you might lose control over yourself, lose your sanity, and jump.

It is absolutely not okay to lose sanity, or this familiar world you've set up, because you'll be exposed to vulnerability all over again.

Yet there's nothing you can do about it, really. Everything you love— whether it's people, passions, objects, states of being, or your sanity—will be taken away from you at some point, and not on your terms.

And that's just downright terrifying.

FEAR OF REJECTION AND THE INEVITABILITY OF RISK

What is the greatest thing you could possibly lose?

For just about everyone, it's the people in your life. This is why rejection, in my opinion, is the greatest Fear you'll ever have.

To the Lizard Brain, rejection is like death. And, as we know, death is scary.

This is why if anyone threatens to undo whatever comfort, connection, or certainty you've created, as a way to get back to control and limit vulnerability, you immediately reject them. Rejection also being their greatest Fear, they reject back. Back and forth it goes—the cycle of self and other, the unfamiliarity, wanting to limit vulnerability, loss, and rejection—until all 7.5 billion of us are in a co-created prison of mutually escalating Fear.

The ideal, you might think, would be to stay away from other people entirely. But alas, there's not enough room. Plus, we humans need each other to survive. It's unbearable, isn't it—that feeling of separateness? You constantly crave that connection you once had, like a lost, starving child craves home.

Eventually, the fear of staying separate forever overshadows the fear of rejection, and you pursue relationships despite the fact that you may be rejected (which, at some point, you will be). Similarly, you pursue a sport, an experience in nature, or a new challenge, despite the fact that you may get hurt (which, at some point, you will). You pursue a gift or talent you have, despite the fact that you may fail (which, at some point, you will).

Again and again, you put yourself out there, trying to connect—to people, to things, to experiences, to your true nature—taking on unfamiliarity, vulnerability, potential loss, possible rejection. And maybe, just maybe, it pays off. Maybe you like the new restaurant. Maybe you do find love. Giving a speech is one of the greatest fears I have, yet again and again I go for it. I stand up there terrified, with the hope that afterwards I won't feel rejected but instead loved. Appreciated. Connected.

Why is it that fear of speaking in front of groups is the biggest Fear we have? Even bigger than fear of death? Yes, fear of rejection plays a part, but there's more to it than that. The fear of speaking in front of groups is similar to the fear of heights. You feel so close to the edge of your own sanity—it's the fear that you may go insane up there and accidentally tell the truth.

And God forbid you do, because the truth is that at every moment of your life, especially this one, you're scared to death.

Nobody wants to believe it's this "bad," that Fear is that big a deal. I certainly wouldn't have believed it during my ski career. I didn't feel afraid of anything.

You probably don't want to believe life is that uncomfortable, either. You're born and then you die, and in between you experience Fear every moment of every day? What? But life is also wonderful. Magical!

And it is. Yet here's exactly the point where you start to repress Fear. If you *only* want life to be magical, anything that doesn't fit that preference is deemed wrong, and not what life is meant to be about. Fear, the uncomfortable end product of everything I've outlined, is now deemed wrong.

Go all the way back to the beginning, though, and you'll see how this separateness—not the Fear—is the "problem." The Fear is just the ultimate result. Like if you ate a bad burrito and got sick: The burrito was the problem. But instead you focus on managing the sickness, while the burrito gets forgotten.

Separateness is the unpleasant reality about life. Not Fear.

But Separateness is our human fate, the very nature of life. And because you can't make life itself wrong, you make vulnerability, rejection, loss, unfamiliarity, other people or things, the Lizard Brain, the Ego, the Thinking Mind, and/or change wrong. Most of your experience here on earth is now wrong.

And especially Fear, which is the final emotional discomfort you feel from all this.

THE THINKING MIND SPEAKING FOR FEAR

Emotions were intended to ignite simple, immediate action based on intuitive, thought-free sensation. With the Thinking Mind as COO, however, emotions instead become complicated and confusing. It's to the point where you too often don't have clear, undistorted access to your basic emotions anymore. They no longer appear simple or move you like they were intended to.

This is most unmistakably seen with Fear—to the point that no one listens to Fear or considers what it has to say anymore. What matters is only what the Thinking Mind *thinks* Fear is, and we consider only what *it* has to say about it. The Thinking Mind, therefore, has become the flesh, the skin, the bones, and the innards of Fear. It speaks for Fear—but it absolutely, unequivocally is *not* Fear.

When one voice speaks for another, this is a problem, because it will get it wrong every time. It's like how, if someone asks a friend, "Tell me about Kristen," and she speaks for me, she will get it wrong every time. There's no way she can know what it's like to be me. She can only run my style through her looping filter and come up with a judgment.

And when the interpretation is that Fear is bad—like when someone tells you a person is awful before you even meet them, and not to bother— you don't ever get to explore your own truth about that person or emotion. They may actually be okay.

FEAR IN THE BASEMENT

There is nothing either good or bad but thinking makes it so.

—SHAKESPEARE

Imagine a dog lying on the floor. The Thinking Mind might judge it a good dog or a bad dog. But look again: The dog is just the dog. It's neither good nor bad. But if it acts in a way you don't like, it's a bad dog.

It's the same with emotions. There is no such thing as a good or bad emotion; there is only emotion. But if an emotion feels uncomfortable in a way you don't like, you call it a bad emotion. Fear is just Fear; there is no good Fear and bad Fear. There's only Fear. Yet people treat Fear far worse than they do most dogs.

How do you feel about Fear? Is it a bad emotion? When it shows up, when you just hear the word "Fear," what happens? Do you get tense, want to change the subject, try to leave the room? In noticing your reaction to Fear, you can begin to get a sense of your own personal judgment or belief of what Fear is.

Are you among the billions who have determined it to be "bad" and seek to shut it down? Do you deem it unnecessary, uncomfortable, and unwelcome? Do you want to protect yourself from it? Do you buy into the rampant belief that it needs to be controlled and overcome?

Granted, you may declare it natural and want to face it. Many do. Yet, in your next breath, do you contradict yourself, claiming to also want to overcome it, to let it go and not let it get the better of you or hold you back? These are clear signs you're not fooling anyone, least of all Fear.

You're not alone, of course. There's a legitimate reason for all this repulsion. When you were very young, you likely experienced the discomfort of Fear as "bad." And it is! Next to Joy, it feels terrible. It feels like termites chewing apart your hopes and dreams. As a child you may have decided to ignore it or push it down. That action may have allotted you some relief, and the termites went away.

Success! The Thinking Mind and that whole department then weaves a success story and belief around pushing down Fear, which grows in thickness and durability over time: that the way to successfully deal with this bad dog called Fear is to lock it in the basement.

The result is a feeling of power. Look at this amazing mastery you have over the Lizard Brain! Over Fear!

Enjoy it while it lasts, though, for you have just rendered yourself very, very weak.

I'm standing in the living room, looking at my parents and thinking, "These people are nuts." I'm six years old.

Mom is screaming. Dad is growling in defense. They do this all the time. Only this time they've dragged me into it. They're fighting about me.

But I didn't do anything worth fighting over. This doesn't make any sense. How could they not see that this doesn't make any sense? I start to cry, then start to yell in anger, then off I run, out the front door and over to the abandoned building next door. I sit on the crumbling cement step and feel better.

There. That showed them. I ran away and I'm never going back.

I sit there for six hours. At least that's what it feels like; all I know is it's a long, long time. Long enough for me to really think about this family I'm stuck with, and wonder what exactly I am going to do about it.

Obviously, I'm going to have to raise myself. These people can't do it. They're too caught up in their own lives and don't listen to me or even see me. In fact, everyone seems to be this way, not just my parents. The kids at school are blind, too, and mean. I'm a good, kind person. Can no one see that? I feel alone and invisible. There's clearly something wrong with other people and this world. No one is ever going to love me. Screw them. I hate them.

I'm just going to get tough and take care of myself.

At dusk, my seven-year-old brother, Ed, comes over to sit by me. He tells me dinner is ready. *No*, I tell him, *I'm never going back*. I tell him what I've concluded about my parents, the world, and what my plan is. He sits quietly and listens. Ed's good like that.

When I'm done, he says he's hungry. I am, too. We go back inside. But I will never be the same again.

THE CONTROLLER

Let's talk about another high-action employee called the Controller. Its job is to control everything and everybody. Whatever it can't control, you are vulnerable to, which is never OK.

Externally, it tries to control the people in your life, strangers, politics, traffic . . . hell, it would control the moon and the stars if it could.

Internally it tries to control you, too. It controls how you spend your time, what you say or don't say, what you do or don't do, how you perceive yourself, and how others perceive you. It's a big, big deal in your corporation, upper management for sure.

The New Age "train your brain" crowd thinks the Controller is an even bigger deal than the Thinking Mind. They insist it has the ability to cage that monkey called the Thinking Mind, put that wild horse out to pasture. Control your thoughts, they say, and you control your reality. Your life. Your destiny!

We all look to the Controller to solve most problems. Anger management classes teach us how to control Anger. Sex addiction classes teach us how to control sexuality. Fear classes teach us how to control Fear. It even seeks to control the amount of Joy or Gratitude in our life (more!). Control your life, they say, and you control your destiny.

If we do a good job and get all of your 10,000 voices under control, promoting the good ones, like Joy and Gratitude, and repelling the bad ones, like Anger and Fear, the belief is that you'll finally be who you were supposed to be, and have the life you want.

It also strives to get the world and humanity under control, all through little ol' you. Lordy, if it pulled that off, wouldn't *that* be something?

IS THE CONTROLLER EFFECTIVE?

An old man and a young man decide to climb a mountain. The young man takes off with vigor, pushing himself hard for five hours before collapsing on a rock halfway up, exhausted.

Pretty soon, along saunters the old man. He hasn't even broken a sweat.

Shocked, the young man asks, "How is it possible, me being so young and fit, you'll beat me to the top?"

The old man pauses, then explains, "You come here to conquer the mountain, but it is more powerful than you, so it will conquer you."

"I come here to merge with the mountain," he concludes. "And like lovers in a dance, it lifts me to the top."

The Controller can be great for getting you out of bed in the morning, your teeth brushed, and to work on time. It's also useful for not dropping F-bombs during job interviews. But beyond that—when, for example, it tries to control other people—you have the makings of a disaster. And this may be bad news for the "train your brain" crowd, but if you look closely, you'll see that it also has limited success controlling your Thinking Mind. According to the Laboratory of Neuro Imaging at USC, your mind has about forty-eight thoughts a minute. That's 2,880 in an hour, or almost 70,000 a day. Quite a relentless stream of thoughts. Controller, you may as well try to control individual drops of water coming out of a fire hose.

As for Fear, sure, the Controller can slow it (and you) down by managing how much skydiving you do, or walk you away from a twerking opportunity. But when Fear shows up the next moment anyway (which it always will), in another form (e.g., the fear of being lame for not twerking), the Controller can get pretty overextended, fast.

Why? Let me remind you that Fear has been around since the first single-cell amoeba. The Lizard Brain has been developing in wisdom for 500 million years. By comparison, the Thinking Mind and the Controller have been around for only about two to three million years, a mere hiccup ago.

Fear will come back again and again—Fear if you do, Fear if you don't—and will outsmart you every time.

Yet the Controller's job is to control; it can't help itself. When Fear shows up no matter what, the Controller still wants to get to work. So it does whatever it can.

And what has proven to be wildly effective? It's called dissociation, or repression.

CONDITIONING AND THE ORIGIN OF REPRESSION

In Bali, there's a majestic temple. Upon entering it, you encounter an unfortunate pothole. Locals like to sit and watch tourists enter the temple grounds, because so many of them trip and fall into the pothole. It's better than TV. The Americans, apparently, are the worst. They get the biggest laughs. The locals believe that Americans, because they are so in their heads, have lost all other senses and awareness found in their bodies, and thus they have the best crashes.

We humans have a long history of avoiding anything unpleasant. It's how we spend most of our time. That includes ignoring, pushing down, or repressing, emotions.

Avoiding or repressing emotions, until recently, was even considered a necessity. Our great-grandparents, great-great-grandparents, and generations going back as long as we can remember have a history of seeing emotions as frivolous. Life was just something that happened to you. Joy was a novelty, and Fear wasn't an option—and certainly not an invitation or a chance to grow. Emotions were a hindrance to what really needed to be done, which was survive. With generation after generation leading to you, no wonder you've lost the ability to be in touch with emotions—not to mention sensations and feelings—or to be in touch with your body, period.

I have a theory that there are two types of people in the world: those who unconsciously wind up exactly like their parents (who wound up exactly like *their* parents) and those who consciously work hard not to wind up like their parents . . . but still wind up exactly like their parents. Which means: Your grandparents' and parents' issues, or in this case their refusal to own their issues (Fear, Anger), always become your issues.

It works like this: When you were growing up and had an emotionally painful experience—which we all do—what happened next? It's normal, as a survival mechanism, to close down. Then, if the people in your life— especially your parents but also a neighbor, a teacher, a friend, even a stranger—reinforce this shutdown, it can become an unavoidable pattern.

It's possible that up to a certain age, you felt emotions just fine. Nothing had been categorized as good or bad yet; you just felt. You were well on your way to being in touch with them and having them move you, as they were intended. But the first time you say "I'm afraid," and Mom says back, "There's nothing to be afraid of," her language sends a clear message that Fear is unnecessary. It's just false evidence, not real, and there's no reason for you to feel it.

Don't be hard on Mom, though. Even when intentions are great, with a million generations of repressed emotions trickling down to this moment, our society, and every mom in it, are now dysfunctional—especially when it comes to emotions.

And now, it's your turn to become dysfunctional. Even though Fear is neither good nor bad, if Mom says it's bad, you will believe it, too. *Candid Camera* once played a tollbooth prank on drivers entering Delaware. An actor in the booth told them, "I'm sorry, Delaware is closed." A full 90 percent of adult drivers believed the actor and turned around. One woman even said, "Well, is New Jersey open?" It's funny, sure, but also very telling. You believe what others say. If you're this susceptible to having your mind hijacked as an adult, you can imagine how it went as a child.

Throw in the fact that it's natural to want to please your mom, friends, and society, at all stages of life, and you're doomed. We humans are very social creatures, with a basic need to be valued by others. Certain emotions make people feel uncomfortable, so you adjust and accommodate accordingly. It's a nice way to be. Plus you get a big payoff: Getting it right makes you feel good about yourself, worthy of respect, and worthy of love.

So when an influencer in your life says either directly or indirectly that Fear is not necessary, you form a subconscious belief that if you live without Fear, you're a good girl. A special boy. The Storyteller (another one of the 10,000 voices) then takes this information and gets to work spinning a big tale around it. It grabs on to memories—perhaps bad experiences with Fear, because these hold your attention better than good experiences—and turns them into a loop confirming over and over that Fear is bad. Round and around, year after year, the story builds, until your belief in the story becomes your habitual reality. That belief can drive your life.

With the Thinking Mind judging Fear as bad, the Controller is then inspired to halt the emotion when the energy of Fear is building, much like you can put a hand over the fire hose for a spell. What follows is a visual representation of how that repression works.

Perhaps there's a hissing snake or angry in-law (same thing to the Lizard Brain). Fear shows up, and the energy of the emotion is supposed to build, peak, then decline. The whole process should take between ten and ninety seconds (proven by science), or however long the snake or in-law is around.

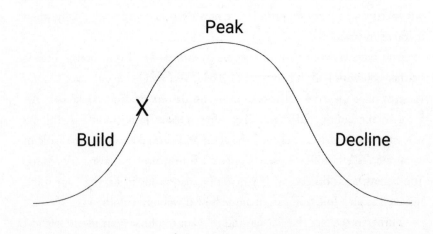

But the Controller stops that unnecessary "weakness" short to keep it from appearing to either you or the in-law.

Masterful at doing this, the Controller employs many tools to halt the rise of fear, not just in the moment, but in life in general: overanalyzing, alcohol, antidepressants, TV, shopping, work, sarcasm, illness—pick your style (see "How to Know If You're Repressing Your Emotions"). It uses many tools to distract you from the emotion or block it from your consciousness altogether.

HOW TO KNOW IF YOU'RE REPRESSING YOUR EMOTIONS

Here's a list of some of the things we do instead of feeling our emotions. It's much easier to distract yourself for years with food, work, drama, the Internet—whatever is your chosen flavor—as a way to avoid Fear and pretend it doesn't exist. Perhaps you recognize yourself in this list?

Criticizing

Controlling

Lecturing

Getting righteous

Being sarcastic

Interrupting

Gossiping

Intellectualizing

Getting wordy

Complaining

Getting confused

Being misunderstood

Getting shy

Getting distracted

Procrastinating

Withdrawing

Watching TV

Eating

Shopping

Cleaning

Organizing

Rushing

Analyzing

Getting busy

Working out obsession

Smiling or laughing a lot

Trying hard	Injuring yourself
Being a good student	Drugs
Caretaking	Alcohol
Getting silly	Worrying
Getting enlightened	Being disorganized
Coughing	Hoarding
Yawning	Daydreaming
Getting sick	Getting bored
Getting tired	Not breathing

This is what we do rather than allowing ourselves to feel.

Over time, the Controller represses that emotional rise again and again, all day long, year after year—until it becomes automatic. And, voilà, you don't have to feel that emotion, seemingly ever.

Thus, at a funeral, the widowed wife can remain stoic while family members marvel, "Wow, she is handling this so well!" In a bar, a man with clenched fists walks away from a fight as friends admire his integrity. A skier can throw a front flip off a forty-foot cliff and become legendary for his lack of emotion.

This ability, and ongoing support from a society rewarding control, confirm that the Controller is on the right track. The water seemingly stops. The emotion goes away. Your life is under control. You can walk around feeling and acting calm, stoic. Fearless.

The thing is, in repressing our emotions, the Controller may as well be trying to control the moon and the stars.

For you can control emotions about as much as you can control breathing: a little bit, but not for long. You couldn't commit suicide by holding your breath—you'd just pass out, and breathing would resume. The same applies to Fear. The moment you drop your guard, Fear will come back. It's as innate as breathing. It cannot, will not, be denied for long.

But no matter, this long-held negative view of Fear has wrapped its tendrils firmly around all of us. It's gotten so societally entrenched that if someone asks how we are, all we reply with is "Fine." We're at the point where any unpleasant voice, whenever it tries to speak, is halted, is thrown down into the basement, and deemed not a part of you. This makes Fear now an "other"—something you are vulnerable to, and perceived like a virus (*Fight it! Take drugs!*) or a leech (*Get it off!*).

Generation after generation, we reinforce hiding away Fear, controlling it, drinking it away, taking a pill so you don't have to feel it. No one wants to deal with their emotions.

And you don't want to have to deal with theirs.

They called me fearless—the media, the ski industry, my peers. Did I believe them? Was I actually fearless?

Two years later, I was back in Squaw Valley, standing on top of the Palisades again, this time attending a party with 100 or so other hard-core skiers. It was late spring during a low snow year, so it was pretty bony up there, more rocks than snow. It had been sixty degrees all day, and what snow remained was twelve inches of mashed potatoes. That and the amount of booze present made it obvious that no one planned to ski off the cliffs.

I'd just spent six hours shooting with a photographer for a *Skiing* magazine article titled "How to Catch Big Air! With Kristen Ulmer."

The article was a prestigious assignment because it was meant for a male audience. In 1993, women weren't known for big jumps (even today women still under-jump the men). Women were known for being particularly bad in the air, so to be recognized as an expert on how to jump big jumps made me feel like a badass. Sure, I acted coy on the outside, like it was no big deal, but inside, my heart was swollen with pride.

Now we were done. Considering how mucky the snow conditions were, I felt really good about my performance. I'd jumped about twelve medium-size natural waves and lips. Some of the airs were pretty big, too. One ledge I flew off five times, flying about twenty feet off the ground for thirty feet before landing, which was big back then. I'd stuck the landings all day, too, didn't crash once.

Now, relaxing and basking in the glory of being the famous, fearless skier chick from out of town was my reward. I was twenty-four years old and lived for this.

"Kristen, come over here," the photographer beckoned. He was standing at the edge of the cliffs. Leaving my group of cute, attentive guys, I skied over. "You should jump this," he said, and pointed to a line below.

I looked over the edge and laughed, assuming he was joking. Below was a ten-foot-long ramp in the shape of an abrupt duck bill, only one foot wide. It looked about to collapse. Then came forty feet of open air before hitting the steep slope of bottomless mush below. If that wasn't bad enough, littered about the landing were giant cinnamon-roll-shaped swirls of frozen ice, some almost three feet tall.

Sometimes we look at an unskiable mountain and joke to each other absurdly: "Hey, there's my line—two turns on rock, then a 500-foot cliff jump, landing on that knife-edge before straight-running that vertical frozen waterfall . . . And by the way, I'm so good I plan to do it without skis." For sure this was one of those times.

But he shook his head. "No, I'm serious. I think you can do it."

I laughed, said, "Yeah, right," and skated off to rejoin the party.

But it stayed on me like a mosquito. This photographer thought I could do it. Could I? Five minutes passed. I couldn't pay attention to what anyone was saying. I skated back to take another look.

Ugh, awful. It looked even worse this time. It was a guaranteed pair of broken legs, even if I were to get off the skinny ramp without it collapsing and throwing me headfirst into a cliff wall. And those ice chunks below? I'd land in them going, what, fifty miles an hour? No. Nope. I went back to the party.

I still couldn't hear a word anyone said, though, so I crept back to the edge and looked over a third time, expecting to see the same mess. Instead . . .

Bam. I saw it. I saw that the ramp wouldn't collapse if I was light and fast, and squeezed my skis together. I saw where to aim for the perfect landing. I recognized that I should land slightly back so my tips wouldn't dive into the mushy snow. I saw a clear path to the bottom through the ice chunks. I could do it.

Then everything stopped. A switch flipped and I went blank. Thoughts, feelings, emotions—it all stopped. My personality died. I died. I didn't feel alive, I felt nothing. That vision was frozen in me like an icicle, and if I moved too much or took too deep a breath, I would lose the certainty, break the ice. So I held as still as possible.

The photographer had seen me go back and forth from the edge and suddenly was there beside me. Without looking at him, I mono-toned, "Okay, I'll do it. But I need to use your longer skis, and I need the bindings set on 14 (the tightest the bindings go, so they wouldn't release in the mush). Used to working with professional skiers and in-tense situations, he knew to keep his mouth shut and got to work. He took off his skis, lined them up next to me, pulled a screwdriver out of his pack, knelt, and adjusted his bindings to fit my boots.

Once he was done, he climbed out onto another cliff ledge to get the best angle for his photo.

Trusting that the bindings were right, I kept staring off into the distance, not noticing if the other skiers from the party saw what was going on. I didn't smile. I didn't joke. I just stayed paralyzed in the cer-tainty. I confirmed to the photographer, "Are you ready?" then turned my body and counted down the usual "Three, two, one—going."

The ramp was fast and slick. It launched me straight up and out like a cannonball into forty feet of open air. The ground was abruptly far away, but I felt nothing. I jammed my hands forward to balance. My skis warbled in the sudden wind and empty space as I accelerated toward the ground. In the last moment before impact, I reached for the landing with both poles, then hit with a shock.

Whatever quiet had been present ended, and the violence began. The snow was fast, thick, and uneven. My skis smacked around as if they were in a blender (still skinny skis back then, 210 centimeters). My eyes vibrated so much from the jarring, I couldn't see.

Gathering even more speed, skiing straight down the steep slope between the death chunks, I was going faster, faster, and then *Ahhhh, I can't hang on!* But I did, and saw a chance to finally make a long turn to the right and took it: subtle . . . delicate . . . careful . . . , and 400 feet later I came to a complete stop, still on my feet. I made it.

Then everything went quiet again. The moment didn't move. There was no wind. My back to the scene behind me, I looked straight ahead to a beautiful mountain off in the distance.

And burst into tears.

REINFORCED IN MEDIA

Self-help magazines often seem to support repression. "Don't let Fear win. Don't let it get in your way!" I've read. However, on the next page the magazine can contradict itself: "All stress comes from resisting what is," or, "We're all spending too much time and energy trying to fight the stuff we can't change."

Which is it, then? Is Fear "what is," or is it something we can change?

Perhaps you buy into this notion that Fear is something you really *can* change or get rid of. (But have you ever been successful at changing *anyone,* much less someone as old and established as Fear?) The more you consider yourself "spiritual," the more this belief can arise. I heard that 4,000 well-intentioned people once tried to sign up for a New York workshop entitled "Live Without Fear!"—all wanting to learn how to overcome, conquer, or let go of Fear. That's a lot of support for this belief.

Mahatma Gandhi once said, "The enemy is fear. We think it is hate; but, it is fear." He suggested that Fear, which is an innate part of you, is an enemy.

Nelson Mandela said, "I learned that courage was not the absence of fear, but the triumph over it. The brave man is not he who does not feel afraid, but he who conquers that fear."

Business gurus such as Whole Foods CEO John Mackey suggest, "Take away the fear, only love remains."

Great writers such as J. R. R. Tolkien write, "Fear nothing! Have peace until the morning! Heed no nightly noises!"

Some books separate Fear into good Fear and bad Fear. Their message is along the lines of "Keep the good, fight the bad." Yet the dog is just the dog. There is no such thing as good or bad Fear; that's just the Thinking Mind judging it. There's only Fear.

And what about "No Fear" T-shirts? They sold millions. Don't get me started.

You can't sneeze without spraying someone who says, "Once you get rid of Fear, then you really start living. Then and only then can you be your true self."

This book seeks to challenge it all.

WE WANT TO BE OTHER THAN WE ARE

Man is the only creature who refuses to be what he is.

—ALBERT CAMUS

A man is sitting on a park bench and a bird hops up to him. He looks down and says, "Oh, no, you're not the bird you're supposed to be."

He takes out clippers and picks up the bird. He trims the tail feathers, thins out the wings, and clips off the front inch of the bird's beak. Then he puts the bird back down and announces, "There! Now you're the bird you're supposed to be."

Kind of a ridiculous story, isn't it? But this is what we humans do. Leaves may fall in exactly the right spot, and we think, "I'd better rake." If you were a tiger, you'd probably spend your whole life trying to get rid of those damn stripes.

WISHING WE WERE DIFFERENT

I once started a speech in front of 1,200 teenagers with this question: "How many of you feel the world is exactly as you like it?"

No one raised a hand.

Next I asked: "How many of you feel you are exactly as you want to be?"

This time there was laughter, and again, no one raised a hand.

These answers show our innate sense of dissatisfaction. We're always on the lookout for things we wish were different. Even if you get the life you want someday, you'll still wish it were different, thanks to the Thinking Mind.

Wanting to be better, different, and other than yourself offers, on the one hand, great motivation to improve yourself. But there's a dark side to this drive. When we want Fear to go away or be different, this suggests it's a problem that must be fixed. And since Fear is a part of you, that means *you* must be fixed. If you need to be fixed, that means you're broken. So your attention becomes focused on how broken you are and what's wrong with you, which leads to toil, struggle, and shoddy self-esteem. That's the heart of this artichoke. If you have a problem embracing life as it is—which is a life that includes Fear—then you have a problem embracing yourself. Basically, if you don't like Fear, you don't like yourself.

But not to worry: There are books and workshops available, promising, "You're broken, but you can get better." Teaching that Fear is bad is indeed great for business. *Fear is bad, and when it shows up (which it will), that means you're broken, which makes you feel like crap. But buy this pill, drink this alcohol, attend this workshop, read this book, and you'll feel better.*

And, heh-heh, I'm sure it even sold you this one.

FLEE FREEZE FAINT FIDGET FIGHT

The skiing? It almost didn't matter. I became a great skier, sure, dramatically better each year, but what I was exceptional at, even more than the skiing, was my ability to repress Fear. Pure genius.

No wonder, then, that I became famous. The fascination people had in their belief that I was fearless kept sponsors calling, took me around the world, made me a sex symbol, gained me flights in F-16 and F-18 fighter jets, and, by the time I retired, had set me up for life financially. It still opens doors to this day. It's probably the very thing that landed me this book contract.

Fight or flight used to be Fear's protective wisdom. It led to immediate action without having to engage a time-consuming extra step: the Thinking Mind. But with the Thinking Mind firmly in place today as COO, micromanaging and inserting an opinion about everything, the wisdom of Fear now gets delayed and distorted.

The distortion is this: Fear has now become the *other* that you need to fight or take flight from. Instead of the snake (the situation) being the problem, Fear is now the problem. The discomfort is the problem. This uncomfortable emotion has become a bigger problem than the situation itself.

No longer, then, do you fight or flee the situation; you fight or flee the Fear.

Fight or flight, then, for us humans, has to be redefined in today's terms. How you used to react to a scary situation is now how you react to Fear itself, and it can even manifest in more than these two ways:

FLEE: As a way to avoid Fear, you may run from anything that may result in your having to feel it. Some examples include: You don't say a word to the colleague who stole your idea. You don't get on the scale. But if you notice from the "How to Know If You're Repressing Your Emotions" list, it can become even more nuanced than that: If your home life is scary or dysfunctional, in order to not deal with that Fear, you work sixteen hours a day. Or you run ten miles a day so the Fear you've repressed can't catch up to you. To avoid vulnerability, you stay single. To avoid how out of control you feel about Fear, you micromanage and control everyone else. Or you overanalyze every move you make, ensuring that your business stays small and you don't have to deal with fear of success. To avoid loneliness, you travel constantly. To avoid change, you stay in a bad relationship or job. To avoid the belief that you may not be as talented as you think, you hold back from pursuing your gifts, because then that belief won't have to be explored or possibly confirmed. The list could go on for hundreds of pages. All these actions are done in order to run away from Fear.

FREEZE: I see this a lot in skiing. A skier will freeze in place when the slope gets to be too steep, then blame Fear for causing that reaction. Freezing is your highly ineffective, unconscious reaction to a perceived threat, which in this case isn't so much the slope as it is the Fear. *Stop breathing and don't move. Then maybe Fear (way worse than the slope) won't notice me and will go away.* Fear finds this to be quite silly: "I know you're there. I'm standing right next to you."

FAINT: Popular with drama queens, Fear shows up and you come unglued. All Fear has to do is say "Boo" and watch the soap opera unfold.

FIDGET: One of my favorites. Horses in captivity who can't run away do this to express their emotion instead. For humans, in the captivity called politeness, it can show up as nervous laughter, talking too much, excessive yawning, fiddling with your hair, or your leg bobbing like a sewing machine. And finally . . .

FIGHT: The big one, and what many if not all Fear teachers help you do, because this is their most "powerful" way to deal with Fear. "Fight" is where all the language of success comes from: "Be a warrior and fight that beast! Don't let it win! Confront and conquer it! Overcome it! Take out as big a sword as you can. Win the war, and then—and only then—will you be free from the snake called Fear."

None of this happens in nature, of course. Can you imagine Bambi fretting, "What do I do, what do I do?" Or avoiding: "Oh, for crying out loud, it's just rustling in the bushes. Stop being such a drama queen." But that's what we do. We have become afraid, most of all, *of being afraid*. And because it's Fear's job to be afraid, that means Fear has gotten confused about its job, too, and is actually now afraid of itself. This is true insanity.

And a whole lot of trouble over just one simple voice in 10,000.

Jumping that duck lip was one of the most memorable moments I've ever had on skis. The question is: Was I magically in the Zone that day, or was it one of the stupidest things I've ever done and I just got lucky?

The answer is: both.

Skiing magazine chose that photo for their big-air article. Pretty validating. Again, the town of Squaw talked about me into the night. Eric Perlman heard about the feat and called asking if I would do it again the next day for his latest ski movie. I told him sure. That's another story.

So what happened up there? Where's that missing step where Fear creeps in like a greasy sandwich clenching my stomach? Where's the usual emotional component found in this equation?

Is this, then, what "conquering Fear" looks like? "Overcoming Fear?" Would I make a great example for the self-help–reading, Gandhi-quoting, spiritually oriented crowd? *Do it like this. Be like this. And you, too, will be magnificent!*

For the next ten years, the media kept calling me the best in the world at sketchy skiing experiences. Or the craziest. Or the most spectacular. Red Bull called. Nikon called. Hell, Prada even let me go on shopping sprees just like the movie stars for my ability to do this . . . this thing. With Fear.

I had fans. I had stalkers. I wasn't just a world-class athlete, either—there are loads of those. I risked my life for my sport. That's a whole other level of intrigue.

Did I deserve all the attention? Was I accessing Flow, or the Zone, or whatever we like to call it? That place where you stop being a separate drop of water and instead become one with the whole ocean, the snow, the mountain, the universe? What the hippies call Nirvana? What the Buddhists call Enlightenment?

I had no idea. Back then, who cared, really? Not me. Cripes, I was twenty-four years old and had a huge Ego. Sure!

Today, however, I care. Having reflected on thirty years of experience, I recognize that I was indeed in the Zone that day. But I realize that there are two ways to be there: the hard way and the easy way. The hard way involves repressing Fear—and I was about to learn the severe consequences of that choice. For it was to be at the cost of my future aliveness, relationships, passion, happiness, and health. It was also at the cost of possible femur fractures that day, and on at least fifty other days when I went to the next level and skied death-defying lines, at the risk of my own life.

The easy way, on the other hand, involves embracing Fear, which I was also doing. That means there existed a strange paradox. I hated and repressed Fear, yet I also loved and pursued it like a woman pursues her lover. I would do absolutely anything to be connected to Fear, to feel that intimacy and aliveness when I was around it—even jump off a seventy-foot cliff or ski a you-fall-you-die mountain, for a single taste of it.

Fear must have thought I was crazy then. *Come here! No, wait, go away!*

Back then, that was okay, though. I was wild and free and getting loads of attention. Everything was on my terms, and frankly, I loved feeling crazy.

WE GIVE IT EVERYTHING WE GOT

One night a man was crawling on his hands and knees around a huge parking lot, looking for his lost keys.

A woman, passing by, offered to help. They set up a grid pattern. The woman started at one end of the parking lot, and the man started at the other. For a half hour they zigzagged the whole parking lot, then met in the center. Still no keys.

"Okay, let's try this instead," she said. "Where did you last see them?"

He responded, "You know that bar over on State Street? I parked outside the bar, walked inside and had a quick beer, and when I came out, no keys."

Stunned, she exclaimed, "But that bar is half a mile away. Why are we looking for your keys in this parking lot?"

He replied, "The light is better here."

Having no interest in the dark side of life, have you ever ramped up your efforts to embrace only the light side, launching a noble self-improvement project with the *Rocky* theme music playing in your mind? Will and Determination (two other employees) kick in to help you strive to become a better you—a you who is free from Fear. You want to be fearless!

Get the mind more involved, the teachers say. The Thinking Mind may create all your problems, but it can solve them, too. Simply figure Fear out, and learn how to rationalize it away.

Or maybe you should ramp up your spiritual practice. Meditate. Do yoga. Talk to a therapist, life coach, or your wise aunt Judy. Become one with your truth. Give a promotion to Love and Gratitude. Become one with the universe and the 5,000 lovely children will thrive and the 5,000 unwelcome children will magically go away. Those nasty little voices have nothing to do with being a healthy human being, right?

Or perhaps you build walls, thicker and stronger all the time, denying Fear access to your castle. Maybe you overcompensate and walk around being cocky and self-righteous, avoiding vulnerability, locking out the Fear. (This I personally found to be very effective.)

Or another classic strategy: Fake it until you make it! The crowd is large, and lots of people are watching. This is not a time to show "weakness." Just think positive thoughts and pretend—*I ain't afraid of nothing*—until even you believe it.

All of this in order to avoid saying these simple words, as natural as wind on a warm, sunny day: "I feel afraid."

AND IT HAS WORKED! (A LITTLE)

If you have a fork sticking out of your eye, simply take three peaceful deep breaths in, and breathe out the pain. Then, for fifteen minutes, meditate in the voice of Gratitude, focusing on all the parts of you that don't hurt. You are guaranteed to feel better.

But you'll still have a fork sticking out of your eye.

You're empowering Love and Fearlessness, and I'll be damned—it works! When you meditate, think happy thoughts, or practice with a teacher, you feel better, happier, more clear. *Hurrah!* you think. *This is the path.* You're more aligned with the truth of who and what you are. That neocortex actually bursts through the clouds more often and gives you the grandest view you ever imagined.

The Will is indeed a strong force. It may have gotten you to the top of that sky-high ladder by empowering your 5,000 good voices, which is quite an accomplishment. If the top of that ladder works for you—if you feel everything is wonderful and you've sufficiently gotten rid of Fear and all those other ratty children—by all means stay there.

But when the view doesn't feel high enough anymore, or if you notice that people are pissing you off, or you seem overly protective and defensive, or you don't feel real intimacy with your partner, or you're burned out, or a million other things that don't make sense given that you have such a glorious view, then start to reconsider your efforts.

When you're ready for something new—a role change, a new level of achievement, or a desire to stop doing good things in favor of doing *great* things—contemplate descending the ladder. When you realize that the ladder is sticky like flypaper and you can't move off it on your own, open this book and continue reading.

Whenever you're ready, let's get you focused on what really works, what is really going to take you even higher up to the truth about Fear as nature intended, and thus the truth about you and your life.

For your intention is in the right place. The only problem is that the ladder has been leaning against the wrong wall.

CHAPTER 3

RUN, BUT YOU CAN'T GET AWAY

NOW WE'RE MODERN

We like to talk about how life used to be simpler, and it truly was. Either it rained or it didn't. Or maybe you caught two fish instead of three. Today you have the same body and brain as your ancestors did. Your genetic makeup is no different. What *is* different, though, is that you live in modern times. *You* may not have changed, but things certainly have. You have iPhones, base jumping, and *really* fast cars. More happens in twenty-four hours than used to happen in twenty-four years. The music is louder, the colors brighter, the days fuller than a zit about to pop.

The state of the human experience is better than ever compared with any time in history, yet still you endure boundless hatred, blame, despair, and ignorance, plus weapons and enemies never encountered before. You also face unique challenges, such as overpopulation, political hostilities, and climate change.

So hey, Lizard Brain, *how's it going with all this?*

Lizard Brain is manufacturing fear faster than Joey Chestnut eats a hot dog—that's how it's going.

What you're experiencing is more of everything, including thoughts firing like a machine gun, and emotion flowing through your system like Class V white-water rapids. To repress Fear today, you have to build twenty dams a day. And that's on top of all that other stuff you've got to do.

Bills, job, food, kids, remodeling, banking, taxes, traffic, laundry, aches and pains, diseases, and 500 e-mails a day. Throw in your primary energy source coming from deep-fried GMOs covered in ranch dressing. Is it working? Do you still have the energy to avoid, ignore, or fight anything negative, especially Fear? Can you still remain expressionless while holding your pitchfork, sweet as June Cleaver, smooth as Don Draper?

The word *survival* was recently on the cover of *Time* magazine twice in one month, so I'm guessing no.

TROUBLE IN THE BASEMENT

At age twenty-three, the summer before I first jumped the Palisades, I did an odd thing. Instead of training for moguls on glaciers like my peers, I decided to create my personality anew.

Having been insecure since childhood, whatever confidence I had as an adult was based on being pretty and being a decent skier. Not wanting to feel insecure my whole life, knowing I wouldn't always be pretty or ski great, I decided to spend four months traveling by myself in Asia to work on my self-esteem.

With this in mind, I had two rules for the trip:

1. I would make myself as ugly as possible: wear my Coke bottle glasses instead of contacts, not bathe much, and wear only frumpy clothes.
2. I would not talk to anyone about skiing.

I didn't know it at the time, but I realize now that this trip was a deep dive into Fear. Not only was it scary to go to Asia by myself; I didn't even know what or where Asia was when I called the travel agent. I also plunged into every scary situation presented, traveling eight days through Bangladesh just to witness real human suffering and volunteering for Mother Teresa's Home for the Dying, in Calcutta, India. Off the tourist path in the Philippines, I wound up being scammed by a group of thirty people over three days and had to leave the country at gunpoint. And the worst? After enduring hundreds of leech bites while trekking in Nepal, I almost lost my right leg to gangrene.

This trip was the most high-impact four months of my life. I came home in time for winter a totally different person.

After not having thought of skiing in months, something alarming happened. Not only did I jump the Palisades that season and become recognized overnight as the best woman big-mountain extreme skier in the world, but I also went from last place in little local mogul competitions the year before to making the US Ski Team . . . within three months.

Now, let's do the math. It wasn't because of training; I hadn't skied all summer, plus I'd never actually had any formal ski instruction besides a few lessons in elementary school. And it wasn't because of commitment: A mere three years earlier, at age twenty, I was still skiing in jeans. I wouldn't even spring for a pair of ski pants.

It was my willingness to go on a Fear quest that led me to become world class in two different sports in one season. This while competing against kids who'd gone to high school ski academies and had the best trainers in the world their whole lives. It was staggering how good I got, how confident I became, and how fast, only by forging a love affair with Fear and being open to the lessons it affords.

This makes it all the more sad that, as with any relationship, the love affair was about to end. A year after that trip, the honeymoon over, Fear and I then entered into a fifteen-year battle. Our relationship, which had always been strained, was about to get ugly.

When energy in motion stops, it does not get destroyed. It has to go somewhere. And that's when things get messy. Thanks to years of repression, Fear is now trapped, unexpressed, in the basement. Welcome to the primary source of all madness.

Let's be clear. What you've now done is taken an employee you can count on and alienated him. You've locked him away. He's down there in the dark, he can't see, he can't breathe, and feels he has no hope for a better future.

Imagine, for a moment, what it's like for Fear to be down there. How would you feel if you were rejected, ignored, and hated, not just by yourself but by damn near everyone on the planet? No one cares about you. No one considers what you have to say. They call you annoying, an enemy, an embarrassment. Certainly not a welcome part of their life.

My guess is that you'd feel terrible and wonder what the hell happened. You're here to help, not hurt. You have not only this self's but also humanity's best interests in mind. They wouldn't *exist* if not for you. And you've been . . . discarded? It doesn't make any sense.

Down in the basement, you are in darkness—there are no windows, no light—and you're upset, anxious, angry, confused, disoriented, blind, and groping for breath and clarity.

And remember, you were hired to do a job: to be afraid. The corporation still needs you. You desperately want to find your way out and fulfill your responsibilities.

But under the circumstances, you're no longer merely afraid, like you're supposed to be—now you're terrified.

Fear is now trouble for three reasons:

First because Fear is a part of you: Whatever it feels down there, you feel.

Second: The basement is actually the Body. The Body has become the dumping ground and storage area for unfelt, unwelcome Fear. This is not what your Body was designed for.

And third, the big one, which is about to become very obvious: *Fear will not be denied.*

The US Ski Team! I felt like you can fake most things, like pulling off a few spectacular cliff jumps one morning for the cameras, but when it comes to weekly competitions against other world-class athletes? No way.

About to have my photo taken with the team, I put on my new

jacket with the USA logo for the first time and stood next to people I'd only read about in magazines, smiling and wondering, "How did I get *here*? And how long before they find out I'm an impostor?"

Of course, I had to ski really well to have gotten there. Even still, I felt like a fake as the photographer snapped away, which raised the question: If not the skiing, what exactly, besides this idiotic smile, *was* I faking?

FEAR WILL NOT BE DENIED

A whining child is trying to get her mother's attention. The mother ignores the child, and the child goes away. The mother thinks, "Success!"

Later, the child comes back, whining louder than before. Again the mother ignores the child, and the child goes away. What a relief!

Again and again the child comes back, each time sooner than the last, whining louder and louder, staying longer and longer. Looking to gain that same relief, all the mother does anymore, all day, is ignore the child. Soon she has nothing left for anything else but this effort.

Thirty years later, the child is permanently by her mother's side, now screaming, hysterical, dysfunctional, and immature, trying again and again to get the mother's attention. The mother sits there, now withered, sick, and weak. A shell, lost in her efforts to still make the child go away.

If you squeeze a balloon, it'll bloop out wherever there's an opening.
If you plug an erupting volcano, it will explode out the cracks.
If you abuse a cat, it will crap on your pillow.
Abused Fear will also eventually act out. Usually in one of two ways:

1. You didn't get its message the first time, so Fear feels desperate to make sure you do now. Whenever it sees a chance, it will seep out any and all cracks and be as loud, irrational, uncomfortable, whining, or moody as possible—so that you cannot, will not, ignore it again. As a result, you will feel pickled in an unreasonable amount of irrational Fear, Anxiety, and Stress.

2. If you're really guarded and hold enough controlled tension in your body during the day—keeping the cracks tightly filled—you may remain unaware of Fear's presence, like I was during my ski career. It then comes out only in covert ways, when your guard is down—say, when you try to sleep at night. Fear never sleeps, so it will use that time to finally speak and keep you up. Or when you're on autopilot or tired, you may say or do things not in line with your self-perception. Or emotions like Anger and Sadness, or seemingly irrational ones like Jealousy or Unworthiness, might keep erupting, and you'll have no idea where it's coming from.

There are as many pathological ways in which repressed Fear either obviously or covertly runs your life from the basement as there are people. How it shows up will be different for everyone, of course, because everyone is different. As we explore these characteristics of repressed Fear further then, prepare to be shocked. For if there's a problem in your life, any problem at all, I guarantee that your putting Fear in the basement has something to do with it.

After my big breakthrough year, I blew my knee out the very next season. It was pretty violent, a real knee-in-a-blender moment that would have made a great scene in a horror movie. My first reaction, though? I wasn't horrified. I wasn't pissed.

I was relieved.

Relieved? What an odd reaction. I didn't know then, but I see it now, that once Asia was over, I went back to repressing Fear. Competing in moguls on a world-class level or jumping off bigger and bigger cliffs on skinny skis apparently proved scarier than Asia, and I couldn't handle it. Reverting to childhood success at being tough and unafraid, I put Fear back in the basement in order to do what I wanted to do in those mountains.

I had no idea at the time that smothering Fear was both physically and emotional abusive to my body. Where does all that Fear get stored, anyway? I see now what happened that day. My body, and Fear, exhausted from being abused, said, *Screw you, I need a break,* and blew out a knee.

All the voices in my basement were that desperate for a break from the Controller. They were relieved by the injury and, thus, so was I.

||||||||||||||||||||||||||||||||||||||||||||||||||||||||||||||||||||||||||||||||||||||||||||||||||||||||||||||||||||

REPRESSED FEAR SHOWING UP AS "NEGATIVE" VOICES: YOUR SHADOW

Much like how red, yellow, and blue—our primary colors—form the basis of the entire color spectrum, we also have primary emotions: Anger, Sadness, Joy, the Erotic, and, of course, Fear. Together, these are the emotions from which all your human experience is created. Fear is the flour making up the cake called Guilt, the sugar making up the cookie called Unworthiness. Or, if you prefer Popsicles: Fear is the ice, Jealousy is the flavor.

What I'm saying is that Fear is the primary ingredient behind all 5,000 "bad" voices. Behind Jealousy is always Fear. Behind the Villain is always Fear.

It makes sense, then, that if you're unwilling to feel or acknowledge Fear, you're likely unwilling to acknowledge the Abuser, Guilt, Shame, Inadequacy, or any "dark" voice in your life. So down they all go. "Not me," you say on the surface. "I'm all love and light."

But if Fear—one lone employee out of 10,000—trapped in the basement can covertly sabotage your life, imagine now what 5,000 can do. Jealousy, Guilt, Shame, Delusion, Powerlessness, Unworthiness, Inadequacy, the Abuser, Negativity, and thousands more, trapped down there together— what's their relationship to Fear? you may wonder. What happens next?

Good questions. Are you ready for the answer?

It's crowded down there, for one. There's only so much storage capacity, and once you exceed it, things start to seep out the cracks.

These emotions are also collaborating in supportive, strategic, and mutually beneficial ways. They compensate for your choice to ignore them by enabling and empowering one another, then use this greater power to accomplish their shared goal, which is to get out and do their jobs in any way possible.

Fear, being the ringleader, sees this as a massive opportunity. It can align with Jealousy to hijack the mind, spin a good tale, and together they will ride each other like missiles to the surface to express themselves. Fear can ride any of them to the surface, whether it's Gossip, Shallowness, or Gluttony. The result? You may not even be aware of Fear anymore; instead you're just crazy jealous, gossip a lot, are shallow, or overeat. That's still Fear expressing itself, but in its twisted, covert way. Which is the only way it speaks if it's in the basement.

Over time, this can be a reliable solution for unexpressed Fear, a repeatable habit or implant it can use again and again, so that it, and all these voices, can get out and do their jobs. And the longer they've been down there—since childhood, perhaps—the more conjoined, clever, and covert they become.

Over time, they may even become so clever that they put you in situations that are ideal for allowing them to emerge. Maybe you date only men who cheat on you, so that Jealousy can always speak. Or you leave late for work so that when someone inevitably gets in your way, anger can emerge. You look for evidence to support what a victim you are, how unworthy you are; or you seek out opportunities for Self-Righteousness, all so that trapped and these other Fear and these other Voices can express themselves.

This is what happens when you're unwilling to allow negativity, discomfort, or unpleasantness into your life. It's a big, big deal to repress a voice. Any seemingly unpleasant "bad" voice you won't look at becomes your shadow, the darkness that follows you everywhere, messing up your life. And while you may have stopped noticing it, make no mistake: Everyone else can still see it.

When you're unwilling to recognize that sometimes you're a real jerk, or you feel unworthy, or you're afraid, and you deny these "negative" voices, they generally express themselves in one of three dark ways:

1. You're aware of the voice itself, coming out in an irrational way, as an obvious part of your life. If you repress Jealousy (*I don't want to feel this!*), you feel more and more irrationally jealous over time. If you see Sexuality as bad and repress it, it comes out as any kind of deviant sexuality, such as addiction to porn or unhealthy fetishes or attractions. This explains the behaviors of priests who have fallen from grace. If you repress feelings of Unworthiness, you feel more unworthy every year. And on and on.

2. The voice cannot be found—you don't experience it at all—but it comes out redirected in other, unexpected ways. One way is that whatever voice you repress, you then judge harshly in others. If you repress your own Weakness, you can't stand people who are weak. If you repress Judgment, you are very judgmental toward anyone who is judgmental. Or you hate people who are haters. You show off how much you're not into showing off. You may even growl, "I'm not rude. You're the one who is rude." You actually take on the very flavor of the voice you repress, but you are completely blind to it, in denial and delusional.

3. Or the repressed voice shows up as a form of compensation that can even take over your whole personality. Disowned Jealousy—"I'm just not a jealous person"—comes out instead as Criticism or Impatience toward your partner. Disowned Unworthiness comes out as Entitlement, or making demands. Disowned Powerlessness: You act very aggressive and cocky. Here's a funny one: Disowned Snarkiness may make you overly kind, but then you walk around feeling superior in your Kindness, which is another form of Snarkiness.

Which is how, thinking that you have controlled these "bad" parts of you, you've only succeeded in unconsciously falling under their power. You have inadvertently become their puppets. Whatever you try to control will always wind up controlling you.

The other side effect is that you're also not aware anymore of what you're feeling, or who you truly are. You're instead focused on what you *don't* want to feel and who you don't want to be. Your focus is not "I feel afraid" or "I feel unworthy." Instead it's "I don't want to be afraid" or "I don't want to feel unworthy." Before you know it, the refrain of "I don't want! I don't want!" becomes your life.

Which is why focusing on what you *don't* want to feel instead of what you *are* feeling is the first thing I address when a client is stuck for any reason. And I mean *any*. If something is going wrong in your life, the only question to ask is: What dark shadow about yourself are you unwilling to look at and own? And, more important, what latent Fear are you refusing to acknowledge? Look at this and all of your problems and behaviors can finally be explained—and addressed.

THE PARTNER THEORY OF FEAR

Here's another dark way that repressed Fear can make its mark. If you don't feel Fear, and your partner or another family member feels it to the extreme, it may inadvertently be your fault.

Not owning Fear is like leaving laundry all over the house: Someone has to pick it up for you. Someone else must deal with it on your behalf.

A classic example of this is the laid-back husband and the over-anxious wife. The more laid-back he becomes, the more anxious she becomes. In his refusal to own his own Fear, she has to own not only hers but also his. Someone has to be the responsible one who deals with the discomfort of life, right?

IT'S CYCLICAL

A ferocious samurai known for picking fights demanded to see a famous Zen master. He was granted entry and, once he stood before the master, barked out a question: "Teach me about heaven and hell."

The master, looking him up and down, firmly replied, "Absolutely not. You're rude and aggressive. You're closed-minded and pathetic. Leave immediately."

Stunned, the samurai pulled out his sword, raised it, and was about to cut off the master's head when he heard the master say:

"That . . . is hell."

The samurai paused, dropped his sword with a clatter, fell to the ground, and in tears of realization started kissing the master's feet, saying *thank you* over and over.

The master whispered, "That . . . is heaven."

You're living in hell whenever you want to cut the head off one of these "bad" voices.

In Zen tradition, the word *hell* in Japanese can be translated as "no space." The word *heaven* can be translated as "spaciousness." Meaning that if you open up space in your life for Fear or any other Basement Voice to come out and do its thing, you'll be living in heaven.

For none of these voices, including Fear, are a problem if they're owned and honored. They're a natural part of you, and you would be incomplete without them. Owned and honored, they offer wisdom and an honest perspective that includes a full vision of who and what you are.

Imagine how much easier life would be if you could just allow yourself space to say, *I feel afraid. I feel inadequate. I am being abusive. Sometimes I, too, am rude.* Do you see how much tension you must hold to remain shut down to any part of your "dark" side?

But it's not so easy, is it? Due to repression, the wisdom of Fear and these other "bad" voices have become more lost over time. Now all you're aware of is their dark and hellish ways of communicating from the basement. Which makes you, ironically, avoid these voices more, and commit to keeping them even *more* repressed. Year after year this happens, until Fear and all his comrades become even more covert, more blind, and even more desperate.

Yet Fear and these others, if you would drop the sword and take the time to contemplate them, are truly not dark voices; they just appear that way after generations of repression. It is merely that the light of consciousness has not been shined upon them. As the Beastie Boys sing, "Dark is not the opposite of light; it's the absence of light." Shine the light on any dark voice and it, too, becomes light. The shadow of the voice goes away. The light appears.

Are you starting to see the madness and complications from all this thinking and controlling away a "negative" voice? And realize that shouldn't blame these voices for being dark, when it is you who have caused the problems by putting them in the dark?

So here's where we stand. Humanity is stuck on a racetrack of repeating this problem, going round and round, with no exit in sight. It feels as if there's simply no way out. You can't find exits because, frankly, until now, you don't even know you were on this racetrack.

But now you do. And here's the exit: You cannot deny that Fear isn't tied to these other voices. And you cannot deny that shutting down Fear is causing you problems. Your current relationship with Fear simply must be addressed.

If you have an irrational Unworthiness, Guilt, Ignorance, Anger, or Shame problem—you name it—you will be unable to get off this racetrack until you look at or feel the underlying Fear. It all comes back to that unwinnable war you created, and your strained relationship with Fear.

ANGER

You also have a major employee called Anger. Anger is another emotion from which your human experience is created. Just as no one is without Fear, no one is without Anger. Also manufactured by the Lizard Brain, it's used alongside or instead of Fear for specific situations. For example, if a caveman encounters a saber-toothed tiger, Fear is the right choice. Fear is flight. *Run!* If, however, the caveman encounters a dude trying to steal his woman, Anger is the better choice. Anger is conflict, battle, *fight!* It makes him throw a vicious punch. The Lizard Brain, being all about running or punching, sends out Fear for running and Anger for punching.

Anger, much like Fear, is simple, with a deep, ancient wisdom. Sharper than Fear, abrupt, more active and specifically targeted, its intention is to push away whatever is in its path. It's a "not on my watch" burst of energy felt in the body, with an unmistakable and purposeful message: Take immediate action and protect against boundary violations. It's supposed to right all wrongs.

Sadly, this wisdom is rarely available anymore in its pure form because of social conditioning. When you're young, Dad says, "We don't do that" about Anger (I call it Anger shaming), and the madness begins.

You think controlling Fear is tough? Try controlling Anger. It's intense and mighty, and the Controller has to really step it up. It takes its biggest sword and three of its deepest breaths to tame that dragon. The Controller can successfully monitor your tone, choke back what you really want to say, or walk you away from an argument. Then, after a spell, you can come back more peaceful, feeling pretty good about yourself for calming Anger down.

Yet consider: If you were the voice of Anger—whose job it is to be angry, not joyful or playful—and you were told, "Go away and never return" by billions of people every day, told to shut the hell up, dismissed as unwelcome, unwanted, embarrassing, and childish, would that make you less angry, or more angry?

Exactly.

Because so few people have a welcoming relationship with Anger, at this point all we know is its repressed version. It shows up, and holes get punched in walls. People get thrown out the window. You get attacked. Or go on the attack. Drama, violence, rage, and angst ensue.

Tell me to go away? says Anger. A few days later it comes back, holding a mightier sword than before, and cuts your silly little peanut head off.

It's a vicious cycle. You repress Anger, it seemingly departs, but now it runs amok in your unconscious world. It's down there gathering strength, until it sees a chance and, alongside Fear, explodes out in weird, disjointed, often embarrassing ways. Which makes you want to never, ever let it out of the basement again. So you repress it even more.

Every therapist, self-help course, and mentor supports your doing this. They may start out saying, "Anger is natural; you must allow yourself to feel it," but they inevitably finish with "Okay, now let's get it under control." That's like saying, "A child is a blessing; now let's beat her." So you take three even deeper breaths, sign up for more Anger management or meditation classes that promise a better future, and repeat mantras like "I am calm. I am peaceful," which makes the emotion go underground further, becoming even more covert and twisted in ways you can't see. And the war between you two is reignited again and again.

Until, after all these years, Anger is pretty pissed off. Its pure, wise form long forgotten, Anger no longer represents its natural intelligence and purpose. Today, it mostly represents its own angst.

SERIAL KILLER SIAMESE TWINS

Why, in a book about Fear, am I writing so much about Anger?

Because behind the Anger is always Fear.

With Fear, adrenaline starts the heart beating faster, providing more blood as its energy comes up the spine and out the limbs, propelling you to action. Thus you have the strength to run (legs) or punch (arms).

Like the mama bear protecting her cub. She stands up with arms high and wide, flooded with energy and blood, claws out, ready to rip your head off. She looks angry, right? But look again: It's Fear. She's afraid you'll hurt her cub. Add a drop of intensity, though, and it's Anger.

Because they are so intimately tied together, it's hard to differentiate between these two emotions. So here's where things get sketchy. The chilling truth is: If Anger is made up mostly of Fear, and the Fear behind the Anger is pathological and twisted, naturally the Anger will be, too. If you have rancid flour? The pastry is gross. Fishy ice? The Popsicle is repulsive.

No wonder the Anger you see is so dramatic and vicious. Anger not only represents its own angst at being abused; it also represents Fear's angst. So at this point, probably 95 percent of what you consider Anger isn't Anger at all; it's Fear from the basement asserting itself. Anger gets mistaken for Fear most of the time.

Which is why today, a man punching someone is a clear sign of repressed Fear. Modern violence is repressed Fear.

And this is why Anger management courses seeking to help you control Anger are just a Band-Aid. These courses rarely address the disowned Fear behind the Anger. Plus, teaching repression and control of Anger itself, which is the only resource that seems to "work," actually *exacerbates* the problem further, as we've learned.

If I were in an Anger management course, I would be really pissed off about this.

All this repression and abuse toward Fear and Anger has thus turned two otherwise nice kids into serial killer Siamese twins. Similar to other shadow voices, these twin emotions currently express themselves in one of two ways:

1. You may be very aware of Anger as the bubbles of Angst, Violence, Blame, and Accusation percolate through your day. Or it may be mostly dormant, building until the moment your guard is dropped, and then out it comes, roaring, sudden, and explosive, in the form of externally directed rage.

I say "externally directed" because, often working alongside Blame, Drama, or Self-Righteousness, Anger starts its sentences with the word "You." It comes out as "*You* are making me angry. *You* are doing this to me." It points fingers and feels justified. You feel justified, which seemingly gives you a free pass to do or say whatever you want.

This is how Fear and Anger work together from the basement, intending to control and manipulate other people. Anger wants a reaction so it can continue its rampage, and it *will* get one. We're all familiar with the cycle of abuse: If a parent is abusive to the child, that child tends to grow up abusive toward the world. It's called displaced aggression. The same thing occurs with emotions: When you try to control and manipulate Fear and Anger, they will in turn come out trying to control and manipulate others. They're very good at it, too.

And usually the people you're pointing fingers at get engaged with the drama, because they're repressing Fear and Anger as well.

2. On the other hand, if you don't identify with this first style and think, "Oh, no, I'm simply not an angry person," this second pattern is for you. Of course, no one is without Anger. If you think you're an exception, likely you're just really good at refusing to feel it, and Anger (and therefore Fear) now gets contorted and comes out in other covert ways.

Here's a short list of what you may feel instead of Anger:

> NOTHING. Numb, bored, and lacking motivation. Passion and fire are severely limited.

> POWERLESS. Like a doormat. You're shy and meek. If you run away from Anger, you run away from power.

> SOCIALLY RECLUSIVE. You retreat far inside yourself, building thicker walls to protect you from having to deal with Fear or Anger, and you won't allow yourself to get close to anyone.

> INDECISIVE. If you don't even know how you feel, it's very hard to make clear decisions.

> EXCESSIVE SADNESS OR DEPRESSION. In society, we're taught that Sadness is more acceptable than Anger (or Fear), so that is what you feel instead.

> EXCESSIVE JOY. You cling to that one experience. An overcompensating smile on your face, this can come across as inauthentic and prevent you from having a deeper life experience.

> HELPLESS OR HOPELESS. Which feels awful, so you kick the dog or yell at a stranger, because even a wee bit of Anger feels freeing.

> STRESSED, ANXIOUS. You feel it all the time, like you're in prison—

tight, confined, not free. One must hold a lot of tension to not have any cracks.

> NEGLECTED OR HURT. Being a victim feels safer than being a perpetrator.

> PASSIVE-AGGRESSIVE, MANIPULATIVE, CONTROLLING. More politically correct than Anger, but it's still looking for a reaction, and, like Anger, it *will* get one.

> JUSTIFIED FOR BAD BEHAVIOR, LIKE CHEATING ON A SPOUSE, STEALING, OR LYING. Don't get mad, get even, right? It's an action you can take that indemnifies the rage.

I could write a whole book on this subject. You may also act judgmental, gossipy, or condescending. You may complain a lot. You may become dominant, self-righteous, and impatient. You may act conceited, or cocky. You may become defensive, which is much easier than being offensive.

This last one is interesting. Have you ever said in defense, "I'm not an angry person," or "You're the one who's angry"? Many don't see themselves as angry (and therefore afraid), and while they might never raise their voices, or feel afraid, they appear to others as the angriest (and most afraid) of all. So often, how you see yourself is not what others see.

Ask your friends, or better yet a newly acquainted stranger, if they see you as an angry or fearful person. Hopefully they can be honest. Other people usually see what voices are running your life covertly and coming out in dark ways. They see your shadow immediately, for either you wear it like a cloak or you project it onto others.

The first one, numbness, is also interesting. Chronic pot smokers often get high in order to not deal with Anger. How do I know this? Because among my clients, chronic pot smokers—when they decide to quit—often report feeling very angry. Anger finally has a chance to come out of the basement. Which suggests that they smoke to self-medicate, so that they don't have to deal with Anger (and the underlying Fear). Basically they opt for stupidity (it's called dope for a reason) to not have to feel Anger.

Are any of these a good trade? I don't know. It's up to you to decide.

A GOOD TRADE?

While staying at a friend's house in Maui, I was awakened every morning at four by roosters, and again at six by a hysterical dog. By the fourth day, I was stabbing pillows.

Behind my Anger, though, as we're learning, was Fear. Fear of not getting enough sleep to write well. Fear of getting injured later while kiteboarding because I'm dopey from lack of sleep. Fear that my entire vacation was being ruined. Fear of being out of control, which was how I was beginning to feel.

I didn't lie there in bed afraid, though. I was aware only of Anger. Anger jacked me up to potentially deal with the situation by killing the rooster or talking to the dog owner (I didn't). But here's the thing: Because Anger was present, I never had to feel Fear. Anger is like Fear's big, burly brother, hopefully taking care of everything. That's why it's so intoxicating.

Which makes it seem like an excellent trade for Fear. Anger is meant to right any wrong. It even rights the "wrong" that is Fear. So congratulations! You did it. With Anger, you seemingly don't have to deal with Fear. Anger is a much more safe and powerful feeling than Fear.

Being so righteous, Anger also makes it so you don't have to deal with any of the shadow voices. It projects them onto others; *they* made you feel and act this way! It's *their* fault. "*You* are making me jealous. *You* are making me feel helpless." It projects your hurt, weakness, doubt, insecurity, and vulnerability onto others and saves you from having to look at your own delusion and ignorance. And, voilà, not only do you not have to acknowledge Fear—you don't have to acknowledge any of your crap.

Anger can also make it so you don't have to deal with Sadness. You see this in kids a lot. If things aren't right in their lives, Anger is a safer, more powerful feeling than Sadness, another primary emotion from which your human experience is created. No kid wants to feel sad—there's too much victim in it. There's no power there. With Anger, there's power.

Is it a true power, though?

"Kristen, I'm driving from Oregon and I'm coming back to kill you. I'm going to f*&^ing kill you," he said. Shivers ran through my entire body. How exciting.

My ex-boyfriend was violent, volatile, and threatening, and I simply loved it. Not him as much anymore, but it.

It started in Tibet, of all places. I had snuck into the country over a 20,000-foot pass in the middle of the night to try and illegally climb and ski the sixth-tallest mountain in the world, Cho Oyu. The Chinese authorities found out about me and two other Americans also there on the mountain illegally. Fortunately, we evaded arrest by abandoning most of our gear and running toward the Nepal border in the middle of a night time blizzard.

I lived for that kind of thing. I simply loved Fear. I loved the way it tasted, smelled, felt. I would have licked it if I could.

High from the excitement of this adventure, back in the safety of Nepal, about to fly home and wondering about my next fix, I wrote in my journal, "I'm attracted to bad boys. I need to get this out of my system. I need to have a dangerous relationship with an asshole."

Within a week I had met him. He was perfect. His name was Aaron.

Wild, curly black hair, reckless, totally in charge, he had a darkness to him that made me melt. I called my parents the week we met and said, "I'm going to fall in love with an unstable guy for a few years. It's going to be horrible, and I'm probably going to barely survive. Just know this is a phase I'm going through and eventually I'll be okay, okay?"

Ooookay, they said.

It went exactly as planned: two years of rabid lust and love, followed by an absolutely thrilling year of drama and terror while we broke up. I cultivated the whole experience like a horticulturist.

Unconsciously I said all the right things to trigger the experience I wanted, and my bad boy didn't disappoint. He broke into my house and destroyed journals, coffee mugs, furniture, and windows.

I called the police exactly the same number of times I had the phone ripped out of my hands and thrown against the wall (seven). He never went so far as to hit me, but he did threaten violence, often daily. He threatened to kill me multiple times. He pointed guns at me, he shook me until I passed out. And I simply loved it. I'd never felt so alive. The drama was delicious.

It felt exactly the same as when I skied. Better, in fact. Less injury. It barely occurred to me that this was an odd way to be.

WHO HAS THE POWER

If the only Fear and Anger you know is the disowned, immature kind, these emotions cannot, will not, ever be a healthy part of your life. A fish-flavored Popsicle will always make you gag. The abused child will always self-abuse and also abuse others.

But what if you were to take your power back? Not by repressing Anger anymore, which is a false sense of power, but by making a choice to stop repressing these voices.

It works like this: Each voice in your corporation has great wisdom, and great delusion—every single one. As you're learning, if a voice is repressed, only its delusion comes out. But as you'll learn next, when any voice is taken out of the basement and owned and honored, only its wisdom comes out.

So what if, instead, you became curious about Fear and Anger and all the other "bad" voices? What if you were to let them out of the basement and give them an honored role in your corporation? Anger would then have a chance to just be angry when the right situation arose. Sadness would have a chance to be sad. Fear would have a chance to be afraid. There would be no overcompensation, contortion, cross fire, or chaos swirling around in your unconscious world. There would be no angst brewing under the surface. Anger would come in and do its job when needed, in the wisest and most compassionate way possible, righting wrongs with integrity instead of drama or violence. Then it would be done. (You may remember from chapter 2 that scientists suggest that this build-peak-decline happens in about ten to ninety seconds.)

In my experience, if this were the case, 95 percent of what we know as modern Anger would dissolve. So, too, would the Anxiety, Defensiveness, Blame, Judgment, Manipulation, Gossip, Depression, etc., and the irrational Fear that goes along with it.

But in order to get to this place, and to get your power back, you do realize you'd first have to recognize that you're powerless over Fear and Anger. Could you do that?

You'd have to stop trying to control and instead feel and experience these emotions when they show up. Is this even a possibility?

It would involve trusting the process. You'd have to let them out of the basement, assuming they wouldn't turn into viscous dragons, threatening everyone around you or biting the head off every dream or hope you ever had. You'd have to consider that they're assets and allies with your best interests in mind, and that they would immediately forgive you for decades of abuse.

Hard to do.

The universe wasn't going to let me get away with any of this repression nonsense. That much is now obvious.

Remember that knee injury? Unwilling to let it drag me down, now running like Sadness and Anger, five months post-op I thought, *What's the most radical thing I could do?*

Why, riding my bike across India, of course. So that's what I did.

Then came two months of being stared at, followed, or tipped over by children hanging on to my panniers and dragging their feet on the ground. I don't think a single kilometer went by without a parade of locals running or biking after me out of curiosity. Add to that hourly near-death experiences as black-smoke-puking diesel trucks ran me off the road. I even had a near-death experience being chased by a fixated bull.

Each day, I rode until I was tired, put my feet down, looked to the right, and slept there, wherever that was. It was often a friendly but very poor, crowded family home. In the middle of the night, rats jumped on me, or an uncountable number of biting or splatting bugs (where the %$#@ did they even come from?) used me as a trampoline. Wild packs of dogs howled most nights.

I could write more about this journey, but what really matters is the end. It all leads to one single moment on the last day, when I simply lost it. I finally put my foot down—literally and figuratively—turned to the crowd on their bikes behind me, and howled at them like a rabid dog: "Stop following me! Leave me alone!" Complete with sobbing, spittle, hysterical gestures, and childlike stomping.

Ohhh, they loved it. I may have even gotten a standing ovation.

The next day, back in Kathmandu, where I'd originally started, my surgery knee swelled up to the size of a grapefruit, for no apparent reason. Clearly my body knew the ride was over and it was now safe to implode. I flew home and found out that my new ACL had turned the consistency of wet toilet paper and disintegrated. I needed to have another surgery. It was October. The Olympics were that coming February.

I called the US Ski Team and quit.

WHY FEAR CAN FEEL OVERWHELMING

You are a divine elephant with amnesia, trying to live in an ant hole.

—HAFIZ, FOURTEENTH-CENTURY PERSIAN POET

Just about everyone on the planet feels overwhelmed at times. Even people with slow lives get overwhelmed. We consider these moments unacceptable. When you "let" yourself become overwhelmed by emotion, it seems like a massive failure. That damn Controller lost control and let Fear, Anger, or Sadness flood your system! Until you "get it together again," you are now out of control with your emotions. Better hide.

Why does this happen?

With your good/bad discrimination, you either like an emotion or you don't. You either want to be with it or you want to separate from it. Wanting to separate from it is why parents, who truly can't help themselves, will say, "Turn that frown upside down" whenever you're sad, or "No need to be scared" whenever you're afraid. We want to rush not just ourselves but others through the feelings.

An extreme example of rushing through emotions is people who forgive a murderer for his crime not long after it's committed. At first glance, it seems so lovely. On second glance, they do this by rushing the now big voices of Fear, Anger, and Sadness out of their lives, quickly replacing them with the voice of Forgiveness, because they don't want to—or don't know how to—deal with them properly.

It's not just the unpleasant emotions, either. Any emotion, even Joy, can be overwhelming and distrusted in big doses. Tom Cruise jumps for Joy onto a couch—and everyone says he's weird and unstable. Have we gotten to the point where, if something moves us, that's simply not okay? We hide or rush past the feeling to accommodate others' opinions, needs, and expectations about emotions, and this, oddly, is deemed heroic. Never mind that it's at the expense of your own mental, spiritual, physical, and emotional health.

Here's what happens next: If you reach for a cookie—which is a natural urge—and stop mid-grab because you don't want to get fat, you short-circuit your brain. The Fear-manufacturing Lizard Brain, the emotion-processing limbic brain, and the higher-state neocortex are all working together, a complicated and elegant system with many voices in play. Like any complicated system, it needs to be in Flow. But if you short-circuit it, you stop the flow, and that unconsumed cookie will either consciously or unconsciously consume you all day.

Similarly, if Fear shows up and you use your Controller to short-circuit the process by stopping its rise, you also short-circuit the emotional system.

Like when you want to yell at the neighbor and don't, or want to cry but stiffen instead.

The energy of the cut-off emotion now has to go somewhere, and it sure as heck doesn't go into the atmosphere. Emotion is felt in the body, so when halted, it temporarily gets stored in the body (what we've been calling "the basement").

As more and more repressed Fear energy backs up, as with any blocked system, other parts of the body start to compensate. It's like if you have a blocked vein: All your other systems have to step it up. In the case of an emotional blockage or a kink in Flow, breathing gets shallow, tension shows up in your muscles, or you may start to feel numb. Adrenaline eventually shows up to push the blockage through, and the feeling that you just want to get out of here grows—*flee!* Or you want to fight, but you don't, so it builds and builds—until the body and the central nervous system can't handle the percolation any longer, and it all finally explodes into your system all at once.

Imagine a balloon. As energy gets stored inside it, the rubber of the balloon slowly gets bigger and bigger until it's the size of the state of Alaska. It finally pops, and *blammo,* you're overwhelmed. Or, even worse, overcome by a panic attack.

But don't blame Fear, Anger, or Sadness. That's merely what fills up the balloon. That's not fair to them. It's your blockage that is the problem. It's your unwillingness to go all the way with Fear through build, peak, and decline, over and over, that leads to this problem. You think you've gotten rid of the emotion, but it just gets stored in the balloon until it explodes.

This is why there's no such thing as overwhelming Fear. Fear is just Fear, it's not overwhelming. But if you've been in a battle with Fear that you can't win, the battle is what becomes overwhelming. You're trying to squash a bigger and bigger balloon, which is an overwhelming task, and then it explodes.

None of this would happen if you just felt your emotions as they showed up, through build, peak, and decline, though fully and with consideration. For when you're open to them, nothing is overwhelming.

WHAT ABOUT BEING OVERLY EMOTIONAL?

Feeling emotions is healthy. If you cry when you're sad, get angry when it's warranted, and feel afraid when things are scary—that's not repression.

But you probably know someone who's *overly* emotional, like in a soap opera. Someone you could point to and say, "She doesn't repress her emotions at all. She feels them all the time—too much, in fact." Being overly emotional is actually a clear sign that you're repressing Fear (and/or Anger or Sadness). The question is: How can you tell the difference?

Easy. It's not a healthy, owned expression if one or more of the following occur:

> You don't feel moved or alive in a crisp way by the emotion; instead it feels devastating.

> You wish the feeling weren't so, or resist it in any way.

> You apologize for it, or are embarrassed by it.

> You blame others for making you feel this way.

> You feel like a victim to others, or a victim to the emotion.

> You feel excessive emotion that seems irrational or out of proportion to the situation.

> The emotion seems problematic in any way. It shows up as a disorder or a phobia.

> It shows up at times that don't make any sense.

> The emotion, and therefore you, seem to act very immature and childlike.

The last point is interesting. When you were four years old and Mom first told you, 'There's nothing to be afraid of," that's likely the age when you first put Fear in the basement. As with any child kept in a basement since age four, Fear hasn't had a chance to grow up and mature properly. It will only have the skills to communicate at a four-year-old level.

That means your corporation is now being unconsciously run by an uncomfortable, angry or sad, terrified, stressed-out, misunderstood, abused four-year-old. And what do we know about them? They're very emotional.

Thus, when I see a man throwing a childlike, angry tantrum, I know he's been repressing Anger for a long, long time. The same applies to a woman who cries a lot. I'll bet she hates that about herself but doesn't know how to stop. That's not her having a healthy relationship with her emotions; that's a symptom of repressing Sadness (and likely Fear and possibly Anger).

For remember: Whatever these emotions feel from the basement, you feel. However they act is how you act. Sadness can become very sad indeed when it's locked in the dark, cold basement.

MANIFESTATIONS OF REPRESSED FEAR

Next, let's dissect in greater detail how repressing Fear affects your life in so many varied and complicated ways. In today's world, there simply is no need to be in the dark anymore about why you are, or act in, a certain way. We have finally arrived. Here are the reasons for many of your problems.

Judgment of Self

There are 7.5 billion people on earth, all of whom want the same things. Fresh air and sunshine, of course, but also to be seen, heard, loved, understood, and considered. Basically, they want to be a welcomed part of society.

Our 10,000 voices are the same. Fear is the same.

This is why when people proclaim, "Love yourself," I'm hoping they mean love *all* parts of yourself, yes? For you can't love everything about yourself *except for Fear* and still call that love. It's like saying, "Love yourself, but not your eyeballs. If only I could get rid of my eyeballs, then I could love and be myself." Or "Love the world, but not alligators. The world would be a perfect place if not for that fatal flaw, alligators." Would you do that? Would that seem reasonable?

Of course not; it would be ridiculous. Yet when you say you want to overcome Fear, that's what you're saying. You may as well aspire to overcome food and water, too.

The most important relationship you will ever have is the one you have with yourself. Which brings us to the irony: If you don't love Fear, which is with you on a cellular level, you are not truly and completely loving yourself.

Whatever your relationship is with Fear, then, Fear being at your core, that's the relationship you have with yourself.

If you're judgmental against Fear, you're judgmental against yourself.

If you abuse Fear, you are abusing yourself.

Hate Fear, you hate yourself.

Avoid Fear, you avoid the truth of who and what you are—you avoid yourself.

Are you starting to get that Fear—being a fundamental part of you—whatever you do to it, you do to yourself?

Judgment of Others

When you fight Fear, you fight not only yourself, but the very nature of life itself, which leads to inevitable failure.

"Why can't I do this?" you'll think. This failure will wreck your self-esteem. This is made worse if you don't learn from such recurring failure and just keep doing the same thing over and over.

When the discomfort from feeling bad about yourself then gets to be too great, you will also start to feel bad about the world. Because you hate the thought of yourself being lame or wrong, you will start to instead see the world and others as being lame or wrong. We all know that if you don't love yourself, you can't love another.

Therefore, mistreat yourself by repressing Fear and you will eventually mistreat the world and others, even abuse them.

Here's what this looks like:

> The highs and lows of self-esteem become tied to your ability to control Fear.
> Control it and you feel good about yourself. Don't control it and you feel bad about yourself.
> Being able to control Fear, of course, is unstable and leads to inevitable failure.

> When you inevitably fail, "I'm afraid" translates to "I am worthless, I am a failure."
> This is followed by "I should be better than this."

Here's where things diverge. "I should be better" can now either be the train that takes you where you want to be, or clobber you like a train. Either path shuts you down into a belief system that involves making others wrong. If you're motivated by "I should be better than this" . . .

> You try harder to overcome Fear.
> Which leads to promotions of the Will, Determination, training your brain, mind over matter, and the Controller.
> As a result, you have more control over Fear, and you no longer feel as much Fear. You hold tension now and calcify whatever worked in order to preserve it.
> Your success leads to an Ego trip. *I'm amazing! I did it!* This leads to feeling superior, and then judgment of other people, especially ones who feel Fear: "I controlled it—why can't you?" They're seen as weak, stupid, victims, inferior. In being so right, you make others wrong.
> This results in your having no compassion, being annoyed by others, or excessively judging them for any weakness.
> Alternatively, you become a rescuer, seeing everyone as a victim who needs your guidance on how to live their lives so that they can be more like you.

If you're clobbered by "I should be better" . . .

> You now worry, "What if I get scared again?" *How embarrassing! I can't stand the discomfort of looking bad or feeling bad about myself.*
> The threat of failing again at controlling Fear becomes intolerable, so you choose an excessive form of control over your actions instead: You become unwilling to risk.

> Because people seem threatening unless they also buy into your process. Unwillingness to risk leads to excessive control over others. Others, who are not shut down, need to be.

> This makes you feel off, embarrassed about who you are—weird or too controlling—which leads to more excessive self-judgment: *I'm not who or what I want to be . . .*

> Which gets projected onto others . . . *and neither are you.*

Either path involves shutting down and making others wrong. This results in alienation, power struggles, and conditional loving of others.

If all this seems complicated, well, it is. And here's why: Fear is really simple, but with repression, the chaos that ensues within the unconscious depths of this corporation called You will always be complicated.

Blame

A man was in his canoe on the lake one morning. He dipped his hand in the water and, to his shock, found an oil slick. Disgusted, he jerked his hand out of the water and looked around furiously to identify the culprit. Was the nearby man, paddling his own canoe, dumping something? Was that factory alongside the river breaking a law? Was it coming from that broken Jet Ski?

Then he realized it was sunblock on his own hand.

When you decide it's wrong to feel Fear and you seek to control that emotion, you get really lost in that effort. When you are not successful and you refuse to blame yourself, you wind up blaming everything and everyone else.

You'll eventually believe the world is causing your problems and doing this *to* you, and that it's everyone else's fault. And you're adamant about it. What does this look like? Here are a few examples:

> If, deep down, you're afraid of something like therapy, or skiing, you call these things stupid, a waste of time and money. You're not wrong—it is wrong.

> If, deep down, you're afraid of rejection, you label the person doing the rejecting as wrong, an idiot. You're not wrong—he is.

> If you lose your job, you blame the career choice, the employer, or the industry as being flawed. You're not flawed—it is.

> If your marriage fell apart, rather than dealing with the Fear that you did this, that you ruined the relationship, you insist that you're not wrong—marriage itself is wrong and you're never doing *that* again. Or you'll argue that the person you were married to was wrong.

You project all your Fear onto others, whether it's people, creatures, systems, or things, whenever you're unwilling to own it yourself.

Of course, love relationships aren't immune to this process. When you're in love, there's always a powerful, prevalent fear of abandonment present. If that is repressed or unacknowledged, it will covertly take over your relationship. Repressed fear of abandonment can show up instead as demands, entitlement, wall building, immature Anger, power struggles, accusations, blame, etc., leading to feelings of separateness, victimization, villainization, defensiveness, and on and on. All this craziness to avoid the simple universal truth, which is "I'm afraid of being abandoned." Or "I'm afraid of being alone."

Conditionally loving yourself only leads to conditional loving of others. Abusing your bad voices leads to abuse of others. Now, I get that *abuse* is a strong word. But I don't think it's inappropriate. Anytime you try to get others to live according to your internal repression and struggle, and you blame your actions on them, that's abuse.

Of course, you don't do this to everyone and everything. This power struggle may just be with certain people or things in your life, and will come out in your own unique way.

Just know that if you have any struggles with yourself or with others, it's hard to see the correlation between your repression of Fear and these behaviors while you're in it, but it's there.

Crazy Mind

How does Fear accomplish all this brilliant masterminding? you may wonder. That's easy. Remember: Anger and other shadow voices have become puppets of repressed Fear. It's to the point that you may not even be aware of Fear anymore; you can't see that it operates these voices. Yet it runs *everything* from the basement. Including, of course, the Thinking Mind.

Yep, we're back to that wild monkey, the Thinking Mind. Your COO.

Fear, often using its buddy Anger, has the marvelous ability to hijack any of the 10,000 minds, but it knows that if it takes over the COO's job, the rest is easy. By hijacking the Thinking Mind, it can use thoughts, stories, ideas, and beliefs and create evidence to justify whatever it wants.

For example, if fear of rejection is not being dealt with, suddenly you'll notice everyone you come into contact with appears to be rejecting you. The evidence is right there. *That person just said no! Couldn't be more obvious than that!*

Fear can use the hijacked Thinking Mind (because it's so clever) to look for evidence to support anything Fear has to say—that you're ugly, you're stupid, your neighbor is a jackass, your wife is cheating, or the world is a bad place. These stories and thoughts are easily regenerated, again and again, since the Thinking Mind is the prism by which you experience everything, and any evidence to support whatever it seeks is easy to find. In doing so, Anger and Fear can talk again and again. And to you it all feels so justified!

Not only that, but the bigger the repressed emotions, the bigger the stories behind them. So if you have a huge story about why you should be jealous—and mind you, it may even be warranted—just know that the madness behind it is repressed Fear, working together with repressed Jealousy and Anger, all hijacking the mind. Complication ensues. Suddenly your Jealousy isn't a wise and compassionate tool warning you that something is wrong and it's time to reexamine your partner's commitment or make a change. Instead you're yelling, stalking, frantically looking for evidence, accusing, awake all night, riddled with Anxiety and Stress, and miles away from the truth of who and what you are.

This is an extreme example, but the point is that when Fear is in the basement, none of your employees are doing their jobs anymore as nature intended. Everyone is hijacked, especially the Thinking Mind. The shadow voices get weirder and more hidden every year. Anger is covering for many of them (including Fear). The Storyteller weaves crazy stories that may or may not be true. The Thinking Mind is trying to figure out what to do about all this, yet can't see its own part in the problem. Meanwhile, the Controller is exhausted, working his ass off, nights and weekends.

Internally, the fishy Popsicles are now all stuck together. They're just a big wad of melted-together, confused, sticky mess. All this because of your unwillingness to feel a simple, primary emotion called Fear.

A few years into my ski career, when I was twenty-six, one of my sponsors, Nikon, asked me to give a half-hour speech about Fear at its annual July sales meeting. I was thrilled. I decided to show them a video of my latest ski movie footage, then talk about how to get Fear under control. Which is what everyone talks about when they talk about Fear. It was a no-brainer.

Such a no-brainer that I didn't give the speech a thought. I was KRISTEN in capital letters, I was Fearless! Surely I knew about controlling Fear. I'd just speak from the heart.

The two weeks before the event, two friends were in town and we stayed up all night, every night. We slept only during the day. It was two of the best weeks of my life.

By the time I got on the plane the final morning, after pulling the last of our thirteen all-nighters, my speech, scheduled for that evening, still wasn't on my radar.

Having three seats to myself in the back, with the hum of the airplane comforting me, I promptly fell into a sleep coma. Only to be woken up ten minutes later with a punch to the stomach. It was Fear screaming, *Ohmygodyouforgotthevideo.*

I forgot the goddamn ski movie, the whole basis for my speech. They had a screen all set up, they'd paid me well, all I had to do for them all year long was this one speech, and I *forgot the video*? I was going to be sick.

The next day, with twenty-four hours of horror and shame behind me, Nikon rescheduled my talk for a day later and paid to have the video FedExed overnight. I was now following a professional keynote speaker who made a living at this. He was really good, too. There I stood, watching this guy work his magic, up next, still with no plans for what I was going to say, even more exhausted after twenty-four hours of Stress. Speak from the heart about controlling Fear? Suddenly I realized I had absolutely no idea what went on in my heart about Fear.

After thunderous applause for the guy, I was finally introduced. I stepped up onto the stage. Shaking, blinded by lights, I muttered that I had a video to show them. It started rolling. Five minutes later, the lights came back on and there I stood, looking out at the crowd.

My mouth went completely dry, so dry I couldn't speak. I just stood there, this fearless warrior, to speak about Fear, opening and closing her mouth like a fish in a bucket.

All I could make was little peeping noises.

―――

Keeps You Awake at Night

Ever wake up in the middle of the night with your mind doing backflips, Anxiety surging, and you can't get back to sleep? That's when this mind hijack is most obvious.

Fear, you see, doesn't sleep. When your guard is dropped, it's the perfect time for Fear to go on a major "I want to be free" joyride.

The funny thing is, what do sleep specialists teach? Feng shui your sleep environment (promote Peace to overshadow Fear). Get up and do something else, something relaxing (distract Fear, replace it with Calm). Meditate (breathe in stillness and Fear will dissipate). Take anti-anxiety medication (designed to repress emotions). Use cognitive behavioral therapy (reprogram your mind as a way to reprogram Fear). Or take sleeping pills, which will shut anyone up.

Such "letting go of crazy" helps you sleep a little better, which is encouraging, and keeps you trying these methods. Yet it's only treating the symptoms that come from repressed Fear, temporarily masking them, while inadvertently exacerbating the underlying cause.

Want to treat the cause instead? Feel and experience your Fear during the day; then you won't have to deal with it at night. It's so simple. Or, even better, just turn to whatever crazy voice is fretting in the night and, like any good mother would, ask it lovingly what it needs to say.

HOW TO FALL BACK ASLEEP AT NIGHT

If you have a problem, be it Depression, Insomnia, Anxiety, Anger, Jealousy, Guilt, Snarkiness, Passive-Aggressiveness, etc., try these words out: "I'm not dealing with my Fear."

Say it again.

Now be curious about the Fear you're dealing with. Or, even better, allow yourself to feel it.

Is that so bad?

This is a good thing to do if you have any problem in your life. And I mean any.

Stress and Anxiety

Here's a monster subject, especially in today's modern world. It's clear that Stress and Anxiety have run amok. Why? Excessive Stress and Anxiety are, of course, 100 percent the result of repressed Fear. I'll say that again, because it's a big, big deal: *Excessive Stress and Anxiety are 100 percent the result of repressed Fear.*

Let me explain: Stress and Anxiety are Fear. Men don't like to call it

Fear, because it's embarrassing. Women are more willing to call it Fear, although some call it Nerves, but make no mistake: This is Fear. Or rather, how Fear communicates. It's the language it uses. Fear speaks Stress and Anxiety. Fear uses the discomfort of Stress and Anxiety as language to get your attention.

As you know, Fear stuck in the basement feels threatened, even more stressed out and anxious than ever. It is going to communicate, then, not just as normal Stress and Anxiety but as excessive Stress and Anxiety. It is screaming from down there, *"Pay attention to me!"*

So not only will you experience excessive Stress and Anxiety by putting Fear in the basement. If you then *also* put its messengers—actual employees we'll now call Stress and Anxiety—in the basement, you have just stacked madness on top of madness.

Imagine for a moment life without Stress. And I mean all Stress. No Stress in love: *Is he or isn't he into me?* No Stress at work: *Will this or won't this succeed?* No Stress at the movies: *Will they or won't they make it?*

It would be dull, right? Without narrative Stress at the movies, you would walk out within five minutes and demand your money back.

Similarly, have you ever met a person bathed in pure inner peace, totally free from Stress? (Yeah, right.) Do they seem authentic? Is there much to talk about? Honestly, how soon before you roll your eyes and make some excuse to bolt?

Not only are Stress and Anxiety (and therefore Fear) natural, but we want some in our lives. Without it we would feel bored, less human, inauthentic, without highs and lows, without contrast—and frankly, little would get accomplished if the whole world was sitting around all blissed out on pillows. Where would progress come from? Where would drive come from?

Some people even suffer from too little Stress in their lives. But chances are, that's not you. Too much Stress is by far the bigger problem. How can you tell the difference, then? What does too much Stress look or feel like?

Ha! That's easy. You know it when you feel it.

We seek to reduce the symptoms of Stress and Anxiety, learning relaxation techniques like deep breathing, being fully present, laughter, dancing, meditation, and the like. Anxiety specialists also teach simplifying your life. This is all good stuff that makes you feel much, much better on the surface.

But look again at that first strategy. Do you recognize that the Controller uses these very same tools to repress negative voices? That means that, deep down, doing all this good stuff actually inadvertently *causes* even more excessive Stress and Anxiety. You may not feel it today, but you will over time.

Another problem with relaxation techniques is that they make the symptoms more tolerable, so who then bothers to address the underlying cause? If you have daily pain and deal with it only by using painkillers, it makes it so you don't have to look into what is causing the pain. It obliterates the symptoms but never addresses the underlying problem. One shouldn't skip a step. Figure out what's causing your pain, fix the problem (it may be something you've never considered before, like repressing Fear), *then* keep painkillers at the ready, should you ever need help again. Much more effective.

The second advice—to simplify your life—is also troubling. Doing less forces you to pick one thing over the other: Do all you want with your life (kids? Launch a business? A hundred tasks a day?) but have to endure a rat constantly gnawing at your belly—or limit your dreams and calm the rat down?

What if you want to accomplish a lot right now and have the energy to do so? The world is an amazing place, with so much to experience; you want to make your unique mark. Sometimes having to make this choice is, well, tragic.

What if there was another choice, though? An alternative that's not just a treatment for symptoms, that actually addresses and fixes the true underlying problem?

It works like this: Overactive Stress comes from the Controller trying to control something it can't ultimately control, or trying to solve a "problem" it can't solve, usually Fear. Trying to control and "solve" Fear and Stress is, frankly, stressful. Trying to calm down Anxiety is like trying to calm down a volcano.

Doing the exact opposite—going belly-up and admitting that you can't control, calm down, or solve these things—leads to relaxation. "Honey, the volcano is erupting and I can't fix it," you say while taking your pants off, flopping onto the couch, and opening a bag of Doritos.

For Stress and Anxiety are not the actual problem—trying to control or "solve" the Stress and Anxiety is the real problem, and the underlying cause behind the excessive symptoms. So long as you do this, and continue to believe that Fear is a blight and that Stress and Anxiety are unnatural and need to be obliterated, you will be pickled in it.

Mental Disorders (Depression, BPD, OCD, and More)

When unfelt Fear energy remains in your system, looking for a way out, at best it causes irrational Fear, excessive Stress and Anxiety, and distorted pathologies. All of these things dramatically affect your relationship with yourself and others.

At worst, it can take over your entire world.

The harder you fight this war, as you know, the bigger the explosions. Eventually, it can escalate to rupture your entire system. You can become emotionally crippled, phobic, obsessive, or even institutionalized. At this point, fighting the truth about who and what you are can become your whole world. Your very life may become dependent upon winning this un-winnable war.

Consider depression. Depression—from the Latin for "press down"—is the result of severely pressing down on emotions and a complete unwilling-ness to feel them. Those voices in the basement are depressed, and so you become depressed. If your depression is inherited, likely your parent also had a complete unwillingness to feel his or her emotions, as did one of your parents' parents, and on and on.

The current treatment—taking antidepression medication—puts these feelings in an even deeper hole, a mile below the basement. You can survive or even thrive by doing this, but not without costs.

One cost is anesthetizing the mind—like a modern lobotomy. You may feel incomplete, as in: Where are all my employees? Or anesthetizing your emotions: Where's my fuel? As you continue to avoid or silence these voices with medication, you likely feel further away from the truth of who and what you are. For who you are is a corporation made up of 10,000 employees, not just five or six. If only a few voices ever get to speak, and none of them are emotions, it's like going your whole life with the most beautiful of guitars but only ever knowing and playing a few basic chords. Where's the richness, where's the creativity?

I get it, though—if you've been absolutely convinced that negativity isn't normal and have been fighting this war your whole life, sometimes that belief becomes more supportable through medicated repression. That's totally understandable, and I wouldn't dare suggest taking you off your meds. But there is another choice. There's always another choice. It's a choice for warriors only, though.

In the introduction, I talked about Jacquetta, who had been diagnosed with borderline personality disorder. Here's what she has to say about her battle, in her own words.

I was in my twenties and in school. Honor student headed for a Ph.D. program. I had a lot of negative thinking about myself. I hated what I thought and felt. If I thought it . . . I reasoned that it must be true. I began to think of suicide.

I started cutting my forearms with razor blades. I knew I was in trouble and got help from a good psychologist. My emotional health deteriorated. I bought a gun. There was a thread of sanity that said, "Get rid of the gun," so I did. I overdosed on antidepressants. I landed in a psych ward . . . met there a good psychiatrist. These people wanted to help, they really did. Their efforts were Band-Aids. I rolled from crisis to crisis, even though I was in long-term therapy and on medication.

I made a more robust suicide attempt. That one almost got me. I was sent to a psych ward again. I was expelled from school, because suicide is illegal. Borderline personality disorder had been spoken of before . . . but now it was official and in a legal document. I understood what the diagnosis meant. Borderlines never—ever—get better. I was looking at meds and occasional hospital stays for the rest of my life.

The next ten to twelve years were off-and-on traumatic. I kept employment, never was fired, but would quit and run when I was scared. (I did not understand that at the time.) I firmly believed I was the biggest loser on earth.

I continued with therapists. I was told I needed to learn to regulate my emotions, keep a handle on things. Take medication to help me feel less.

I felt hidden and unseen. Masked, rejected. Imprisoned. I couldn't unlock the lock.

For about fifteen years, I was on my own. Kept it together, more or less. Alienated my friends, was forgiven sometimes. Not always. I stayed employed.

Five years ago, I hit a wall. I was done. It was not dramatic. There was no precursor or event. I was tired. I saw no end. At fifty-one, well, let it be over. It felt calm. I made a suicide plan. I wrote a new will. Simple, efficient, no hurry. Part of this plan was to ski one last time. One more winter. One . . . more . . . winter.

I literally stumbled onto Kristen on the Web. We eventually talked. The first words I said to her in an e-mail were "My life is ruled by fear, it has to go." I had no idea what I was getting into.

She did not know it till later, but I kept my plan as a "safety net" . . . a way out of this. As with everything else I had undertaken, I expected to fail. Because I was always doomed to fail . . .

Engaging in this work . . . has been a whole new ballgame. I had no reference. I could not dodge it or intellectualize my way out. In characteristic fashion, I quit over and over again. I came back, because I felt new things and could not give it up. I felt . . . better. Even when I felt "bad," I felt better about those feelings. My emotions became interesting. Engaging.

Emotion as curiosity. What will show up today? I learned that thoughts are not always truth. Feelings are true . . . very true, and can be trusted. Careful what you think about what you feel.

Science had always been my framework. Structure. Rigor. Replication of results. Feeling, and sitting with feeling . . . How could this be helpful? One must dig, one must overcome. That's what I assumed. One must *think it through*. Human intellectual ability offers all answers.

Not true. The body, where emotions are felt—I now start there. Always return there.

It's been four years. My life is better. My work relationships are better. My personal relationships are better. Fear and Anger are beautiful dance partners.

It's still hard. It's a great deal more fun, even when it's . . . well . . . not fun. Most of my life has been about giving up, about running away. I still faint in the face of fear sometimes, or freeze. Not always. It is not like before. Feel it, move toward it . . . There is much more space to live in. I get to do a lot more. My friends notice. I am aware of a bigger internal world and a much bigger external tangible world.

Kristen didn't save my life; she offered a path, an opportunity to try something different. I was gaining art and skill. I was doing this work, rather than doing something sad and tragic to myself. Allowing the feeling to go all the way . . . is the same art that allows great light and beauty to come in. The path is filled with color, lightness and darkness, and texture you never noticed until you walk with her. I wanted to be in all the way. To learn to feel.

I want all of it.

THE NEXT DECADE WAS A BLUR OF HEDONISM AND THE CURATING OF MY MASSIVE EGO.

After quitting the ski team, over the next three years I had not one but four reconstructive surgeries in a row. It's supposed to be a one-year recovery each time. Yet, because I was so good at repression, I never missed a ski season. Thinking about that now, it seems unbelievable. I squeezed some very aggressive skiing in, between springtime surgeries, ongoing rehab, constant pain, and struggle. The emotions I ignored those years were the size of elephants. I sat on elephants.

I freaking did it, though. I won the first big-mountain nationals competition ever in the United States (with one run that would've placed me fourth in the men's category), complete with what *Powder* magazine called a seventy-foot jump (thanks, guys, but it was forty, tops). I also filmed five ski movies during this time. I couldn't walk very well, but I could ski like the Terminator—masculine, impenetrable. My big-mountain ski career grew like a rainbow across the sky.

I also sobbed in agony every night.

In those three years I had other injuries, too, plus recurring strep throat (twelve times!), but I always made it through. By then my attraction to Fear was hitting its high, and I started eating sketchy outdoor experiences like they were Skittles.

I aggressively took up paragliding, rock climbing, and ice climbing. I dabbled in race-car driving. My favorite hobby became riding my bike at night in Manhattan (wearing stilettos). I seemed to have a constant need for adrenaline and intensity and didn't care where it came from. Fear was intoxicating. The more Fear I felt, the more fiercely in love with myself and with life I became. The closer I came to dying, the more romantic these sports became. The outdoor industry voted me the most extreme woman athlete in North America, beating all women in all sports, not just skiing. I was also voted among the top ten in the world most likely to die by skiing.

I was proud of that. My near-death experiences—of which there were dozens—became my most cherished memories.

Then it all started to fall apart.

I remember on one trip to Canada, late in my career, I got caught in two avalanches on two consecutive days. One of those slides took me from zero to sixty miles per hour in a half second, sifting me upside down through a steep sixty-degree rock hallway. The other abruptly tossed me off a forty-foot sloping cliff of shark-tooth rocks. I had grown up a bit by this point, so for the first time, I let Fear fully flood my system. It was jarring. I almost quit skiing.

It was one of the first steps, though, in taking a look at my problems. As uncomfortable as it was, I ate it, and digested that Fear, because some part of me knew I needed to, and needed to fast. Otherwise I was headed toward being crippled, or dead.

‖‖

PTSD

This is a very delicate subject, because some might take offense at my comparing PTSD from extreme sports (which are supposed to be fun and epic) to PTSD from being in a war (which is horrific and soul-crushing). I want to be sensitive to this obvious distinction.

David Brooks wrote in the *New York Times* that "most discussion about PTSD thus far has been about fear and the conquering of fear." All this bad advice out there about how conquering Fear is the solution to PTSD drives me nuts. In my experience—for I *have had* PTSD—it is the *cause* of PTSD. More specifically, not willing to feel Fear, or any emotion, is the cause of PTSD. It's unfelt Fear turned into stone in someone's mind and body, weighing them down.

Everyone is so afraid of examining that stone, especially the soldier who has experienced tremendous trauma, because it seems it'll be too dangerous—it might erupt out and roll over everything in its path. That may even be true if someone has a lifelong, calcified history of not knowing how to feel. Or a lifelong history of having it come out as rage.

I've spent several years now being fascinated with wounded warriors who suffer from PTSD. I want to help them, and have gotten to know that world enough to comment, the caveat being that I know that sports and war are obviously very different, and I'm coming at this from a respectful place.

Both pro extreme athletes and pro soldiers start at the same place, consciously signing up for a high-risk life/career, and they also commonly end up in the same place: lifelong injury and PTSD. What they experience in between, however, is very, very different.

Yet, as a Fear educator/facilitator, I see that what's true for an extreme athlete and what's true for a soldier, in the end, are often the same thing: They suffer.

And suffering, no matter where it comes from, is suffering.

Tragically, in school, learning how to feel your emotions is not taught. And then, in the military, becoming stoic is *explicitly* taught. The image of the soldier standing there blankly as the drill sergeant yells in his face is hard to forget. *Repress. Repress. Repress.* And you will pass your training and be ready for action.

I get it. It works. Anything else might put their lives at greater risk.

Same with extreme sports: While there's no drill sergeant, repression of Fear is still standard. And it also works. I know it did for me, for years.

But at the end of a military career, at the end of an extreme sports career, you'll find more and more soldiers and athletes who are struggling. They saw a lot of their friends get violently hurt or killed. They miss the high of the battle. They may suffer from chronic injuries. They may suffer from adrenal fatigue from living in a state of excessive Fear and adrenaline for too long. The body doesn't know the difference between getting chased by a lion, getting shot at, and jumping off cliffs every day.

They also may feel dead inside, depressed, as though life has lost its meaning. And yes, they may have PTSD. I know I did. Which is probably why I wanted to work with wounded warriors.

Yet if emotional intelligence—your ability to experience and feel your emotions in a healthy, productive way—were taught in schools and in the military, my prediction is that there would be no PTSD.

It would also severely reduce depression, mass shooting rampages, and other mental disorders.

Feeling Dead

After his daughter died, Bobby Brown was asked how he felt. He said, "I am completely numb."

Familiar, yes? After a tragedy, we often go numb. Repression is certainly one way to not "deal" with your emotions during a tough situation. The ramifications of doing this are, of course, what we're reviewing in this chapter.

Add this one to the list: Speaking of numb, if you spend enough time trying to not feel a voice, it can become a permanent situation. You may become habitually programmed to be unable to feel Fear, ever, and thus frozen in your ability to feel anything, period. Basically, by going numb today, you may become numb all the time.

Living numb is just fine. If you're unwilling to feel Fear—or any emotion, for that matter—you can still walk this earth and even accomplish a great deal, but not without consequences.

Consider this. I asked 500 people this year: "If given the choice, would you rather feel happy or alive?" Four hundred and ninety-nine answered "alive." I believe people choose "alive" because it includes "happy" but isn't limited by it. Aliveness is what we seek. It's why we're here: to feel *alive*. But if you're unwilling to feel Fear, Anger, or any of the unwelcome 5,000 voices, it not only means you're half alive—it also means you're half dead.

For you can't selectively repress an emotion without inadvertently repressing all emotions. That high, thick wall you've built to block out Fear and protect yourself from having to see the truth of what you're feeling also keeps out everything else. It blocks out or dulls Joy, Gratitude, and Love, until you're left feeling nothing. (And not the good Zen nothing, either.)

Inside the safety of the wall, you're not just blank, either, but also blind. You are too blind to see outside your walls, and too blind to see your truth inside—the truth of who and what you are.

For the truth of who and what you are is what you're feeling at that moment.

Thirteen years later, having just returned from my first Burning Man festival in Nevada, I came home and finally admitted, "I'm tired of living an inauthentic life." Even though I had by this time four different monthly columns in ski magazines on three continents around the world, was hosting a TV show, and was fully sponsored and living the dream to the point that I didn't even have to ski anymore if I didn't want to, I wrote an e-mail in twenty minutes, saying to everyone, "I quit."

As usual, I wore a mask that day. The letter was pleasant and thankful. Written with a smile.

What I really wanted to say, though, was this: "See you, suckers! I'm done. Screw all y'all. I hate this sport. I hate this industry. I think big-mountain skiing and other dangerous sports are the most pathetic display of human insecurity I've ever seen. Anyone who does this is transparent, stupid, and lucky to be alive. And I'm the stupidest one of all. I'm embarrassed about who I've been, who I am, and I can't take it anymore.

"Oh, and thanks for all the free shit."

That mask, at least internally, was off, and I was finally able to admit that something felt off. Had always felt off. What was it, though? How is it possible that the thing I most loved in the world—skiing—and an industry that had treated me with nothing but respect had been rendered as bad as, well, alligators, flesh-eating viruses, and forks in the eye?

Three months later, I met a Zen master and finally found out.

Burnout

Repressing Fear leads to burnout in three distinct ways.

1. It's an unwinnable war that takes all your resources.

By repressing or trying to overcome Fear, you're fighting the very flow of your life. You're trying to swim against the current, and you'll swim and swim and swim until you're utterly exhausted. With so much energy spent keeping these voices in the basement, over time you simply don't have energy left for anything else.

2. Whenever you're not living your truth, you eventually crack.

Emotions and what you feel right now are the gas in your tank. They're supposed to power and drive you to creativity and self-expression. They're the only sustainable fuel source behind energy and passion. Anything else, such as adhering to goals set for the future, Perseverance, or the Will, works for a while, but without this fuel source behind it, you won't make it to your destination.

Consider the kid whose parents want him to be a doctor. He can go very far by ignoring his truth for the sake of theirs. He may control, push through, or go around what he's feeling, projecting and grinding with tunnel vision toward a future goal. He may even go all the way to being a doctor. *Hurrah,* his parents say.

By ignoring his feelings, he becomes who and what his parents want him to be. But how intimate is he now with who and what he actually is? What kind of future does he have?

Eventually, we hope, that system will crack.

3. Whenever you're not learning from something anymore, you burn out.

Anytime you hate something—be it Fear, your partner, your marriage, your job, Anger, anything—that means you're not open to learning from it. And while you may stay with the person, or keep doing the job you hate, once you're no longer open to the lessons found there, you burn out.

Which is why I need to remain, always and forever, a student of life. Otherwise I burn out as a teacher. I become like an empty hose: No new water flows through my system, and I dry up and become brittle inside.

This is what happens when you stop learning.

What nourishes you and keeps your sparkle is staying curious and open to learning and growing from this person, sport, marriage, job, or, yes, this emotion.

So if you're willing to learn from Fear—despite the inevitable pain and discomfort of it—you remain a student of it and thus connected to the water source. Do this and the water will keep flowing; stop and you will dry up.

I will say, though: Drying up can often be a good thing, because it's the alarm that wakes you up. Alas, this is not an easy road. For example, we're at a crazy point in humanity where even a seventeen-year-old gymnast can already be burned out. If parents, coaches, or even you push yourself to be fearless, making you deny the truth of what you're feeling, eventually bad things start to happen that will force you to look at it. Things like: un-derperforming, injury, injury that won't heal, relationship conflict, making some huge stupid mistake, or growing to hate your job, life, partner, or, in this case, sport.

As much as all this sucks, that's often what makes you stop what you're doing and start growing in the right direction: to finally look at Fear.

Like any plant growing in the wrong direction, inevitably it will be drawn toward the light. At some point, your truth will come out. You will always, eventually, be drawn back toward what you're feeling.

WHAT IS THE WILL?

I'd like to now introduce another voice that I hinted at previously, called the Will. The Controller may activate the Will to bulldoze Fear in pursuit of an ideal. The Will is indeed a powerful employee to have on your board of directors. It's long been considered the most useful employee to promote if you want to accomplish goals.

Alas, the Will, in its effort to succeed, tends to act like a slave driver, with no regard for any other employee. It often sees the Body as a resource to be consumed, demanding that it do what the Will wants—sleep only this much, survive on this food, run this far—until it's an exhausted resource. It overpowers other minds, too. If, say, Laziness or Resistance shows up, the Will stomps them. It represses these voices, and we all know how that goes.

As for Fear, the Will rarely has use for it—or any other emotion, for that matter. It's a rough approach, but wow, does it ever work. The Will can crush all "negativity" and make you a star, helping you avoid discomfort or distraction along the way. For about twelve years tops, that is.

Then everything starts to fall apart.

For if the Will runs your life for too long, bad things will eventually happen.

Flow Stops

What is Flow? I'll talk about this more in chapter 12, but for now, just know that it's the 10,000 minds running their 10,000 thoughts, feelings, or agendas like water through a hose. Primary emotions show up often: Fear, Anger, Sadness, Joy and the Erotic. All 10,000, though, show up in the hose as circumstances warrant, running into, through, and out the other side. Because you're constantly changing, faster than the speed of light, everything moves through very quickly. It's a great system, and works such that space always remains open for the next thing to enter.

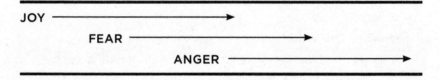

But when Fear shows up, or any voice not in line with what the Controller or the Will wants, it kinks the hose. And Flow immediately stops.

A voice may kink a thought or belief as well, trapping it in the hose where it will have no choice but to recirculate, forsaking any new information coming through the hose. Let's say, for example, the thought "I'm beautiful" comes through the hose. Great, there it goes, flowing along. Next comes "I'm ugly." Uh-oh. That's not in line with the ideal snapshot of yourself. With a giant NO from the Controller, a burst of effort from the Will, the hose gets immediately kinked.

Suddenly you're stuck in a repressed belief, story, or opinion that keeps circulating. No new thoughts, ideas, or learning can enter.

Along with your mind, your body is also now kinked. Emotions are meant to be energy in motion, felt in the body. "I'm afraid" comes through the hose. "Nope," says the Will. "I demand instead 'I'm unafraid,'" and the hose gets kinked. The unexpressed energy, along with the Fear or thoughts associated with it, has to go somewhere, so it floods the basement. It floods your body and pools there.

This leads to serious physical problems as this water turns stagnant, then rancid, and eventually poisonous.

Physical Problems: Aches, Pains, Injury, and Illness

Almost every physical problem you have is in some way tied to the repression of Fear. How's that for a statement?

Where's the proof? you may ask. With so little time or money spent on such studies, few doctors are willing to acknowledge the effect of repressed emotions on the body.

But you'd have to be willfully oblivious to not see a correlation between repressed emotions (especially Fear) and physical problems. You can't kink the flow of your body for decades and not expect to suffer physical consequences.

Start with this: Can you see that repressing Fear leads to Insomnia, excessive Stress, Anxiety, and Monkey Mind? It's also tied to overeating, overscheduling, overcompensating, and on and on. All this is known, of course, to compromise your health.

These conditions not only make you feel awful; they also cause or worsen nearly every single health problem there is, including high blood pressure, heart disease, cancer, Alzheimer's, diabetes, headaches, stomach problems, asthma, and many more. They make you feel older faster, gain weight, and increase your risk for heart attack, stroke, immune disorders, early death, and so on.

But oh, no, it doesn't stop there.

1. How repressed Fear leads to aches and pains.

In order to keep the hose kinked, you have to be doing this from a rigid place: bracing and holding tension to keep form. Resisting the natural flow of life is hard work.

This makes you a tight person, both mentally and physically. Over time, clinging tighter and tighter to protect yourself from emotions or other bad voices causes your body and mind to become less like water and more like stone. A stone in your head is very heavy and shows up as weariness and dullness. A stone body is very tense. It shows up as stiff shoulders, a tight back, and knotted muscles.

Until you deal with the unwelcome, kinked thoughts, your head will remain very heavy. And you can massage those kinks in your neck, shoulders, and lower back all you want, but they also won't go away until you deal with the unwelcome emotion behind them.

2. How repressed Fear leads to Injury.

What do we know about rigid trees? If they can't move with the wind, eventually they break.

I see it all the time in humans, too. Athletes who resist Fear get injured quickly and often.

So whenever you have a new injury, or a recurring injury, or an injury that won't heal, you should ask yourself, "How am I rigid in my thinking and beliefs? What am I unwilling to feel? And how does this contribute to the occurrence (or recurrence) of this or a new injury?"

Do this, stay curious about the answers, and, like magic, you'll notice that you've started to have less injury, and old injuries will finally heal. I know they did for me.

3. How repressed Fear leads to illness.

Louis Pasteur noted, at the end of his life, that it's not bacteria that results in disease; it's the combination of bacteria meeting the ideal host environment that results in disease.

If your host environment, then—otherwise known as your body—is not in flow, what do we know about rivers that get backed up? They become stagnant, putrid, murky cesspools, ideal for bacteria, viruses, and more to thrive in.

If your host environment is using all its resources fighting wars against unwanted emotions, it becomes weakened and doesn't have much fight left over to ward off, say, the flu.

If your host environment has a massive wad of unfelt Anger and Fear lying around, these slowly turn to poison, which leaches out into your entire body.

4. How repressed Fear leads to eating too much.

Fear is often felt in the belly. It's a sickening, uncomfortable feeling meant to get your attention and warn you that something's wrong. But if you eat in response to it, in an attempt to feel better—and it works, even faster than alcohol—you succeed in covering up the discomfort.

Therefore, snacking is you unconsciously distracting yourself from the feeling of Fear, and the problem it's trying to warn you about. How can you tell the difference between eating for sustenance and eating to cover up Fear? Stop eating and really pay attention to that sensation in your body. Is it hunger or is it an emotion you're trying to avoid or cover up?

Additionally, the weight you subsequently gain often becomes a secondary wall of defense against having to feel the Fear or deal with the problem. It's like a thick layer of security separating you and the basement door, behind which lives Fear. If you lose the weight, that crazy son of a bitch might get out. That is not an option.

Adrenaline made me feel alive, yet my body didn't know the difference between adrenaline from skiing an Alaskan mountain too fast and from getting chased by a *T. rex*. It was all the same.

I suppose if a *T. rex* chased you every day, even if you (oddly) loved it, after ten years your body would be exhausted by so much drama.

After I ended my ski career, I was immediately diagnosed with flatlined cortisol levels—complete adrenal failure. The doctor put me on steroids for three months. Then, over the next ten years, every decision I made, be it where I lived, who I dated, or whether I had kids, was run through an "I need ten hours of sleep per night" filter. I was simply exhausted. I couldn't schedule more than two things a day (lunch with a friend, a fifteen-minute conference call) before spending the rest of my day facedown in a puddle of drool.

It wasn't until I addressed my underlying Fear that my adrenals finally recovered. It wasn't until I admitted how Fear was behind every decision I ever made that I finally started blooming again.

Unworthiness

Underneath all our masks, deep in our unconscious, if we're willing to be honest with ourselves, we will always find a feeling of unworthiness. What did we do to deserve being alive, anyway? Nothing.

Many of us spend our lives looking to feel worthy of this incredible experience of being a human being. We desperately want to be "worth it." And the only thing that makes you feel worthy is if you really live. If you go all the way.

We are here, then, wanting—*needing*—to feel and experience life all the way.

The good news is, with Fear being such a deep, innate part of our life, if you're willing to feel and experience it, you'll feel worthy. For you'll have gone all the way.

On the other hand, if you avoid Fear, then you avoid life. And you'll feel bad, as if you spent your whole time here not really living. What happens next—as I've witnessed it—shows up differently for each individual, so this is but a short list:

> You may feel inauthentic, like a fraud.
> You may feel alienated from the world.
> You may not feel connected with humanity, nature, or life itself.
> You may not feel confident of your worth.
> You may not feel in charge of your life, but more like a victim to it.
> You may not pursue your gifts and talents.
> You may feel guilty or ashamed for not doing more, living more.
> You may feel like you're not living the life you were meant to live.
> You may feel like you're only existing.
> You may feel like you're not growing, only shrinking.
> You may never have a chance to explore your true self.

All this is no life. It's agonizing. Robbing yourself of emotions is robbing yourself of your very life.

For if you hold back on experiencing emotions completely—the good and the bad—life, in return, will hold back on you.

YOU ARE NOT A VICTIM. YOU DID THIS.

If a dog is vicious, blame the owner, not the dog. The dog's true nature is loving and kind. It's the same with Fear. But if you beat the dog for being itself, it will start acting out. You should never train a dog by beating it.

The more you beat the dog for being afraid, the more afraid you'll make him. The more you beat the dog for being angry, the angrier he'll get.

I can't tell you how many times I've heard "Well, if I could just get Fear under control, overcome my Fear, all my problems would be solved." I even hear this after working with people for a whole weekend on the subject of Fear. It's weird.

Let's pause, then. If at this point you still ask, "Why can't I get a break from Fear?" you're missing the point. The point is: No one gets a break from Fear. No one.

Not only is saying such things disrespectful to Fear, and not only will it cause Fear to play an even bigger role in your life, but it is a guaranteed failure.

You. Will. Not. Win. This. Battle.

So please stop saying these things. If you keep doing it, here's what to expect:

> › The more you try to get rid of Fear, the more afraid you'll feel. The more you try to get rid of Anger, the angrier you'll feel. The more you try to control your appetite, the hungrier you'll be. It works that way with everything.
> › The more you try to control anything, the more out of control you'll feel.

> The more beaten down you'll become: *This is exhausting.*
> The more confused you'll become: *Why isn't this working?*
> The more controlling you'll become: *I just need to work harder.*
> The more blind you'll become: *I'm stuck but can't see where.*

You won't be fooling anyone, either, no matter how big your smile. The people in your life will clearly see that Fear, from the basement, has set the house on fire in order to get out. This is especially true if you feel you've mastered Fear. Your greatest Fear will remain obvious: being perceived by yourself or others as afraid. *I rule my life like a hero!* Hero strength is great, but holding the form of a hero at all times? That's no way to have that connection with yourself and others that you desire, and no way to live in freedom and Flow.

If you acquiesce to your powerlessness over Fear, if you admit that this dragon can't be slayed, then and only then will you be on the road toward health instead of sickness.

Easier said than done, right? Not to worry. That's what chapters 6–12 are for.

But for now, just know this: So long as you are in denial of or avoid these voices, you will have to limit who or what you want to be, and continue to try controlling things you cannot control, until Stress and Anxiety grow so strong that you have no energy or time left over to fight any battles besides these. Your own personal growth evolution, if you continue down this path, will eventually come to a halt.

So get this now, or put this book down for another time. It's not Fear that stops you; it's your unwillingness to feel Fear. That's what stops you.

Once you understand this, then and only then can you stop being a victim to Fear. You can start to own your power. *You* did this to Fear, not the other way around. You abused this child of yours, beat this dog, banished this employee, fought the moon and stars. You and you alone turned a mere rain cloud into a hurricane.

This should be great news. It means *you* erected the prison walls, not Fear.

Which means you also have the ability to take them down.

It started with a simple question from the Zen master. The question was: "Allow me to speak to the voice of Fear."

I shifted in my chair and looked for this part of me, this voice. Finding nothing, eventually I raised my hand and admitted, "I seem to have no Fear."

Chuckling, he replied, "Yeah, I'm not surprised. Let me help you."

He started talking, and ten minutes later everything—my career, my personality, my problems, my relationships—made sense. How had I not seen it before?

My whole life up until then had been one massive paradox, where two opposites existed at the same time. I both loved and hated Fear. A paradox, said G. K. Chesterton, is "Truth standing on her head to attract attention." Well, it worked. Suddenly it had my full attention.

Experiencing Fear, I realized, was my reason for being. The skiing was just the portal. Yet the things I subsequently did were so dangerous, so threatening, I then had to strangle it to keep a tight hold on myself. If Fear was my lover, I played that game that goes "I want you, I need you, come here, my precious . . . No! Too much, you're crowding me!"

This must have been very confusing for Fear. I know it was confusing for me.

Can you love and hate someone at the same time? Well, sure. I both loved and hated my parents most of the time. Doughnuts, life, my cat who scratches the couch—love them all, hate them all. A paradox gives any experience rich contrast. When you love something, that love feels richer and makes sense only because you've also experienced hating it.

Just as a painting can't be made using only one color, having light and darkness gives contrast, perspective. Only then can it become a masterpiece.

My painting of Fear, though, was no masterpiece. It was very messy. For I had painted it while in the darkness of my own delusion.

It was time to turn the lights on, to wake up and start a whole new canvas.

WHAT IS THE BIGGER PICTURE?

As you can see, there are infinite personal consequences for repressing Fear. My husband and I have a joke that anytime someone has troubles, whether it's a fifty-pound weight gain, a car accident, an inverted testicle, anything, clearly it's the result of repressed Fear. (That and gluten.)

Joking aside, can you see that by repressing Fear, you lose the deep connection to your Self, and you lose a deep connection to other? Not just people, but the sunset, the air you breathe, your dog, money—it's all other. And whatever energy you have left after fighting this unconscious war, how present, curious, vulnerable, and sustainable is the quality of that remaining energy?

Also, here's even worse news: There are global consequences.

We know our intellect evolves through our interactive nature. The ways in which we connect show us where we are in our evolution. If we can't fully connect, we stop evolving.

Knowing this, if we continue prioritizing science, technology, and cognitive thinking, I see humanity on a train headed not toward who we truly want to be—who we innately are at our core, and therefore to the next level of human development—but further and further away.

Sure, our intellect is part of the picture, our true nature, and indeed an important part of our future. But it's not the only intelligence we have. It's limited, and it can take us only so far.

Of course, we don't need to drop the Thinking Mind (as if we could), and slowing down or stopping the train won't take anyone back to the station. But if we aspire to the next level of conscious development, we need to find a way to start bringing along our feelings and emotions. They have their own intelligence, too. Don't they deserve to be on this ride?

Do this, or someday it may even be too late. We may simply stop feeling anything, period. Do this, or we may inadvertently wind up becoming more robot than human.

SUFFERING = DISCOMFORT X RESISTANCE

The Buddha once said, "Life is suffering." He didn't say life is sometimes suffering; he said life *is* suffering. You can't be a human being and go all the way without experiencing suffering. That's just the way it is.

It's actually kind of beautiful. But we'll get to that.

For now, though, let me summarize our entire chapter with a single, poignant equation:

$$\text{SUFFERING} = \text{DISCOMFORT} \times \text{RESISTANCE}$$

It works like this:

DISCOMFORT: What do I mean by discomfort? Fear, of course, is uncomfortable. So is Sadness. Unworthiness. Pain. So are all the 5,000 "bad" voices. Let's say you feel the discomfort of Fear at a level 10.

RESISTANCE: The ol' "I don't want this." Look, it's okay to have a preference for no Fear, Sadness, Unworthiness, or Pain, but when they show up—which they will—and you wish it weren't so, you're now in the voice of Resistance. Let's say you resist to a level 10.

What you have, then, fully resisting Fear, is 10 times 10: That means the suffering is 100. That seems high, yes? So what can you do here with this equation to limit suffering?

You cannot get rid of the discomfort. Fear, Sadness, Unworthiness, Pain . . . that number is fixed. It's innate. Pain is Pain. It hurts to be rejected. It also hurts to break your leg. Similarly, Fear is Fear. It's a primary, unavoidable emotion, and it feels mighty uncomfortable.

What is *not* fixed, however, is the Resistance. That number is totally, completely up to you.

Well, sort of, because as I've mentioned before, Dissatisfaction is innate. No one is ever satisfied for long. Ask Olympic gold medalists how satisfied they are after winning a gold medal—it runs away faster than Usain. Dissatisfaction with Fear is what leads to Resistance, a voice that also has a right to exist. But in reviewing our equation, it is much, much easier to work with than Suffering or Discomfort.

With that in mind, let's say, then, that your Fear is a level 10, and the Resistance is a realistic level 2.

What we have now is 10 times 2—and *bam,* look at that math! The suffering is only a level 20. Much better than 100.

To illustrate this equation, consider tattoos. Tattoos are very painful to get. It's understood, however, that if you embrace rather than resist the Pain, you can arrive at a magical, altered place.

Can you see, then, that life—even without tattoos—is innately uncomfortable, yet the bigger concern, by far, is the Resistance, not the discomfort. Which brings us back to our two choices:

1. Continue to insist that "life isn't supposed to be about Fear." Don't embrace things as they are; fight hard to get rid of that discomfort. In order to keep it up, Resistance leads to Resistance then leads to more Resistance, until your unwillingness consumes your life. Harsh as it is, do this and you will suffer more: 10 times 100 . . . 10 times 1,000. Or you could try and numb the discomfort with drugs or superficial distractions, and never get to fully live.

Or . . .

2. Acknowledge that "life is supposed to be this way." Shift how you approach your discomfort. Seek to look at, reduce, and redirect your Resistance, and arrive at a place of allowing things to be the way they are, including the horrible condition of being human, which includes Sadness, Pain, Unworthiness, Fear, and more. Do this . . . and you will still suffer.

Not expecting that, right? But you *will* suffer less. A whole lot less.

To the point where getting a tattoo can become pure pleasure—or even a spiritual practice. And there is little suffering.

FEAR IS NOT THE PROBLEM. YOU'RE THE PROBLEM.

It comes down to this question: Is it really Fear that prevents you from achieving your potential? Or is it your misguided judgment and resistance to Fear that prevents you from achieving your potential?

I've been saying it's the latter. You have this sword called the Mind. A sword can be used to take a life or give a life. Everything you do, every decision you make about how you use this sword, is doing one of two things: empowering you or weakening you.

Are you using this sword to protect Fear and the nature of your life, which empowers you, or are you using this sword to fight Fear and the nature of your life, which weakens you?

It seems counterintuitive, I know, even ridiculous, to protect or empower a perceived enemy such as Fear. But that's because you're aware only of its immature or twisted version.

I'm sure at this point you also blame Fear for being the problem. If a lover or a friend is awful to you, as I'm sure Fear has been, it's hard to trust that lover again. But what if you were to recognize it was actually you who caused the problem, not the lover? Can you make that shift?

For this is indeed your fault, you know. You and only you are responsible. You can't blame your parents—even if they caused it. It's on you now. You can't blame society or history—over time we've *all* somehow been programmed the wrong way, the reverse of what should be.

You can only blame yourself. Look at it this way: until now, the entire rise of civilization up to this moment—billions of years—has led to you. And the worst war on this planet is not in Baghdad or on the Gaza Strip— it's actually in you. You and you alone have unconsciously agreed to fight the truth of who and what you are. You are at war with yourself, terrorizing yourself. You are, even in doing this, at war with the universe.

Why would you do that? Not only Fear but now the universe will kick your ass if you keep this up.

Until you get the lesson, that is. The lesson that Fear is an employee in your corporation doing its part to create the best you possible. That Fear has your best interests in mind and is ready to make friends, whenever you're willing and ready.

The only question that remains, then, is . . . are you willing and ready?

THE TIPPING POINT

Pavlov's dogs are famous for their patterned behavior. The scientists rang a bell, the dogs salivated. Interesting.

What's not as well known about those dogs is that they were kept in cages in the basement of the building, and one day there was a terrible flood. Rescuers couldn't get to them for several days. You can imagine the horror when they finally made it: Most of the dogs had drowned. A few survived, though not without having endured considerable trauma.

Yet here's where things got really interesting: When the bell rang, those surviving dogs no longer salivated.

Trauma had deleted their habitual patterns.

Sometimes people who hire me are in crisis. It's like they've had an alarm clock in their head, becoming progressively louder and louder, until they finally call me to turn it off. The CEO who is now having panic attacks. The husband in a horrible relationship for twenty years who just can't make a decision what to do. The single mother with dwindling savings who keeps botching job interviews and can't figure out why.

I see them as Ferraris with a stuck wheel, driving in circles. The crisis is the key to unlocking the wheel.

If you're reading this book because you're in crisis, consider yourself lucky. For without a crisis, without becoming so frustrated that you reach out for help and agree to give up what you've been doing, there would be little hope for change.

The crisis may be mild. Maybe you just feel like a clown. Clowns do neat tricks, but if you do the same trick over and over, you get stagnant, redundant. Eventually you get to a place where you start feeling ridiculous. Insane for doing the same thing over and over and never getting a different result.

Or better: The crisis may be bad. The more Pain, Suffering, Angst, and Stress you have, the more fuel you have for this journey.

Best yet is if you feel your life is at stake. Anytime you're truly ready to learn or grow, for *real,* it will feel like your life is at stake.

With any of these scenarios, what makes them great is realizing that whatever path you've been on is obviously the path to nowhere, and despite the investment you've already made, you refuse to go another inch. You finally recognize that you've been missing some sort of truth, message, or lesson that has been standing on its head trying to get your attention, often for decades.

Here's the truth, message, and lesson: There's a resource available to you—it's called Fear. It has incredible value, and you must stop trying to get rid of it, or even thinking you can get rid of it.

A crisis means it's finally time to get this "negative" force working for you, not against you.

WHAT IF I'M NOT IN CRISIS?

And the day came when the risk to remain closed in a bud became more painful that the risk it took to blossom.

—ANAÏS NIN

"My life is great" is perhaps the worst thing that can ever to happen to you, because this is when all learning and growing come to a halt. Stay there for too long and you'll notice that eventually you will feel uninspired, incomplete, or stagnant, as though there's just something missing. The reason is: great isn't enough.

Until you're experiencing all that life has to offer, the good, the bad, all 10,000 voices, employees, children, or instruments—whatever analogy you choose—of course you will feel like something's missing. Because there *is* something missing: not any more learning and growing, but the expansion of the whole rest of you, which is innate and tugging at you all the time. "Everything is fine" is actually a cop-out, a stuck place, an obstruction to the exploration of who and what you are expanding higher and further, not to mention the evolution of humanity.

You shouldn't worry, though, for even if there's no trauma luring you to the truth of who and what you are, it's going to happen anyway. Plants always grow, and they inevitably grow toward the light.

So here's your choice: Do you want to wait for a crisis—which will happen—and be carried to your greater truth on a stretcher someday, or do you prefer to walk there now, on your own?

Either way requires you to go through your own darkness to get to that light. It involves a willingness to look at your shadow voices, problems, and delusions, and to feel Fear, which is there, waiting to be acknowledged.

Given the choice between light and darkness, people tend to choose the light. If continuing to avoid Fear or distract yourself from having to feel it seems a preferable choice, by all means stay there. That's okay. Especially if feel you have no problems.

But if you're willing to go into the darkness, like a warrior, not only will it negate your having to grow and learn the hard way down the road, but I promise you, the other side will offer you a greater light than ever before.

PART II

DROPPING THE STICK

CHAPTER 4

YOUR CAGE

DUKKHA

A dog is carrying his favorite stick. But . . . what's this? He finds a bigger, juicier stick in the bushes. What to do?

First he tries to put both sticks in his mouth at the same time. That doesn't work. Quickly he realizes he must drop the stick he's carrying in order to pick up the new stick. So that's what he does. Thus, the bigger, juicier stick becomes his new stick.

What about humans? How long does it take for you to drop the stick you're carrying in order to take home the new stick?

Good news! You're ready for a new stick. It's time to embrace Fear.

But before you move on to chapter 6, and the specific methods and strategies for embracing Fear, take a moment to read through this important chapter. I've found that most people who say they want to create a new paradigm around Fear actually don't create one. Something gets in their way. So it's important to recognize these obstacles when they show up—because they will show up. Chances are, you will cling to that old, tired stick even when a juicier stick becomes available.

And if this sounds unreasonable, let me ask: Have you ever met a reasonable person?

Back to the analogy of being a Ferrari with a stuck wheel. Can you see that the other wheels are rotating, and there's motion, so it feels like you're getting somewhere? But really you're just going in circles, thanks to that one locked-up wheel. And you don't know you're operating in a stuck way, because until you experience operating in a functional way, you can't possibly know you're not.

The Buddha gave stuckness a name: dukkha. It's recognized as being one of the most important things he ever taught.

It usually takes a while to become stuck. Like the frog in slowly heating water, you can't feel it happening until twenty years later, and by then it's too late: You're boiled alive. Other times, it can take just a second. Either way, whether you can see it or not, dukkha is your life. And it will keep you from realigning with Fear in a different way.

How did you become so stuck? you may wonder. The first half of this chapter explains how. The second half helps you recognize where you're stuck. And the answer is, usually, "everywhere."

UNCONSCIOUS MIND RUNS THE SHOW

I want to establish one thing. Have this in the back of your mind as you read on: What you're aware of is but the surface of the ocean. A lot goes on up there, plenty to keep you entertained and occupied for a lifetime. Yet it's the vast ocean underneath, of which you're unaware, that creates the mood on the surface.

The ocean of voices interacting underneath is called the Unconscious Mind. It's a more powerful employee than your Conscious Mind. It's a memory-gathering, reactionary mind, and it runs your whole being. It fires habitual patterns so fast that you can exist on autopilot and not have to be aware of anything, or make things up anew every moment. Which is great.

The bad news is that you usually can't help but robotically obey it. It's your programming. And the busier you get, the more this mind takes over everything, and the more robotic and blind to its programming you become.

We like to think we have the power and ability to access and change its patterns anytime we want—that we can reprogram ourselves. And it's not impossible, of course. But it's not a natural process to be conscious of this mind. Nature does not want you to become aware. Nature is mostly concerned about safety and procreation (important work, incidentally).

If you're a warrior and make considerable effort, you can try to understand the Unconscious's reactions (of course, the key word here is *try*). The most common way we do this is by asking such questions as: Why do I act the way I act? What makes me feel this way? Most people use therapy for this. And while this can be a fascinating exploration, it's like trying to understand why your cat acts the way it acts. Does anyone *really* know why Kitty likes to sit in a cardboard box, or do we just guess?

Trying to cognitively understand your Unconscious Mind is like trying to cognitively understand the universe. It's infinite, there's no bottom or top, beginning or end, most of it is ungraspable, and you can get lost in the process forever.

Through therapy we also try to use our Conscious Mind (it's similar to the Thinking Mind) to understand or fix problems found in the Unconscious Mind. Many feel they've had great success at this, yet the Unconscious Mind is not meant to be Conscious—otherwise it would be called the Conscious Mind. It's like trying to make sleep awake. Sleep is sleep, and awake is awake. The Unconscious Mind is meant to remain Unconscious.

Thus, the instant something becomes conscious, while you might not be stuck in an old pattern anymore, look again: You're now stuck in a new pattern. Take a cup of water out of that vessel and it simply fills up again. You may not be stuck in, say, Anger anymore, but now you're stuck in the voice of Gratitude—which feels like a step in a great direction (and it is), but it can be just as annoying.

Given this, with little lasting success and such limited tools (twenty years of therapy, and really, what changes?), eventually most give up and just let the Unconscious Mind do its thing.

Past a certain point, I mean, why bother? The Unconscious Mind will always remain one of the great mysteries of life. Which I say is great—we need more mystery in our lives.

THE BARS OF THE CAGE

A man had a pet bird that he kept in a steel cage. The bird hated living in a cage, and felt sorry for herself. When the man went to work each day, he would hang her birdcage on the front porch to give her fresh air and a view.

She felt even worse on the porch, though, for free birds would come by, and she could almost hear their thoughts: "Imagine that. A bird? In a cage?"

Sure enough, one day the man accidentally left the cage door unlocked. As he drove away, it swung open, and the bird, for the first time in her life, saw the world without looking through steel bars. Freedom was hers! The possibilities seemed endless. She began to think about what to do.

Later the man came home, and what do you think he found on the porch?

Don't tell me you think he finds the bird gone, because you know that's not true.

How did this happen? How have we all become so stuck in our cages, unable to leave?

What are these bars in our cages, anyway? And, more important, are they real?

A Cage Bar Called *Beliefs*

Ever see a fully grown five-ton elephant in the circus? To make him stick around, trainers put a little band around one leg that's connected to a little stake in the ground. Why, one has to wonder, doesn't that big elephant just rip up the puny stake and go on a tri-state joy stomp?

Here's why: When elephants raised in captivity are very young and weigh only a few hundred pounds, trainers tie them with a big band to a big stake in the ground. That elephant will try to get away for about twenty minutes. Once he believes he can't, for the rest of his life he'll never try again.

A belief is like a snowflake that starts out merely as a concept, idea, or notion. Standing on a cliff, you watch it fall from the sky toward the great chasm below. Once you say, "That's me," and leap out to grab it, guess what? It will take you down into the chasm with it.

Down into the chasm you fall, holding tightly to your beliefs about the world, other people, Fear, Anger, how to live your life, how everyone should live their lives, and more. This is how beliefs become your stuck places, your cage bars. You have millions of these. Just look around and see all the flakes you cling to.

Yet, what beliefs are ever truth? For example, my husband, Kirk, believes I'm a goddess. My ex-boyfriend Tom believes I'm a moron. Who should I believe? Who is right?

Truth is, sometimes I'm a goddess, other times I'm a moron. The second I lock on to a belief, though, even if I believe I'm a goddess—which makes me feel nice, and enlightened—now I'm stuck. Because when I act like a moron, I don't have the freedom to ponder that new snowflake. I'm lying facedown, clinging to my belief that I'm not.

Here's what's important to remember: It's not just your negative beliefs that keep you stuck; it's *all* beliefs. "Kristen is a moron" holds Tom hostage, too, as much as "Kristen is a goddess" holds Kirk hostage. "Life is beautiful" holds you hostage as much as "Life sucks." Whenever you have a belief about what life is, who a person is, what love is or isn't, it's the same as having a belief about a stock. You invest in it, and we all know how *that* goes.

How to eat, how to have sex, what Fear is, how to grow spiritually, what makes a person a goddess versus a moron . . . I get it. You want and need to trust these beliefs, want to keep them frozen, keep them preserved. They're your constant and comfortable place. Even if you're clinging to nothing, to an illusion, you don't care—*because they're yours.*

A Cage Bar Called *Revelations*

In India, they sell monkeys for food. But where do these monkeys come from?

There are no monkey farms, so clearly they're hunted in the jungle. How exactly do the hunters capture them unharmed, though? Monkeys are famously clever, agile, and quick.

Here's what hunters do: they create a jar with an opening big enough for a monkey's hand to slip in, but not big enough for his fist to exit. In the jar they place peanuts, then leave it in the forest. A monkey will happen upon the jar and think, *What luck—peanuts!* He'll stick his hand in, grab the peanuts, and—oh crap, he's stuck. So long as he clings to the peanuts, he can't get his hand out.

The monkey will be found, having had no food, water, or sleep, often for days, still clinging to those peanuts. All he has to do to break free is release the peanuts, but he won't do it. He'd rather die than release those peanuts.

You're no different. That's how hard you cling to anything you deem yours.

Revelations are the most powerful beliefs that you cling to, for they are often found at critical times in your life, and seem like light you can rely on whenever you again find yourself in a dark forest. If you had a revelation once that Fear is "False Evidence Appearing Real," that's a thick bar on your cage. You get very attached to it. It's yours.

If you had a revelation once that you were able to calm Fear by taking three deep breaths, that's a thick bar in your cage.

This is especially true if you paid a therapist $250 an hour for any revelations, or put a lot of time into a practice that seems to work. Some people even make a single belief, story, or revelation the basis for their entire lives. They seem like glorious flowers, when the truth is, they're weeds. You don't even need to water them, and still they thrive.

Grow enough of them? They choke out other plants that are also ripe to grow.

A Cage Bar Called *Stories*

The stories we tell ourselves, particularly the silent or barely audible ones, are very powerful. They become invisible enclosures. Rooms with no air. One must open the window to see further, the door to possibility.

—SUSAN GRIFFIN

Your stories develop through history and information downloads into your Unconscious Mind. The first time Mom reacted to your Fear is in there. The first time you ignored Fear and felt powerful is in there. Your stories about everything, not just Fear, have been pieced together over the years and circulate round and round. It's hard to see any other view but them.

And they're why, when a stranger at a party asks, "Tell me about yourself," you have an answer. You tell your stories, of course: what you've experienced, what you stand for, and how, as a result, you spend your time.

Where would you be without your stories, right? Nowhere. You'd be nothing. You wouldn't even know who you are. Your stories become who you are.

But look again. It's not you who is speaking to this stranger. It's the voice of the Storyteller.

Yet the Storyteller is not who you are. It's just one of 10,000 voices that makes you who you are. When it speaks for you, then, how could it possibly get it entirely right? Imagine if a friend standing next to you at that party were to tell the story of who you are—do you think they'd get it right? A little bit, maybe, but they're not you. Neither is the Storyteller.

At some point, you'd interrupt your friend and say, "Wait, ha-ha, that's a bit off." But you don't question the Storyteller, do you? And here's where things get sticky. The Storyteller doesn't just tell the stranger who you are— it also tells *you* who you are.

I can't tell you how many people I've facilitated for hours, helping them conclude on their own that an old, tired story of "fearlessness is the goal" holds them hostage and it's time for a new story. As we hug goodbye, they turn around and say, "Thanks, Kristen! I'll be sure to be fearless from now on!" Wait, what? We just spent three hours unraveling this!

They just can't help themselves, because of the Storyteller.

Unless and until you recognize that you're not the Storyteller, and it is not you, you will keep unconsciously coming back to your long-held stories. And that's all they are. Stories. Fables. You could have a single moment in which you feel afraid of your dad. The Storyteller gets involved, attaches to it, and recycles it over and over like a battery getting charged through constant motion. Next thing, the energy of the Fear never leaves your system. If you try to add in a drop of love, it will reject it. That ingredient is not part of its recycled story.

You could have a story that "I can't be caged by Fear." Little do you realize, though, that that story *is* your cage. You could have the story "I like who I am," and that will keep you the most stuck of all, preventing you from growing beyond or seeing any other truth besides it.

If it remains unconscious and unquestioned, you will always believe it, and actually think that it's you talking, telling your truth.

Until you won't even be able to see a different reality if I drop one on your head.

A Cage Bar Called *False Self*

A penny will hide the biggest star in the universe if you hold it close enough to your eye.

—SAMUEL GRAFTON

This cage bar is my favorite. It explains so much. You could even call it the whole cage. The False Self is a voice that is created, starting at age two, as you individuate from others—first from your parents, then friends, peers, the rest of the world—and become a separate egoic being. It's a natural and clever process that helps you deal with the inevitable vulnerability and Fear that ensues, which to a child is shocking and scary. It does you a huge favor, which is to form beliefs that help you frame and make sense of the world as you go through this intense transformative process. It's complete by approximately age twelve, and won't evolve much from there.

No one is without a False Self. Much like any voice, your False Self is unique and has its own style, but because life is Fear-based, it is also Fear-based. And thus, so are you.

As it develops, it will take even a single input, like Mom saying once, "Don't be stupid," and create a lifelong story around, perhaps, how stupid you are. Or it can work in the other direction: It will take a single moment of being called a scaredy-cat by some kid on the playground and create a defining characteristic refuting it—"I'm not afraid of anything!"—that will be the theme of your entire life. By age twelve, you'll have already settled into the False Self as being the core of who and what you are, and it will dictate how you walk and talk, how you carry, see, and express yourself, usually right up to the end. Because it lives in your Unconscious Mind, you can't see its profound influence on you, unless you make a specific effort.

As you get older, its initial purpose—to protect—will no longer serve you. The False Self instead begins to hinder you. Perhaps you have a huge desire to change your relationship with Fear, or with food, or with your mate, and have the Will do it. The Will can be your foot on the accelerator. Yet the False Self's desire to protect the status quo will eventually overpower any other voice—even Determination or Perseverance—and stamp a bigger, firmer foot solidly on the brake. The False Self does not want you to change.

You could drink a Red Bull and crank up the effort to 11, but if left unrecognized and unchallenged—which it usually is—it will shut you down every time.

Every. Single. Time.

The False Self was supposed to be a temporary answer to who and what you are, yet most often it becomes permanent, as solid a cage bar as there is. If left unexamined, it won't just prevent you from realigning with Fear at a higher level; it will also prevent you from ever becoming your True Self.

I remember filming with Eric again a week after throwing my first backscratcher. He assumed that because I could jump cliffs—which is one skill—I could ski great, too. If you recall, I kind of sucked at skiing at that point. Eric had no clue.

First run that morning, wearing snazzy new clothes from a sponsor, on new skis from a company planning to pay me a salary, I stood between a sandwich of rock walls twenty feet apart, with a 300-foot-long, steep nightmare of mogul ledges in the middle.

Three, two, one. The cameras started rolling again.

We're all puppets to the False Self working in our unconscious minds, and I realize now that I was no exception. My False Self said, *I feel invisible. I'm all alone. Nobody is ever going to love me. I'm a good person, but no one can see that. Everyone is too caught up in their own lives to see or consider me. I just have to take care of myself.*

Some people are crippled by their False Self beliefs and stories; others are motivated by them. The difference is very simple: Wish they weren't so and you're crippled. Embrace them and you're motivated. I was the latter, for somehow, even though I wasn't aware of this in the slightest, I had embraced all of this, and it was about to work magic.

The perfect storm was upon me. A camera, a cute guy named Rob also filming that day, just the right fears calcified since childhood, and *bam*—while I felt no Fear again, it drove all of this, and created my fire.

Circulating in my Unconscious Mind was: *If I slay it, Eric will notice me, and Rob will love me and want to be around me. I'll finally be seen, and they'll consider how great I am. I'm independent and strong; I can do anything. Watch THIS.*

I pushed off and skied the way I'd have normally skied, which was okay, but, armed with the motivation of False Self + Fear of being invisible, I did it twenty miles an hour faster.

That's all it takes, really, to go from being an expert skier to a world-class skier. Past a certain point it's not about technique, it's about using your emotions—in my case Fear—and radically embracing and expressing it to the very edge of destruction, without falling. And no way would I fall with so much at stake.

Twenty wild, erratic seconds later, I screeched to a halt and smiled at Rob. He grinned back. Eric stood above, clutching his camera, screaming in ecstasy. My legend grew. And yes, I had just gone from being an okay skier to being a world-class skier. In one run.

THE HABITUAL SELF

Your millions of beliefs, morals, opinions, stories, realizations, experiences, judgments, things you know for sure, things you hold dear, and on and on, together all gloriously help shape who you are. They give you form. Make you *you.*

With them come millions of habitual patterns, or a voice I like to call the Habitual Self. If you believe, for example, that it's weak to cry, with that comes a habit—like going numb in the face of Sadness. If you have a story that you're bad at sports, your habit might be a sharp *no* to anything athletic.

From picking your nose to flicking away Fear, all these habits become your quirks, style, identity, personality, etc. Along with the other bars in your cage, they confirm over and over who you are. *I'm the guy who is fearless. I'm the girl who says no to sports.*

There's a comfort to this, of course. But the cost of knowing who you are is high: a whole lot of bars in your cage. They hold you hostage. They become your programing. Computers get reprogrammed all the time. We don't.

So when I come along to take you out of the cage, even for a moment, and ask you to temporarily leave your beliefs, stories, realizations, and, now, habits around Fear, some of which have been there for ten, twenty, or sixty years, and feel as core as your ethnicity or eye color, how far will I get before your unconscious, habitually patterned Mind swoops in to put you back safely in its cage—to you being you?

Undoing a habitual pattern requires you to become unmolded clay. It requires you to go into a state called bardo—or free fall—and not exist as something real or solid for a bit. Not exist as "you."

It's a state of in-between. You're not *this* anymore, and not yet *that*.

"You mean I'm not the girl who is bad at sports?" You'll argue, "No, no, that's not true," and point to evidence supporting this story. "But I am a fearless guy," you'll argue. "That's who I *am*." It doesn't matter what the details are. You could be in the habit of believing you're a worthless pile of crap, and you'd cling to that like it's a fuzzy teddy bear (albeit a stinky one).

To create a new habit, you have to be willing to drop all this and not know who you are for a while, to stay in the emptiness. And because that's so scary or seemingly ridiculous, you must have a *strong* motivation and desire to change. You must also have a plan or method that actually works to get you to the other side of a habit, or you'll quickly snap back into the safety of your cage.

BOTTOM LINE: EGO

We do not see things as they are. We see things as we are.

—TALMUD

Enter the Ego. Your Ego is your sense of self. It is your home.

And it is your cage. So long as you are you, saying "me" and "mine," and remain tucked in with all your beliefs, stories, and habits, you will be living in your Ego. Your skin is your cage.

Within these bars are housed your mannerisms, talents, loyalties, your ability to jump off cliffs, or your ability to drink ten shots without throwing up. They're yours. *You*.

The Ego has, oddly, come to represent Arrogance or Pride. "That person has a big Ego" is an insult. But everyone has a big Ego, because everyone has a big opinion about who and what they are. Even the girl who "doesn't know who she is"—she knows for sure she is the person who doesn't know who she is. Some people are very aligned with the voices of Arrogance or Pride. Others have big Egos about being humble. It's the same thing.

There's a belief that you can transcend the Ego. You may even think that's where I'm going with this chapter—"Get rid of the Ego, get rid of dukkha"—right?

But those who claim to have transcended their Ego—"spiritual" folks, if you will—you'll notice that they usually have a huge Ego about not having an Ego. The cage bars to them seem gone, but they're not; they're still there, only now they've become tendrils wrapped tightly inside them, which only others can see. The Ego will always find a way to wrap its tendrils around everything, even a state of Non-Ego, and develop a story and belief about it. It is your destiny. And frankly, why would you want to get rid of it? You're here to have a human experience, right? Well, this is it.

Who would you be without your Ego, anyway? *Nothing,* screams the Ego. And no one. That's what. A puddle on the floor.

The Ego is not a voice, though. It's a dynamic of all these voices I've outlined. It keeps you separate from the other—people, nature, the world, even your emotions—and it does not like change. Thus, the Ego has very little power to make you happy, or accomplished, or help you evolve and change to a new reality, because that's not its job. The Ego's job is only to spend its life proving that you, as you, exist.

There are subtle differences, but in many important ways, the Ego *is* your Thinking Mind. This is because the Thinking Mind is how all these cage bars interact. "I have something to think about and believe in, and I have a story, therefore I am." Because of the Ego, you are solid, fixed, and permanent, and the thinking supports that to make you real.

And if I were to challenge that reality, question your thinking or Ego even a little bit, what would happen? The Ego would fight for its life, because that's what it would feel is at stake.

And thus, so will you. Your investment is too huge. Imagine you've been riding on a train track, pumping away on a handcar for 5,000 miles. After all this time and effort, you do feel you've really arrived somewhere. Somewhere significant.

You've arrived at clarity, right? Thanks to the Ego you are more clear about who you are, how the world is. Maybe you even feel less Fear and Anxiety than ever before. You've invested so much in achieving this clarity that you're probably unwilling to lose it.

So along I come, swinging my big book on Fear, asking you to drop all you've accomplished and switch tracks.

You okay with that? I mean, why *would* you turn back when both your track and my track seem to take you in the same direction—toward a better life with less Fear? I say the track you're on is not going to take you to the new place I'm proposing. You say you're not so sure about that, especially because you see my track may even go in a radically opposite direction.

Okay, then, here's the hard truth: There's not always change. There's *only* change. Let me say that again. *There is only change.*

Which is another way of saying, pause and consider this: You are not your Ego. You're always unmolded clay. You will always have an opportunity to fly out of the cage. You can fly and soar with the winds of change and find that you're not even the same person you were five seconds ago, if only you knew how.

The Tibetans say you have two enemies in life: clinging and aversion. Clinging to what is familiar, aversion to what is not. Because of these, you remain molded clay. You stay trapped behind cage bars. In Zen it's called "being tied to a post without a rope." Dukkha.

You cling to everything. Look at how much you cling to the way you dress, to your hairstyle, to a sport, to a car, or even to a favorite color. And these are just little things, never mind things that really matter, like how you deal with Fear.

Your aversion to most things, including divorce, getting older, death, or change of any kind, supports the clinging.

Now do you see why you are stuck, everywhere?

ARE THESE CAGE BARS REAL?

For years, when the horse came and went from the property, he avoided a large tree trunk on the left side of the road.

One day the tree trunk was removed, and the hole filled in with dirt. Yet for the remainder of his days, the horse continued to avoid that spot as if the tree trunk were still real.

The horse remained impeded by an obstacle that was no longer there.

Finally we have arrived. These bars in the cage. Are they real? They sure seem that way. Even with considerable efforts to remove them, they remain obstacles to freedom and to change.

Western psychology, which permeates our culture, certainly supports that they're real. Even though it advertises that it will get you unstuck, Western therapy helps keep you firmly stuck behind these cage bars. Therapists have you talk and think and talk and think about your problems, which confirms your identification with your Thinking Mind. They encourage you to tell your story, talk about what you believe in, give tremendous attention and therefore validation to your False Self, lead you to more and more realizations, and help you create habits that—while many of them are good habits—are still habits.

They even encourage your Thinking Mind to try and solve the problem with Fear, the exact problem the Thinking Mind created.

Even if you don't see a therapist, our culture assists you to live within your skin and believe you are your Ego, perpetually reconfirming the existence of these cage bars. Until the cage bars not only seem as solid and real as steel, but grow thicker and stronger over time.

But seriously, even if you fired your shrink today, flew out of the cage, and went into free fall, would you finally be able to ponder a new reality around Fear? Would that work?

Nope.

Because in only six seconds, your Unconscious Mind, Thinking Mind, Habits, et al. would sabotage the effort. It would bring you back to the comfort and confirmation that you're real and you exist, as these bars prove.

And you're back to your Ego.

Take a deep breath now, and let's go back to our initial question: Who and what are you? Not knowing is, alas, not an option. But for our precious six seconds, contemplate this instead: Maybe, just maybe, you're not merely a collection of habitual patterns, beliefs, and stories. What if this Ego dynamic is actually *not* you? What if you've mistakenly become a limited "Self" attached to only these few voices running the boardroom who have come to speak the loudest?

Their view is not the full reality. It's only partial and, to go further, simply a projection. They are *not who you are*. What these handful of voices are, really, is just habit and nothing more.

You are so much more. Thousands of voices more.

What I'm saying, then, is that it doesn't matter whether the bars to the cage are real or not. What matters is that the Ego will make them real, and will argue that they are real, as if its life depended on it. Because for the Ego, it does. It won't die until you do, and it will argue with reality and win every time.

And no smooth-talking Fear expert like me will be able to crack that unless and until you start observing these voices are employees in your corporation, and that they are not you.

TRY TO LEAVE THE CAGE? WHAT WILL HAPPEN NEXT?

Let's say you're living in a world of mazes and tubes, just like a lab rat. Once, you went down the tube of repressing Fear and were rewarded with a block of cheese. The Fear went away, and you did the thing you wanted to do fearlessly.

Thus, you start going down that channel again and again. But one day you're rewarded with only half a block of cheese. Then a quarter block. But hey, it's still cheese, right?

Until one day it's a pellet. Then a half pellet. Eventually a quarter pellet. At this point a rat will leave to look for cheese elsewhere. But humans? We won't. We'll keep the same damn pattern going down that same damn channel, year after year, decade after decade, and it's only when desperation sets in that we'll go on a search for cheese elsewhere.

The problem is, we then try to leave the Ego and explore new channels the same way we did ten, twenty, thirty years ago, when we were younger, because that's all we know. Often our body, mind, and psyche can't handle it. And so we end up crawling back to the old quarter pellet, resigned, because at least it's something to eat.

Like the guy who spends his life mastering science and technology, making money, having kids, but devotes little time to trying to get along with others or feeling his emotions. After a midlife crisis or near-death experience, or simply because he refuses to take another step as his current self, he may go on a journey to feel his emotions. Without proper guidance, the effort will flop. He alienates his kids the first day. The second day, he weeps in public over a Pepsi commercial.

Of course, he's going to recoil and turn back to his old ways. No one wants to weep in public over a soda commercial.

Best to just keep on keeping on, even though you're starving.

But when your hunger becomes even more intolerable, which it will, and it's time to venture out again, simply allow me to hold your hand this time. We will watch the soda commercial together, and I promise, we will chuckle.

CHAPTER 5

TEACUPS

E very moment you're awake, every interaction you have with any person or situation, every sentence you read in this book: They're all like tea ceremonies.

I've been offering you tea all along, offering you teachings. By reading these sentences, it's as if you're holding up a teacup, saying, "Yes, please," then receiving that tea. I assume your intention is to drink it, to get nourishment from it. Or maybe not.

There are four types of teacups, and the first, crucial step is to look down and observe what kind of teacup you're holding. It may be different than you think.

Now, let's be clear: I don't care what cup you have extended. While you may think you have an open, empty, upright cup, even just realizing that your cup is not empty can become the only gem you get from this book, and that's enough. In fact, that's huge, and it's well worth the effort of having read this far.

Read at least these next few pages, though, so at least you'll know whether it's worth reading the second half of this book—which is about how to engage in the practice of Shift—or if you should wait for a different time in your life to drink this tea.

UPSIDE-DOWN CUP

If you feel you've mastered life, or Fear, look down: While reading this book, your cup is upside down. I can pour the tea, yet it spills everywhere.

You're not interested in tea right now. That doesn't mean you won't be later today, or next year. But not now.

This shows up as negation. "Nope, I don't want to." You may even *say* yes, but all signs point to "No tea, please." You're happy with the way you are and your current relationship with Fear. There's no need for improvement.

It's taken you years to deal with Fear sufficiently. You've empowered No Fear, and it has worked, plenty. You don't want to lose that control you've worked so hard for. This looks suspiciously like I'm asking you to give up those results.

Look, I get it. What if the message of this book is wrong? If you empower Fear, or Anger, or any unpleasant voice—like Unworthiness or Powerlessness, which are also in the basement—it's just too risky. Your whole house of cards could come crashing down.

Besides, you *like* where you've arrived. This is not a bad place to live.

MUD AND DIRT IN YOUR CUP

Zeus is looking down from the sky at a man in rags, walking down the street. He's been down on his luck his whole life, poorer than dirt. Even the man's shoes are falling apart; they're held together by tiny pieces of string. Zeus looks away.

His wife, seeing this, comes over and smacks Zeus. "Don't look away," she says. "Help him!"

Zeus replies, "I can't help him. He's not ready." She smacks him again. With a sigh, "Yes, dear," and a lightning bolt, Zeus sends a bag of gold down to the street, just ahead of the walking man.

They watch from above as the man approaches the bag and stops before it. Ever so carefully, the man steps over the bag of gold, as slowly as possible, so as not to destroy his shoes any further, then continues on his way.

The mud and dirt are those beliefs, habits, thoughts, opinions, stories, revelations, certainties, and more. I could pour the tea, but the tea is too tainted to drink. This is what I described in the last chapter, as it's the most common approach to any tea ceremony. You will do everything in your power to preserve the mud and dirt in your cup. You may even find a way to twist the words of this book to make it thicker.

A HOLE IN THE BOTTOM OF YOUR CUP

It looks like you're interested—you may even feel interested—but what you read goes in and then comes right back out. You never actually get to drink anything. "Okay, I'll do it," you may say. You commit to the tea ceremony. But the funny thing is . . . then you don't do it. You go back to the same old thing you've always done. That's when you know you have a hole in the bottom of your cup.

I see this all the time with skiing. People say, "I want to improve my skiing. I'll do anything!" I say, "Okay, do this." They try the drill for a turn or two,| and six seconds later they become their Habitual Self again. It's like saying, "I'm so thirsty," being handed a glass of water, and then standing there, holding the water and not drinking it, still talking about how thirsty you are.

WHY DO ALL THIS?

Why do you do this? Why ask for tea, or water, and then not drink it? I link this phenomenon to two reasons:

1. It seems like a lot of work to change.
2. You won't change unless you have to.

Seems Like a Lot of Work

Finish this sentence: "I don't want to have to . . ."

Is it: "start over"? "do the work"? "put in the effort"? You know the words. How many times do we say this? It stops us from fixing a marriage, or starting a new career. It also shows up here as: "I don't want to do the work it takes to really be alive."

After high school or college, school's over, right? Learning anything new is okay for tennis lessons on a weekend, or figuring out the latest technology. But at some point you want to be done with learning and just do the thing. Just live.

But you do realize that anything worth doing requires a lot of effort, right? We all know that. It's never *poof* and suddenly you're joy and light, right? Never *poof* and you're a concert pianist, or Gandhi. It requires endless practice. Endless awakening. Not everyone is up for that.

It's much easier to stagnate.

Won't Change Unless You Have To

Renowned actor and addict Robert Downey Jr. was asked, after he became sober, whether it had been difficult to quit drugs and alcohol. He surprised the audience by saying, "No, it was easy."

"Getting to the point where I was willing to quit, though?" he added. "That was very difficult."

You're not ready until you're ready. If your life is rushed, you have too much to do, you're in a hurry, and this is not a priority, then don't read the second half of the book. It's not for everyone. Not for every day.

That doesn't mean you won't ever read it. When the time feels right, this tea ceremony will always be available. If today it's a no, put it down and come back another day, and it will take on a different meaning.

YOU MAY ALSO PUT UP A FIGHT

A memory test was conducted where subjects were flashed pictures of random, unconnected images: a car, a daisy, a house, a toaster. They were asked at the end to list the things they saw.

The test inadvertently offered an unexpected insight into human nature. If a subject got an image wrong—for example, if someone claimed he saw a blender, when it wasn't one of the images—the subject would usually argue, get defensive, and adamantly insist that there was a blender shown during the test. Some even became hostile.

This shows how the Ego (you) aligns with whatever you feel is real and fights for it as if your life and sanity depended on it, even if it's not real.

If you hold any of these first three cups, what happens when someone pushes you to stop this nonsense, read this book, get the right cup extended, and drink the damn tea? Someone who claims to know what's best for you? While they might actually know what's best for you . . . you're unlikely to listen. In fact, you're more likely to react from Anger, Resistance, or even Hostility. Here's why:

1. You'd have to go far out of your comfort zone to make changes or integrate new patterns or ways of being, which is terrifying. And we know how you react to Fear.
2. Trying something new means having to admit you've been doing it wrong until now. That somehow your life has been wrong. Who wants that? Ironically, this acknowledgment is a sign of great intelligence. "A fool thinks himself to be wise," wrote Shakespeare, "but a wise man knows himself to be a fool."
3. It's a scary journey to explore the mysteries found in your Unconscious Mind. What might you discover down there in the depths? Perhaps on the surface you feel there's something wrong with you, and if you go searching down below, you're concerned about what horrors might be revealed or confirmed.
4. Waking up involves shadow work, cleaning up the dark stuff you won't look at—like Fear—and dark things you can't see have never been okay.

5. You like control. It's hard to own your shadow and delusion, but it's even harder to own that you're powerless over Fear. How is it possible that you're powerless over Fear? Nonsense.

6. Asking new questions isn't easy, because you're afraid of where these questions will lead you. Which is away from your Thinking Mind and into your feelings and emotions, where discomfort lies.

7. Owning and having a love affair with Fear requires you to become an expanded, bigger version of your current self. A thirteen-year-old who grows six inches in one year is all gangly and awkward. Growth is never a comfortable or pretty thing. Better to stay the same size.

All these things make sense for why you'll *avoid* change, but why go further and put up a fight? Because when someone challenges you and gets in your face, refusing to back down, or when the Fear gets to be too extreme and you can't escape, you do what anyone does: You fight.

Long before I even get to the subject of Fear, I have actually had people in my courses scream, "How dare you!" and call me evil. "No!" you'll scream. You will fight to the death for your Ego, stories, and beliefs. Some people would even murder rather than see these slip.

‖‖

A forty-something client wanting to accomplish a death-defying feat hired me for a two-hour session. He was a professional extreme athlete—one of the best in the world for more than two decades—attempting a stunt for a nationwide TV show. He'd failed twice already, almost dying in both attempts. The next day, he was going to try a third and final time, and he wanted my help to get over his now crippling Fear.

When working with a client, I ask questions rather than provide answers. I help them explore their unique relationship with Fear and allow them to come to conclusions on their own about how they should treat it.

About an hour into the process, I benignly asked to speak to the voice of Fear. It immediately became obvious that he had been severely repressing it for decades in order to be the athlete he wanted to be. Given that it was a habitual pattern, this was what he was again trying to do, but it wasn't working anymore. Quite the opposite.

I started squirming. What an awkward situation. A man so invested in repressing Fear—could we undo this pattern in one session? I've done it many times before, but those clients' lives weren't at stake the very next day.

Having repressed Fear for so long, of course, he was also a mess personally. His relationships were in ruins. He was depressed. He seemed disorganized and nervous, flaky and unfocused. Yet he was blind about why. *My God,* I thought, *I'm sitting on a simple solution that could radically alter his life and help him do the stunt.*

Yet I paused.

And did . . . nothing.

I left Fear alone. Here's why: He hadn't hired me because he wanted a happier life. He wasn't ready or interested in that. He'd hired me to help him pull off this stunt. If I gave him a juicy new stick entirely, one he may not know what to do with just yet, and sent him out there to the wolves still trying to sort it out? That didn't feel right.

Instead, I nudged awake a few voices like This Moment and Connection and sent him on his way.

Sometimes it's better to keep walking another mile in crummy shoes that are comfortable than put on new shoes and risk blisters.

FEAR IN THE BASEMENT

Three things cannot be long hidden: the sun, the moon, and the truth.

—THE BUDDHA

There's a great deal of power to be found in repressing Fear. Look at my life, for example. I did it and was able to become a world-class athlete. Over-compensation can also be very effective. I experienced fame, money, and massive attention. I'm the first to admit that there's a tremendous payoff. It can even last a decade or more before any signs of trouble appear.

From the outside, repressing Fear can often let you shine. You get to be what your parents and society want you to be. You project confidence. You don't have to deal with your demons, wounds, or delusions. You don't have to be embarrassed in public.

Even the suffering found in repressing Fear can become your home, your special, happy place. You're used to the war, and the Ego can use the drama and pain from it to make you feel invigorated, alive, and special.

The Ego will always seek to make you feel special. But that special-ness may take on interesting forms. Sometimes the Ego says, "I'm such a great athlete!" Or it may say, "I am so depressed!" with the same intensity. Whether you're special in your athleticism or you're special in your depres-sion, it's the same thing to your Ego. Maybe you're more depressed than anyone else who ever lived—the best in the world! "I am miserable, there-fore I am" can be very validating.

And addicting. Soldiers home from Afghanistan commonly report missing the excitement and camaraderie of war. Without it, life can become boring and empty. It's the adrenaline, cortisol, and drama that come from the conflict that they miss. They may feel like they're addicted to excite-ment, when really they're addicted to the drama that ensues from repressing Fear. I get it; I know this one personally.

If you're used to such Stress, the cells in your body were built upon and therefore expecting that ongoing ingredient. If there's no Stress, then you will walk around with your Unconscious Mind and Body scanning the environment—"Where's Stress? Where's Stress?"—like a smoker looking for a cigarette. And you will find Stress on any street corner if you're looking for it.

The analogy to smoking is no accident. Our most major addictions in society are actually not to sex, drugs, alcohol (or even nicotine), but to *who we believe ourselves to be*. You're no exception. Your addiction is to your Ego,

Beliefs, etc., and what you're used to feeling, and you will always go for that fix. Even if that fix is Stress and Anxiety.

When you're younger, you can sometimes get away with feeding that addiction. It ages you fast, though, and will always catch up to you someday. The same goes for repressing Fear.

When it does catch up with you, you'll know. The sensation is unmistakable. You won't know what it is, but there's a distinctive and gnawing discomfort that eventually becomes intolerable.

It could show up in 7.5 billion different ways. Maybe business keeps failing. You never really seem to go all the way with your gifts. Your growth is stagnant. You can't feel anything. You've just never had a sense of confidence. You're getting older and still remain unsure what to do with your life. Your relationships aren't good. You never get to express yourself fully. You know this ain't it, your best life.

Worse, an incurable disease gets triggered, like Alzheimer's or rheumatoid arthritis, or you become crippled by lower-back pain or a shoulder injury that won't heal. Or you get fibromyalgia and haven't a clue why or how.

Your alarm clock will have a unique screech only you can hear.

OPEN, EMPTY, UPRIGHT CUP

A man entered an outhouse. In the toilet he immediately spied a shiny gold coin sitting on top of a steaming pile of maggots, rats, and feces.

He really wanted that coin, but it required him to reach into the hole up to his shoulder. It just didn't feel worth it. Yet he couldn't turn away.

Then he had an idea! He reached into his pocket, took out another shiny gold coin, and dropped it onto the pile. Now it felt worth it.

What will tip over your cup so I can pour you another cup of tea? What will make you drink in this message—that Fear is an asset, not a hindrance—rather than spit it out? What's the tipping point?

There are three of them:

1. THE MOMENT YOU RECOGNIZE TRUTH. It's easy to recognize. There are two fears to choose from here: the fear of dealing with the discomfort of Fear itself, and the fear of never being complete, liberated, alive, and able to grow. Is it more painful to own your crap, or is it becoming more painful not to? Once the second wins, once you recognize your truth, that truth demands attention.

2. THE MOMENT YOU HIT ROCK BOTTOM. With certain seeds, only the intense heat of a forest fire will be powerful enough to crack open the hard, protective shell, allowing them to finally sprout.When your efforts to resist beat you into submission, when your suffering gets to be so profound, when the load finally gets too heavy, when the pain of avoiding Fear becomes greater than the pain of looking at it—at that point, you will become so exhausted, finally, that giving up becomes easier than hanging on. Then and only then will you get out of your own way, put down your load made heavy from your avoidance of Fear, and become who you are meant to be.

3. THE MOMENT OF YOUR DEATH. Is this when you finally climb out of your hole? If this is how long it takes, I wonder, will you wish you'd had another chance with life, one that included a love affair with Fear and all your 10,000 employees, rather than a war?

So which will it be?

Charles Du Bos once said, "The important thing is this: to be able at any moment to sacrifice what we are for what we could become." At some point you won't be able to ignore that you're capable of change, and the idea that Fear is bad will be just that: an idea. That's usually the moment when you start asking important questions and the journey starts. Action blooms from there, and you'll be willing to reach into the discomfort.

Your teacup will finally be open, empty, and upright. From this place you can receive and drink the tea, and be nourished by it.

And so we're about to get started. The solution. And I hope you're on board and as excited as I am. For if you are willing to drink this tea I'm serving, you're about to start living finally as a whole, complete human being, with all the attendant glories, and all the horrors.

PART III

SHIFT

The Game of 10,000 Wisdoms

CHAPTER 6

PICKING UP THE NEW STICK

PLAYING A LARGER GAME

He not busy being born is busy dying.

—BOB DYLAN

You're broken and you can get better" sells a ton of self-help books and workshops. This has been the whole justification behind the "conquer Fear" market. The idea is that because you have Fear, you're broken, but we can help. As you know by now, this is not one of those books. This is a larger game than that.

If you *have* gone this route, though, here's the good news: There is no such thing as the wrong experience, or the wrong path. You're always having the right experience. You are always on the right path. None of it was a waste of time, because it got you to this point. No plane is ever on a straight course toward its destination—it's always correcting. Adjusting its path over and over is the only way it gets where it wants to go.

Here, then, is the next correction you must make:

You must enter into the biggest fear of them all: the unknown. You won't know how it's going to be, or who or what you're going to become. All you know is that it will be completely different.

Choosing this new path requires you to acknowledge your fundamental delusion about yourself: that you don't know who or what you are. It also requires you to forget everything you've ever been taught about Fear, and own and acknowledge your ignorance and delusion about this emotion. Eventually comes a willingness to enter into the discomfort of Fear itself, which is also unknown territory.

What kind of adventure will you have down this crazy, uncharted path? It seems fraught with peril! It means relinquishing your long-held agendas. It means following conflict and discomfort instead of joy and love. It requires you to choose darkness over light, for at least a little while.

Your only assurance is, I promise you will come out the other side with more light than ever before. You've accomplished a lot while encased in concrete. But once you get free from it, there's no telling what you can become.

CONGRATULATE YOURSELF

It takes courage to grow up and turn out to be who you really are.

—E. E. CUMMINGS

If your answer is yes, welcome to chapter 6. This is what's known as a rude awakening. The rudeness is over. You've gone through all this trouble to feel bad; something good has to come of it, right? Now comes the awakening. You know the saying: "With all this crap, there must be a pony in here somewhere." You're about to find the pony.

Congratulations are therefore in order, for many reasons.

First, you're likely here because a problem outlined in chapter 3 caught your attention. Good. That means you didn't let a good crisis go to waste. Crisis drives evolution. If you feel you have no problems, all doorways to a better life are closed. Once you admit that there's a problem, then there's a doorway. The bigger the problem, the bigger the doorway, and the more you'll get out of this book.

Second, this is a scary world, which calls for you to be courageous. Courage is a willingness to feel Fear. Ignoring or forgetting who and what you are is remarkably easy to do, but there's no courage in that. Anyone can do it. It's a path for wimps. Fill your life with good things like paying bills, working, eating, remodeling, banking, repeating "if only, if only," and it's easy to miss your chance to make this important shift.

But great things? They come from taking the much harder and more painful path of looking inside to become a complete human being, studying who and what you are when the time is ripe, and being willing to go into that darkness. That makes you unquestionably not a wimp. It takes a brave person to own one's Fear.

Third, you're ready for a bigger game than the one you've been playing, but also a bigger game than your ancestors played. You're willing to go where your grandparents and your parents couldn't, or wouldn't, breaking the chains of repression that have stretched back as far as recorded history. (Note: This can feel disrespectful to them. If this troubles you, I recommend having a conversation with them, asking if it's okay.)

Last, your patterns of energy impact not only your life but also the lives of people you know and meet. By deciding to take responsibility for who you are, you will dramatically change your patterns of energy, and the effects will ripple around the world in a poignant way. This should be very empowering.

All this makes you one of the brave warriors of our time.

THE FIRST STEPS

The short-term pain of accepting the truth is much better than the long-term pain of believing an illusion.

—CHRISTY ALSANDOR

Eventually a caterpillar will find it impossible to stay the same, and it will anchor somewhere and start the process of becoming what it's meant to be next.

What are you becoming? Whatever it is, it's happening fast. Every field in the world—science, travel, communication, all of them—has changed tremendously in a short time. We have new tools and information available, taking us to what we're next intended to be, whether we like it or not.

The same holds true with emotions, although we're a bit behind with the transformation. We're only starting to look at how repressing emotions can lead to trouble, and that owning them is a more fruitful journey. But it has started, finally. How exciting it must look to you, then, as you take this first step as one of the early explorers, and how terrifying, too. How far will you go? How far will we all go? Where will this journey take us?

The first step involves removing the kinks in your hose, or, if you prefer, getting your wheel unstuck. How do you do this? I'm reminded of a small plastic safe from the 1950s designed to look exactly like a moldy cabbage. You fill it with money and jewels and put it in your fridge, the idea being that it looks so gross, no thief would ever look there.

Our practice involves handling and being curious about your moldy cabbages. By touching the slimiest, most disgusting thing in your house and being curious enough to find the opening, you will discover riches inside. This book is 100 percent about igniting that curiosity.

The key is to simply ask questions, rather than try to fix anything. And that's it! This isn't about thinking and talking about your emotions with a therapist for ten years. And never again is it about trying to control them, either. Focus, instead, on just being curious about what you're feeling in your body, and then allow yourself to feel it.

I will help you become tuned in to your emotions and your emotional patterns—and they *are* patterns. The Buddha was rumored to have been stabbed by a knife one day. It made him grow and grow until the knife was no more than a toothpick, which he flicked away. Be curious: Are your knives making you grow? Or are they killing you? It's up to you to see these patterns rather than continuing to withdraw into your limited experience and view.

Also, this is very important: The noticing is all that really matters. Because of this I'd prefer you didn't have a goal, but if you need one, it would look like this: We are no longer on the track to getting over Fear, or over Anger, or over Suffering of any kind. The goal is only to *embrace* these states, to be content with them, even like them. You're going down this track with the intent to joyously embrace the often horrible condition of being a human being. To love everything about this life of yours, the bad and the good. You are looking to even become content with being miserable.

Some see this as sad, but in this practice, we see it as beautiful. It's a chance to finally realize, *Hey, I'm not broken.* You're perfectly imperfect, and at the top of your potential already. You just haven't seen it yet. You've been like a beggar begging for more, while unknowingly sitting on a pot of gold.

WORTH IT

A woman gave birth to a baby in a village. Everyone in town celebrated. The baby was happy and healthy, until one evening the baby suddenly fell ill and turned green. It looked as if it wouldn't survive the night.

The villagers ran to the nearby city and asked the great master to come help save the baby's life. The master followed them home, looked at the green baby, and instructed them to gather the ten worst thieves and scoundrels in their community and bring them to the house. "We're going to have a ceremony to save this baby's life," the master said.

The villagers were stunned. Gather the worst thieves and scoundrels? That didn't make any sense! Why wouldn't he gather the most wonderful, lovely citizens for the ceremony?

They were deeply concerned, for the baby's life was at stake! But they didn't want to doubt him and his wisdom, so they acquiesced.

The ten worst thieves and scoundrels were rounded up and asked to participate in the ceremony. They, too, were confused; this was a first. But they agreed, and all night they sang and chanted with the master, until, when morning came, the baby was no longer green. Its life had been saved.

As the master departed, several citizens followed him. They stopped him at the edge of town and asked about his strange ceremony, and how it could possibly have worked. To which he replied:

"Sometimes the gates to heaven are so tightly locked, it takes a thief to pry them open."

Let's have a ceremony with Fear. Being willing to sit in a room together is the first step you take to end a strained relationship with anyone, be it a lover, parent, sibling, friend, colleague, emotion, or any of your 10,000 voices. Then own what an ass you've been—someone has to be the hero, right? With good communication, put aside your agenda, show them respect, and apologize. That's when things change, and they change fast.

What is the Golden Rule? "Do unto others as you would have them do unto yourself." All people on earth want the same thing: respect, trust, love, and a chance to be seen and heard. It's the same with your voices. That's what they want from you.

What if you were to start trusting and being curious about Fear, Anger, Sadness, Misery, Shame, Unworthiness, and more? Empower them and show them respect; then they won't have to operate covertly, in a twisted way, from the basement. They will seem radically different in an instant, and come out the opposite of how you've been experiencing them. They'll become wise assets and allies, operating in a mature way, giving you great insight, motivation, and clear vision. Show them respect, and in an instant the gates to heaven will open as 10,000 voices become 10,000 friends, then 10,000 wisdoms.

Fear is the biggie. Make friends with Fear and anything becomes possible. This is why, with new clients, I always start with Fear. Because it's the place where we're most stuck. We can't get to other journeys until your relationship with Fear is healed. It's the main ingredient in all the shadow voices. Deal with it, and you deal with them all.

Thus, a Fear practice is the key to liberation. Have one and you will feel unshackled from Fear, Fear will feel unshackled from you, and your whole being will throw a party. If you disassociate with the thief, the scoundrel, you lack the wholeness it takes to be healthy and amazing. Own the thief, the scoundrel, and you're more complete. The more complete you are, the better you're able to function.

I've spent a lot of this book saying your destiny is your Thinking Mind and the other parts of you that make up your Ego dynamic. That you can't escape them. And it's true. But there's so much more to you than just those few voices. You know this.

But if you try to go on a quest to access, say, your Spiritual Self—the part of you that's pure connectedness, the biggest version of your mind, bigger than this room, bigger than this earth, bigger than the expanding universe—and you don't first start with a great relationship with Fear, which is at the very core of who and what you are, you will fail. It's like trying to build the penthouse without first building the foundation. The penthouse will always collapse, for you'll have skipped an important step. You cannot skip a step. You must first have a great relationship with yourself.

Which means your primary job in this lifetime is to access your emotions, first and foremost, if you want to eventually reach the highest stages of consciousness.

WHAT NOT TO DO

The monk approached the master and asked, "I want to achieve Enlightenment. If I work with you, how long will it take me?"

The master replied, "Ten years!"

The monk was taken aback. "That's a long time!" He asked, "What if I work twice as hard—nights, weekends . . . Then how long?"

The master replied, "Twenty years!"

It's likely you don't even know where to start. You want to go on this journey, but if you've never been good with emotions, it's like being crippled and blind, losing your cane, getting spun in circles a few times and kicked to the ground, and now you're expected to stand up and find your way home. It pays to have a guide, someone to say, "Hey, you're only blind because your eyes are closed—start by opening them," and a map to get you home.

Open your eyes then, and let me show you what direction to travel.

A train needs two things to get somewhere: steam and tracks.

You provide the steam (right heart, passion, desire to make this shift) and I'll provide the tracks (right mind, direction, guidance).

Let's start with where not to go, what not to do.

In the Western world, a lightbulb switching on represents your mind igniting. In the East, the lightbulb switching on represents your mind disappearing. For us, the lightbulb means it's time to use what we call the Intellect (a.k.a. Thinking Mind) and get to work fixing this problem just as we have any other—like fixing a broken car.

For us Westerners, developing this cognitive Intellect gets full priority. So at this point—especially if you have a talent for figuring things out—you've gone quite far on this train down the reasoning-and-intellectual track. You probably believe this version of the Thinking Mind to be so good at anything it can fix all problems, be they psychological, spiritual, physical, or emotional. But it can't.

The Intellect is a beautiful tool, but a terrible master, especially when it comes to love, emotions, or having a bigger experience than your Ego. In fact, it is exactly because of thinking that you can never get to feeling. That mental ride will take you further and further away from the station called your Original True Nature—and further and further from our solution.

The "smarter" you are, the bigger, longer, and harder the journey home. To "fix" this problem with Fear, you need to access an entirely different intellect that exists within you—likely one that you're not familiar with in the slightest. A non-habitual intellect you've never nurtured but that is alive and well and ready for your attention.

So for you "smart" folk then, here's a list of what *not* to do.

THERAPY: When you hire a therapist who, by profession, specializes in "the mind"—and then tries to help you use your cognitive Intellect to solve an emotional problem—it wastes your time. It becomes like this giant, complicated jigsaw puzzle with pieces scattered all over, appearing and disappearing, and you have no idea what the puzzle is even supposed to look like when completed. So basically, fire your shrink. Talking and thinking about this subject—heck, any subject—can be relentless. The second you explore "I need to have a better relationship with Fear," you only get taken back to your Thinking Mind, and you can get lost in that process forever.

RELIVE EVERYTHING: You don't have to go back and feel every emotion you ever ignored, or re-live the stories behind them. You don't have to pound on pillows or talk about the time you lost your leg or was abused, in an attempt to heal. You don't have to contact people from your past to discuss what happened, or get an apology. This kind of work requires a lot of effort and unnecessary pain and seeks only to keep you in the cage, making the bars stronger. It takes you into the past and the stories there, which don't exist anymore except as a loop in your Thinking Mind and Ego dynamic. All that matters is Fear and your relationship with it, as it exists today.

MAKE SENSE OF THE PAST: No need to hash over the past and determine who or what did something to you—your parents, your teachers, the military, society—that resulted in your repressing emotions. It's like having an arrow sticking out of your chest, lying there bleeding on the ground, and discussing who shot you, when they did it, why, where it happened, and whether they might come back and shoot you again. Instead, let's simply take the arrow out and let you heal.

TRY AS HARD AS YOU CAN: This is not a time to put on the *Rocky* theme music and give it everything you got. Here's where the Will also no longer works. I get that you crave a new relationship with Fear, and care a lot about getting it right. But the solution can be as simple or as complicated as being in a river: If the Will tries to push the river or compel you to swim upstream, that gets ridiculous and complicated fast. It's much more simple if you wade out and let it take you where it wants to go.

HAVE AN AGENDA: Stop planning. Plans fall apart. While the outcome of this practice does indeed result in less Fear and Anxiety and more Joy, if your agenda is to "embrace Fear as a way to get rid of it," that's another form of trying to conquer Fear, and Fear is too smart for that crap.

HAVE A GOAL: Ditch these, too. Goals cause tension. Especially having an expectation or goal to "feel better" in the future. Stop reaching for a carrot you think exists outside yourself as you stand here, as you are, today. It will always prove out of reach.

ANTICIPATE AN IMPROVED YOU: Don't expect to come through the other side of this a "better, stronger, faster" version of your Self. This is not about self-improvement the way that you currently understand it. This is about just . . . being. You have to be where you are first. This is how you become better, stronger, faster without much effort.

HOPE: Stop clinging to hope—it just causes tension. It also keeps you focused on a better future. Again, you have to be where you are today, especially if what's true for you today is Hopelessness. There should be some relief in this.

LOOK FOR ANSWERS: Stop trying to "figure things out"—sometimes life isn't about that. The harder you look, the more wondering "how" takes over, and then you're back to thinking instead of feeling. Consider: What would it be like to live in a world where everything has an answer or can be explained or understood? Imagine what you would lose. Curiosity and an open mind, that's what. Instead, stop looking for answers and seek only questions.

LOOK FOR CLARITY OR CERTAINTY: It's all so impermanent anyway. In six seconds it will change. Just go for awareness.

TRY TO DISCARD PARTS OF YOU: Remember how you got here in the first place? Right: trying to get rid of Fear by locking it in the basement. Do not try to get rid of any voice like excessive Fear, Stress, Anxiety, excessive Anger, etc. You'll only drive yourself nuts. Be aware of them, notice them, acknowledge them, and be curious about them. That's our practice.

ASK HOW: The Buddha achieved Enlightenment with a single shift while looking at Venus. He stopped asking how. Do this and the answer will just be there.

TRY TO KNOW ANYTHING COMPLETELY: And lastly, if you have to know anything for sure, it's a form of Resistance. "The only true wisdom is knowing you know nothing," Socrates observed. When you realize that you don't know who you are, and don't know anything about Fear, you have arrived at a *very* deep insight, one of the deepest there is.

In conclusion, here's where you stop trying to make sense of Fear, or of anything. This place is one of Not Knowing, Not Seeking, Not Thinking. Like when you look at the rain, and don't need to know what it means. It's unexplainable, but you can feel it, sense it, or, better yet, at times, even *be* it.

Yet even writing this, trying to use words to explain the unexplainable— do you notice already we're in the wrong place? We're already back to the Thinking Mind working hard to make sense of what exactly it is I'm asking you to be or not to be.

THE THINKING MIND

Train tracks were laid in a remote village. The next day, the villagers stood in amazement as a big black locomotive rolled into town, burping black smoke, and came to an ominous stop.

They ran to grab two wise men from town—Simple Joe and Analytical Joe—to help them with this moment.

Analytical Joe got right to work trying to figure out how the train functioned. He entered the engine compartment, computing how logs added to the fire created heat, which created steam.

Simple Joe, meanwhile, went and talked to the conductor. He asked, "How long have you been doing this?" The conductor replied, "A long time."

"Does it work?" he asked. The conductor said, "Yep. Works great." With that, Simple Joe got on the train.

It started to move.

Analytical Joe quickly jumped off, for he still hadn't sorted out how the tracks and the wheels worked. When he finally decided to get on the train, however, it was already moving too fast and he was left behind.

Your Thinking Mind is not the right tool for the job of feeling your emotions. But you will try to use it anyway. Why is that?

This voice rules your life, that's why. It will try to rule this problem, too, but I assure you it is the wrong voice.

It's like having only a screwdriver in your toolbox. Screwdrivers are great, but if that's the only tool you have to build a whole house, you won't be able to get the job done.

In short, the Thinking Mind, while a beautiful tool, is a terrible master. Put the Thinking Mind in charge of anything and you'll become very limited.

And yet the Thinking Mind, which created the problem with Fear, is also . . . brace yourself . . . *the solution*. It is up to you whether you tap into the delusion found in this mind or tap into its wisdom.

Delusion comes when this mind remains subjective—meaning you think that it is you and you are it. Thus, you remain unconscious of any other perspective.

Wisdom comes from seeing it objectively, being conscious of the fact that it is not you, and you are not it. Thus, you can witness it as the amazing tool it is, become conscious of it, and gain a new perspective. Two different choices: One makes you struggle, the other does not.

Making this shift from the Thinking Mind being subject to object is the single most important step you will ever take in your life. Do this and suddenly this mind is no longer holding you hostage, and other minds/ voices will finally become obvious and available to you—9,999, to be exact. That's a whole lotta new tools in your toolbox.

IT IS NOT YOU, AND YOU ARE NOT IT

No problem can be solved from the same consciousness that created it. We must learn to see the world anew.

—ALBERT EINSTEIN

Before we delve into Shift, let's go back a step and examine how you typically relate to the Thinking Mind. This is important for helping you to recognize when you fall back into your habitual patterns around this mind, which you will.

The Thinking Mind's job is only to think, but you demand a lot from it. You expect it to decipher what's real and what's not, to be clear, to understand and know things for sure, to fill in any gaps with beliefs, to make perfect decisions and then quiet down and be reasonable when your day is done.

Take a moment, though, to ask, who is the "you" that is demanding a lot from this mind? It is actually your True Self who is pondering that question. Pretty neat, eh?

Once you separate from the Thinking Mind, you can see all this. And in that moment, you can also see how maddening this relationship can be. If you're unconscious about it, you're unconscious about yourself and why you act the way you act, and that's a tough, repetitive, robotic life.

But if you're conscious about it, that means you have a relationship with it, and you can start to witness it. Question it. Challenge it. Not believe everything it tells you. With that radically different form of awareness, suddenly you have choices.

But, you must proceed wisely. At this point, many try to discard the Thinking Mind. *Blech. Get it away. It's not going to help me feel my feelings.* It holds you back from love. It holds you back from connectedness. Anyone with a consciousness practice tends to want to keep a distance from this mind as a next step on the path to freedom from the cage. "Quiet the mind" practices also sell a lot of events and self-help books.

This is not one of those books.

Because of such practices, one of the most common pieces of advice about the Thinking Mind and how to discard it—as well as a thought, a belief, Ego, Fear, Jealousy, Anger, etc.—is to "let it go." It's the worst advice I've ever heard. If your friends say it—about anything—please either fire them or retrain them. How do you let go of something, anyway?

Well, you don't.

You don't have that kind of power over the Thinking Mind, much less Grief, Fear, or any of the 10,000 minds. You don't have that kind of power over any river or force.

Take Grief, for example. You can't move forward if you haven't felt the Grief or Fear from experiences or failures behind it. It will still have its hold on you. You have to feel the feeling first. We all know that.

Second, you often don't even know what it is you'd be letting go of. It may feel like one thing (thoughts, Fear, Grief) when it's entirely another (Clinging, Resistance, Control).

Third, letting go is too passive. If you ate a meal, would you want to let it go? No way. (Well, maybe doughnuts.) Instead, use the Thinking Mind, its thoughts, and other voices to your advantage, and extract the nutrients first.

What I propose instead, then, is "let it be." Why not acknowledge and embody the Grief and Fear of any of the minds first, including the Thinking Mind. If it has a crazy thought, which is the voice of the Crazy Mind, stay in the craziness. If it's Grief, stay in the grief. Whether it's Fear, the voice of Suffering, or what have you, stay in it and learn from it. Juice insights from it like you'd juice an orange. Get every drop.

If you do this, all the way, you'll become a student of these thoughts and emotions. At some point you'll even develop a sense of humor about them. That's when you know it's time to move on, but it will require no effort. Do all this, and at this point these voices, including the Thinking Mind, will simply let go of you.

HOW ABOUT CONTROLLING THE THINKING MIND?

What we're doing here is first sorting out the board of directors. They and you need to be clear on their roles before we can start talking to the rest of the corporation. Which leads us to: What about controlling thoughts?

The Controller knows better than to try controlling the heart's pumping blood or the stomach's secreting acid (aside from taking blood thinners and Tums), but when it comes to thoughts, that seems mandatory. Because . . . well, the Thinking Mind is crazy. It chatters on and on at the most inopportune times. It's like the annoying guy at the board meeting with the messy hair and ripped clothing. Let's just say that I've facilitated the voice of the Thinking Mind and the voice of Insanity in the same hour, and there's not much difference.

It has such incredible control over you that it seems radically important to believe you can control it back. The thought that you don't have control over the Thinking Mind is horrifying. We can't stand the idea that we're being run, for the most part, unconsciously by a voice that, more often than not, is insane.

Drugs and alcohol are one solution.

But if you fancy yourself smart, controlling it without vices can often become a test to see how smart you really are. Here are a few tried-and-true ways people attempt to control their mind without drugs. New ones pop up all the time, but the current standards are:

1. **TALK THERAPY.** Setting up an appointment with your shrink is a classic strategy. You attempt to confront"crazy" by being in the same room with it, rather than drowning it out or running away from it. You'll reason with it, hoping you can get a sense of control over it, with the goal of making the insanity of this mind sane. And it works: You walk away from your sessions feeling clearer about your life and more in control than when the hour started—for one day, at least.

2. **COGNITIVE BEHAVIORAL THERAPY OR NEW AGE PRACTICE.** These are different practices, but the same in that they also say you're not a victim to this mind's erratic thoughts. Their strategy is to approach the situation as if your mind were a computer. What do we know about computers? If they have programs that don't work, they get reprogrammed. Thus, just repattern or reroute your mental circuits and things will be very different, simply because you made your mind different. Brain science even supports these claims. You can create your own programming, your own reality. Even "living fearlessly" is possible, the claim goes, if you program it to think fearless thoughts. Or, hell, go for gratitude. Or self-acceptance. You name it! Any new programming is yours if you do the work.

3. **MEDITATION.** Last but not least, meditation is a very popular route. No one would ever argue that meditation is about controlling the mind,

or about discarding it, but if you're doing it to feel better, or be calmer, or be free from thoughts more often—which many people are—it is. The concept is that our mind is like a wild, volatile child who—after he or she finally gets undivided, completely focused attention—calms down. We like calm children.

These all work to control the Thinking Mind. But, alas, they make for a long, hard journey. It can take twenty years or more of therapy or, yes, even meditation to maybe arrive somewhere sane. And take even one day off from meditation and you'll notice a little slip back toward insanity, even if it's twenty years into your practice. Don't even think of taking off a whole week.

For these are old-school maps that will take you on a much harder or longer journey than necessary to your destination. They're like using Rand McNally or asking directions at a gas station to get somewhere, when Google Maps and GPS are available—new, simpler guides that offer a more easeful journey. Today, you don't have to work like a dog, invest years, or remain confused or frustrated to get where you want to go.

What this 10,000-voice game is, is a sophisticated new system and map. I'm a modern guide. What I'm offering is the most direct route to having relief from the Thinking Mind, and to accessing Fear—and your other voices—which comes only once you are free from thoughts. And it doesn't involve controlling the Thinking Mind, or much of anything, for that matter.

WHAT ABOUT CONTROLLING FEAR?

There are two mistakes one can make along the road to truth: not going all the way, and not starting.

—THE BUDDHA

And we're back to Fear. Every book out there talks at some point about controlling or reframing Fear as a path to freedom. But ask yourself if you really think it is possible to think yourself free from Fear, or that Fear can be trained to not be afraid?

As we've explored, looking to render Fear powerless is, as we'll soon learn with the Thinking Mind, a long, difficult, all-consuming battle with devastating results. Along the way you will be beaten into submission by this voice. The more you try to get rid of Fear, the more afraid you will feel. The more you try to get rid of Anger, the angrier you will feel. The more you try to control any voice, the more out of control you will feel about it. The more you try to understand, the further from the truth you will become.

I say again: Do the exact, radical opposite. Therapy, reprogramming, and meditation are limited in their ability to reduce Fear. The quickest path to freedom is so simple: Just realize that, aside from avoiding or repressing it, you have limited control over Fear, the Thinking Mind, or any other voice. Whatsoever. They are not puppies eager to please. You can't change Fear's nature. Fear is never not going to be afraid. You can't calm it down. You can't let it go. And why would you want to? Fear is a very old dog. You are not the authority on how it should or should not behave. If training it to be what you want it to be is your intention, it will only exhaust you.

Give up all hope of ever controlling Fear; only then you can start to feel, and start to heal.

WHAT *CAN* YOU CONTROL?

The Controller needs to have *something* to do. Here's what's possible, then: It can control the situations you put yourself in that warrant Fear. For instance, if it's scary to learn to ski, don't learn to ski—and, voilà, no Fear. But as we've explored, it can't control Fear itself.

Here's what else it can control. Let's say you decide to learn to ski anyway, because you know it would be a tragedy to go through life without challenges. You take your first lesson, and actually ski your first run without falling down. Success! At this point people say they "overcame the Fear" and did it anyway. But that's not true: The Fear is still there. You didn't overcome the Fear; Fear is what made the whole experience thrilling. You overcame *the situation.*

All Fear goes through your mental prism. Thus, it's not the feeling that moves you—it's the interpretation of the feeling. If you interpret Fear as a good thing, you will enjoy the experience. If you interpret Fear as a bad thing, you either won't enjoy the experience or flat-out won't have it. How you perceive your life, reality, or Fear, then, is what matters. Perspective is everything.

So the Controller, while it can't change or control the Fear, can change or control your perception of it. This is one way the Controller can be of great use.

The proper way to describe going through an experience that is challenging, then, is that you *enjoyed* the Fear. Not that you *overcame* it. You are not smarter than Fear. But with the Controller helping out, you are smarter than the situation.

MUCH MORE SIMPLE: LET IT BE

The real voyage of discovery consists not in seeking new landscapes, but in having new eyes.

—MARCEL PROUST

What if you don't try to override Fear or the Thinking Mind, but rather work with them?

What if, instead, you acquiesce: "This mind thinks it's in charge, and so it is"? Its job is to think, not do what you want it to do. What if you don't challenge that, and just admit to being human? Why not stop trying to control, understand, manipulate, calm, mold, cajole, and transform it, and instead let it do its thing, crazy and all?

Let insanity do its thing and you'll be fine. The Thinking Mind is not meant to be sane. We get that wrong.

Think about it this way: For thousands of years, people have been trying to control the Thinking Mind, or telling it to shut up. That's like confining a wild horse in a tiny box. Who wouldn't feel crazy? Trying to control your mind is like trying to control your children, or your enemy. And we all know how that goes.

Keep doing this, and this mind *will* rebel on you. You'll only make it more crazy. You may as well be kicking a hive of hornets that's sitting in your head. May I remind you that "Think positive thoughts" is exactly what caused our problems with Fear in the first place? Same here: You do not want to piss these voices off.

So stop spending so much time on it, and put the wild horse out to pasture. It works great; simply let it do its thing. This will free up energy so we can get down to other important business, like the business of feeling your emotions. Finally.

LET IT DO WHAT IT'S DESIGNED TO DO

A king was rich, but not, he felt, rich enough. In his castle was a four-foot-thick steel door behind which lay riches ten times what he possessed. But he couldn't get through that damn door, no matter what he tried.

Finally, in desperation, he offered to share the riches fifty-fifty with any man who could break open the door. Next morning, a tremendous line formed and, one by one, armed with the latest technologies—cannons, drills, explosives—men tried to bust open the door.

Nothing worked. Until one man approached the door, put his hand on the knob, turned it, and opened the door.

Relinquishing total control is, of course, difficult for the Controller. It's used to thinking there are riches to be found in your Unconscious Mind by ramming down doors or taking prisoners. There aren't. What else can it focus on, then, to make the best use of its considerable expertise?

In order to form a new relationship with Fear, let's encourage the Controller to—you know the prayer—not waste time on things it cannot control, focus on the things it can control, and have the wisdom to know the difference.

By now you recognize that the Thinking Mind is not an animal to be trained. Nor is it a computer that needs reprogramming. This is very important: It's an individual, a very important employee in your corporation. And it works great, so long as you let it do what it's designed for and needs to do. Same with Fear, and the Lizard Brain, which is what this book is ultimately about. These are all big players in your Unconscious Mind, running your show on the surface.

Now, if you want to get the best possible work out of an important and wise employee, what do you do?

Would you drug him? Attempt to fire him? How about put duct tape over his mouth to keep him quiet? Make demands? Try to change him? See him as useful for some jobs, like building bridges or keeping you safe, but to be discarded for other jobs, like sleeping or love?

Do any of these things and you'll have a tumultuous relationship with this individual. This is not just bad for you, but bad for the whole corporation. Not only this employee but others will be on edge. Production will fall way down. Few will be able to do their jobs to their full potential. Most will wind up angry and frustrated and sit around watching cat videos on YouTube all day.

Do you want to be a great manager? Like the ones who get awards and create profitable businesses? Then do as they do: offer your employees consideration, curiosity, respect, and compassion. These are the conditions under which any voice will give you its best work.

Controller, are you listening?

You may think that your way out of the hole is to control or change a voice, which is a huge job. Actually changing the prism through which you view it is much easier and more effective. Take the cuffs off these individuals then, and instead empower them. Listen to them, observe how they work, and remain curious as you watch them do their jobs that only they can do.

Much like when you listen to your children or your parents when they're trying to figure something out, they will appreciate it—and become better people for it. They will be at peace. Don't forget to feed them, too. They like stimulation. In turn, they will love and feed a gorgeous part of you back.

CHAPTER 7

LISTENING TO THE VOICES

OKAY, NOW YOU ARE READY

If you wish to make an apple pie from scratch, you must first invent the universe.

—CARL SAGAN

With appropriate tasks for the Thinking Mind and the Controller to focus on, there is a new kind of freedom at your fingertips. For starters, the Thinking Mind will take care of all the thinking, which (oh my) means you don't have to.

This is huge. You are now outside the cage, or call it "outside the box." What's it like to not be bothered by thinking? Such freedom! What you want can now find you, or you can go find it. Now we can get to the business of feeling our emotions, and solving this emotional problem *emotionally.*

Imagine you've been a guitarist holding a beautiful guitar your whole life, but thus far you've played only a few chords. Look around: There are now possibilities everywhere—in fact, thousands of other chords and instruments you never even noticed, also at your fingertips. Let's move toward experiencing whole-mind thinking, then. Let's engage the full orchestra and finally make some beautiful music.

Emotional intelligence being our next chord. I want you to go find it. What do people who have a healthy relationship with their emotions experience? Let me give you a vision now of what you're going for: that jigsaw puzzle in completion, of which Fear makes up an important piece. Each step transcends and includes the last, and the puzzle comes together like this:

1. Once you realize you are not the Thinking Mind, and you treat it with respect like any good friend would, the Thinking Mind, free to finally be itself, calms down and drops off.

2. Now you can just start feeling instead. This comes by actively paying attention and connecting to the wisdom of the Body, which is where emotions are felt.

3. Fear can now make its presence known, and you can shift to feel it and connect to it as it exists in your Body, allowing it to speak for itself.

4. When you do this fully, connecting with feeling Fear or other emotions, your Body will also become unclogged and open up, so yet again there will be room for other voices to enter.

5. With Mind (and thus Ego) and now Body dropped off, that means plenty of room for something really big. You can now experience voices beyond your ability to grasp like Big Mind, Connected Self, or the Infinite.

6. But it's not over yet. Our ultimate, whole, complete puzzle doesn't stop here, but rather includes coming back to your human side: back to your Ego, Thinking Mind, Stories, Lizard Brain, Fear, Body, and all other employees that make us human. Tapping into all intelligence, including the intellectual, physical, emotional, and spiritual, which I'll go over soon, all the 10,000 voices are now accessible, and you are complete, whole, and free. You are an important, unique, and distinctly different puzzle piece made up of 10,000 wisdoms, within a giant picture of the whole universe. This is the truth of who and what you are.

ASK THE RIGHT QUESTIONS AND THE ANSWER WILL FIND YOU

The unexamined life is not worth living.

—SOCRATES

If you want to arrive right away at number 6, you're already lost. Start with this realization instead: The puzzle is already complete and put together. The orchestra is already playing a beautiful concert. Your penthouse is already perfectly built. You just need to wake up to see that you are already whole, complete, finished, and incredible. There is no place to arrive; you're already there.

What is the secret of awakened people who get this? Is it becoming a monk, being a vegan, being celibate? Nope. Does it transmit to you from a guy wearing a robe at the front of the room? Definitely not.

It's merely that—usually through suffering—a curiosity has been awakened inside of you and you've begun asking bigger questions. Some questions might include:

What am I?
Why do I exist?
What is my purpose?

The journey does not get started until these questions get ignited. The questions are the only things that matter. The quality of your life is determined by the quality of the questions you ask yourself every day.

Here's another big question to add to your list:

What do I feel?

As humans, we were put on this earth for one reason: to feel. So when you ask this question, leading to even a glimpse of what you feel, that's the only question you need, to confirm you're alive.

Once you can do this, all I've described becomes possible.

Here's another big question: What's your relationship with Fear, and is it the best relationship possible?

If you think you've arrived at an answer already, that means your cup is not empty. You're in full-cup Expert's Mind, which is not open to new experiences. Believing you've "figured out" the answer means you are unconscious to the real answer, which is always going to start with "I don't know." The more aware you are of all that you don't know or haven't figured out yet, the more conscious you can become—about this, about anything.

You have to start with not knowing. You have to be willing to first sit in confusion about the answer, about any answer. So figure out some kind of logic that puts you in empty-cup Beginner's Mind, where you don't know anything, which will lower your defenses and allow space for a new experience.

Then say this out loud: "I don't know what my relationship is with Fear." No clue! How could you? The relationship is being carried out in your Unconscious Mind, so finding an answer is like swinging at the moon with a stick. Start with confusion, and stay in curiosity. This is how your mind will be free to fly wherever it wants. Do this and, like magic, you can ask the question "What do I feel?" and you won't need to find the answer. Instead—*the answer will find you.* Soon you'll arrive at a true and fascinating clarity found in the Body.

This is our practice. Not trying to get rid of Anxiety anymore. Not even trying to get along better with Fear. Not trying to get to peace. Just asking questions. Chasing answers, but never catching them. The goal is merely to ask questions and nothing more. Like the greyhound chasing a rabbit on the track, never catching it but happy to do it again and again, day after day.

If this causes you to scream, shove the book into the bathwater, or flip through the pages, thinking, *Come on! I just want to know how I do this!*— okay, I'll oblige you: Find your answer by living the question "How do I do this?" physically. On your own, if you must, or with a teacher if you can find one who offers an embodied practice. But just keep asking it—this or any question—until the answer becomes found and obvious in your Body, merely in the ongoing question.

This is how to have the best possible relationship with Fear—the easy way—because not knowing is where real wisdom lies.

LISTENING TO THE VOICES

The master was given a piece of cake by a student. The student, always curious about the mind, asked, "Do you eat cake with the mind of the past, the mind of the future, or the mind of the present?" The master shrugged and said, "I eat cake with my mouth."

Learning to do anything can be likened to learning to ride a bike (even learning to ride a bike). First you try a tricycle and learn to ride it. Next comes a bike with training wheels. Then one without training wheels. Maybe you fall a few times. And, step by step, you get there.

The practice of Shift is no different. In case you haven't figured it out by now, where we're headed is not just a better relationship with Fear, but going all the way with being a human being, Fear and all—because so much of what makes you human includes recognizing your delusion and sitting in the wretched discomfort of Fear.

Each step involves asking questions and getting to know yourself better with each question. Each step takes you on a path from *becoming* to *being* completely who and what you are.

Here's the step we're taking next: You and the Thinking Mind can now witness and listen to the 9,999 other minds. You can ask, for example, "Fear, what are you feeling?" And get an answer that is from Fear, not from any other mind attempting to speak for it. It may simply say, "I'm feeling afraid," or "I'm feeling ignored." Merely by asking questions, Fear (aka the Fearful Mind) can now speak its truth through it. You can witness and listen to Judgment, which is another voice. Or Joy. Or Anger or Sadness or Hopeless. You can observe all these voices speaking their truth like a meditator watches the clouds come and go, without identifying with them. This is you being aware and having an experience of what is true in this moment—without differentiating good from bad, without distinction or preferences, although that includes being aware of the voice of Preferences.

From this place, any employee can now speak and not feel threatened. Jealousy can advise. Hatred can give you insight. Worry can enlighten. You can witness the wisdom of any of your many minds . . . with a simple promotion to the one listening to them all: Curiosity.

SHIFT, THE GAME OF 10,000 WISDOMS

I like the word "flow" because it suggests a river. The river doesn't leap out to find you, and you can't alter its course to suit your needs. Instead, you need to be more proactive. You must be curious enough to go find it—to find Flow, and jump into the mighty river of it.

Here's where we can finally see the world anew, from a different form of consciousness. You are going to seek out and jump into these voices. You are going to become them. Starting with the Body.

Up until now, you have been observing a few of the 10,000 voices flowing through the hose. Shift can offer you that: the perspective that they are not you and you are not them, and thus you can witness their roles in your life. Now, this is a major turning point in the book, where the next step is learning how to first connect to, then feel, then *become* them. Any of them, even the ones we haven't yet explored. You will learn how to speak as them.

Look at the language I'm using. Words are important. Thinking about

Joy is one experience. Experiencing Joy—that's another. Then there's feeling Joy, which takes you into your Body. But notice the separation that remains in these between you (subject) and Joy (object). *Being* Joy is another experience entirely, when all separation is gone and you know you've gone all the way.

Be the Controller. Be the Thinking Mind, or Anger, Jealousy, or whatever it is that shows up in your hose. Feeling your emotions is only partway there, while being your emotions allows you access to the core truth of what they have to say—their wisdom, and how in return *they're* experiencing this corporation called You.

They are going to become your states of being now, no longer just voices. You will not be doing an exercise pretending to be the Body. You will not be acting like the Body. You will not be aware of it, the way you're aware of a cat. You will become the Body. There is a *huge* difference. You'll know it when you get it right. Welcome to Shift, the Game of 10,000 Wisdoms.

It works like this: to recognize and then be what you're feeling right now, whatever it is that shows up, simply speak as that voice. Do it out loud if you prefer. Speak in the first person as the voice ("I"), and refer to yourself in the third person ("he" or "she," or your name). And do it one voice at a time. "I am the Body." Now "I am Fear." As with a ham radio, if you move the dial too fast, you hear only gibberish. You must instead move one frequency at a time to access clarity.

Witness a single voice, notice your cognitive needs to understand it, and drop yourself just as you would drop a pen, and jump as you would from one train track to the other. In an instant, shift out of your current self and become this voice, without trying to understand. It's like breathing: I cannot explain how to breathe other than to say just open up and breathe. Same here. Jump track, without need for further explanation, and be there now.

You can't understand this place. You can't get to this place. But now you can *be* this place. Once you get that there is nothing to get, you're there. There is no other way. Just step to the inside of a voice as simply as you'd enter a room, and speak as that voice.

Standing on the steep slope, I pressed my forehead into the snow in between ice axes, presumably to rest. Breathing into the snow heavily, emotionally, as Love, I heard my rhythmic gurgles echoing back in my ears like whispers. A bit of drool started falling slowly from my mouth. Abruptly, I stood back up to face the sunshine.

In a triangle extending up from either side of my backpack were my skis, strapped together at the top. They were heavy. I started climbing again.

This was my second attempt to ski the Grand Teton, in Jackson Hole, Wyoming.

It was rumored no one had ever skied it on their first attempt. Three weeks earlier, I'd found out why. The Grand is a mountain without a bottom—like an ice cream cone. You climb straight up the edge of the cone, and once you get to the ice cream, you look up: the ice cream isn't ice cream at all, but rather nasty freezer burn. Then you look down. The drop-off below is so shocking and abrupt, you say, "This is ridiculous," then rappel back down and go home. At least that's what I did.

Now I was back. There were four of us. Climbing the cone requires first stepping above a 1,000-foot drop-off in one move, then climbing a second 1,000 feet of nearly vertical ice. We'd had to move fast because of the avalanche danger above, and, since belaying each other takes forever, we climbed all but 20 feet of it without using ropes.

Getting to the lip, this time the ice cream was three-foot-deep slushy, like from a 7-Eleven, perched on a tipped fifty-five-degree sheer pane of glass. Not quite ready to slide off, but close. There was also a five-foot-deep runnel made of hard, white ice, deeply grooved in the middle from where prior avalanches had shucked their paths. This was what we would climb up next.

I was about to make history.

WAKING UP THE WISDOM OF YOUR BODY

A man walked past the Buddha on the street and stopped in shock, taken aback by his light. Incredulously, he asked the Buddha, "What are you, a god?"

The Buddha said no.

"A wizard?" Again no.

"A man?" No.

"Well, then, what are you?"

The Buddha replied, "I am awake."

It's the Body's job to feel, not the Mind's. Get this at your core. Your mind thinks. Your Body feels. Which is why you must stop thinking about Fear, in order to feel Fear.

The best way I've found to do this is through our game. Using Shift, not only can you have an eagle-eye view of your patterns, and witness how much and how fast you change as these voices come and go, all from a different form of consciousness, but you can actually have a physically embodied experience of being a voice.

We search for truth and wisdom everywhere. We take classes and go to the best teachers. We look so hard for freedom. Maybe it's found in this man? Or this divorce? Or this ski trip? It's rare that we look internally. This game helps you do that.

It provides a map of your Unconscious Mind. Like a map to Paris, say. But you must play the game. For if you only study that map, only think about going to Paris, only talk endlessly about Paris, visualize it, watch a movie about it, that does not mean you've been to Paris.

You actually have to physically go there. Similarly, you do not awaken by thinking about spirituality; it is something you must physically experience. You do not feel your emotions by thinking about them; you have to travel to and live in the place where they exist. Which is in the Body.

Are you still thinking about what this means? If yes, that's the Thinking Mind still creating separation. You cannot trust the Ego or the Thinking Mind, because it argues with reality. These minds lie, and do not take you to what you feel.

Your Body, however, does not lie. Which is why, when you ask the question "what do I feel?" and you have the tool (Shift) to travel to where the answer lies—which is the Body—you can live the answer and be free to access the voice of Fear in an authentic way.

The Body is the only place where true awareness is accessed. You can trust what you find there to be real.

<hr>

On my first traverse across the top of the tilted slushy, a two-foot-deep fracture split off to the left and right between my skis, loudly and abruptly like a lightning bolt.

Avalanche!

The wad of mush moved slowly the first few feet, and I rode it down the mountain. Just before it accelerated, I gently stepped uphill with my left leg, shook my right leg out of the avalanche, then watched it accelerate to seventy miles an hour in an instant. My friends called it "the move." I was like the Road Runner when he finds himself three feet off the edge of a cliff, pauses, then quickly steps back onto the cliff. *Did that really just work?*

Sure did. Within seconds, the avalanche hit the edge of the cone below, exploded into the air with a roar, then disappeared abruptly over the edge. We could hear it crashing violently down the mountain, out of sight, for a full minute.

I hadn't even taken my first turn.

Over the next hour, when I did turn, that caused even more slides. It was very steep. The snow above me was a wall I could easily touch with my elbow bent. With each turn I shaved off another six inches of slush and rode it each time for about seven feet, curling my toes, before clawing to a stop again. Then I sewed my mind back together and prepared for the next turn. This was how I skied the first female descent down the Grand Teton. I averaged about two turns per minute.

Crossing the runnel was one of the hardest things I've ever done on skis. Equally steep, it was pure ice, and so concave that as I crossed it, my skis seemed to bend almost in half. I held my breath, put my hand on the upper slope for balance, and, in one dynamic, quick move, squirted my way to the other side. All above that 2,000-foot cliff.

This is what's called no-fall skiing. If you fall, you die. And it's really hard not to fall.

My heroin this day was Fear, as it had been for years. It's not excitement, it's not adrenaline—those are just after-effects. I was high on Fear. It was as much of a problem in my life, by this point, as heroin. People who are addicted to Fear don't live very long.

But I didn't care, because this heroin was so good. I'd rather feel this one moment of Aliveness, Presence, Focus, Intensity, and Lust in my Body—all which come from Fear—than decades of nothing.

HOW DO YOU DO THIS?

Ask the question "What do I feel?" To answer, please, now, allow me to speak to the voice of Body. With a physical shift, you're there.

ME: Hi, whom am I speaking to?
YOU: The Body.
ME: What is your job in this corporation?
YOU: I am here to sense things. And to feel things. I also pump blood, breathe, digest food, and much more.
ME: What do you feel right now?
YOU: I'm tired. I can feel it in my neck. And hungry. I've run out of energy.
ME: How can the self support you?

YOU: Listen to me. I need sleep, good food. Also, I want to move. I want to be touched. I want to feel. Pay attention to me. I am you, after all.

Here's how to tell when you're *not* there:

> If you think you've succeeded and think you are the Body, you are not the voice. You're still some sort of mind. You can't *think* you're something and be it at the same time.

> If you try to understand, question, or doubt—*Is it really true that I'm the voice of the Body, or am I still "me"?*—that's not the voice.

> If you pretend to be it, you're not it.

> If I ask you, as the Body, "How do you feel?" and you respond, "I think I feel . . ." you're not there. You're still the voice of the Mind. Anytime you say, "I think . . ." when playing this game, the Thinking Mind or one of his friends is speaking, and won't be saying a voice's truth, but rather its own.

> If you're trying to get to any kind of solution, or realization, you're not the voice.

The tipping point is this: Much as with Paris, you have to be there to be there. Not trying to understand this place. Not trying to get to this place. Just be in this place. Get that there's nothing to get, and you're there.

Here are a few drills you can use to land. These drills allow you to embody, and therefore become, any voice, not just the Body.

> Stand up and stretch open space in between your thoughts, bones, ligaments, etc. A voice needs space to enter, or else it won't.

> Many spiritual traditions seek to make the Body so uncomfortable (fasting, excessive heat or cold, slapping) that you can't help but become it. So imagine being thirsty. Not just any kind of thirst, either—you're in a 110-degree desert for days without water. Can you see you are now your Body? Now, imagine that it grows and grows until you become the Thirst. Every cell in your

body is the Thirst, until the mind or Self no longer exists. This illustrates the full embodiment of a voice.

› In Zen, there's a riddle: How do you fall into a thousand-foot-deep well? The answer is: You just take a step over the edge, and down you go. You just do it. Same here.

› It's hard to think and breathe at the same time. Get out of your head by breathing as the Body for a spell, *then* talk as the voice of the Body.

› If you're thinking about a past injury or where a pain comes from, that is not the voice of the Body. The body has no recall of past or future. Its truth exists only in this moment.

› Put your hand on your head; speak from there. Now put your hand on your heart. Or your solar plexus, your belly, etc. Speak from there instead. You are now the voice of one part of the Body.

› If I ask you, as the Body, "How do you feel?" start your sentences with the words "I feel . . ." You may say: "I feel cold." "I feel sad." "I feel afraid." Or whatever it is you are aware off. And that's it. That's your truth.

› Stay curious. The second there's a judgment (like "I should put on a sweater") or a need to know (like "Why am I feeling sad?"), you're back in the Thinking Mind. If this happens, simply add another drop of curiosity and ask the question again—"What do I feel?"— and in an instant, answer the question anew as the voice of the Body.

› You must be fully present. Visiting Paris means nothing until you allow yourself to feel the wind on your face and smell the flowers in springtime. Until then, you're not really in Paris. You must integrate and fully experience these sensations to really be there.

Then, notice, and nothing more.

DO OR DON'T DO THESE VOICES

Doris approached me after a speech and said, "My husband recently died, and I'm lonely. Can you recommend a community I might join?"

I happily talked to her for twenty minutes and made several suggestions. She thanked me and left.

Her friend came up afterward and asked, "I saw you talking to Doris. Did she ask you to recommend communities she might join?" I said yes. To which he said, "Her husband died seven years ago. She asks everyone who comes through here to recommend communities, yet she's never once joined any of them."

Don't be like Doris. You know that feeling your emotions is important, but at some point you will get stuck trying, seeking, and being curious about them, all of which feels like movement because you're being proactive. Same with asking how to, thinking about, intending to, committing to feeling your emotions. Just know that these are not right efforts. Do all this and notice: There isn't any movement.

This is why "Do or don't do this practice—be or don't be these voices" is all that matters. The rest is a waste.

A MUCH-NEEDED PROMOTION TO THE EMPLOYEE CALLED THE BODY

I hear and I forget.
I see and I remember.
I do and I understand.

—OLD CHINESE PROVERB

Congratulations. No longer focused on thinking, you're now in the business of feeling.

The Body is where your emotions are authentically available, both the ones showing up anew and the recirculating ones you've neglected in the past. They are all available to you, as they exist in this moment. Joy may be experienced in the heart, arms, or rib cage and feel very expansive. Fear may be experienced in the chest, throat, forehead, and shoulders, among other places, and feel constricted. The Body will speak to you and give you access to these emotions without confusion, anytime you're available to listen.

What was your relationship with your Body before now? Has the Body been little more than a life-support system for your mind or a storage facility for repressed emotions? If so, I'm glad we've given it a promotion. This employee offers so much, yet remains so often an underutilized, overlooked resource. It's called physical intelligence.

The heart pumps blood without thought. A child learns to walk without having to ask, "Do I start with my left or right foot? What do I do with the knees?" The child just starts walking. This is the wisdom of the Body. Did you know that a woman who is brain-dead can still grow a baby? Did you know, because it changes more slowly, the Body is more who you are than the mind?

Try this cool trick: Slump your shoulders and say, "I feel great." Now throw your hands in the air and say, "I feel miserable." Which wins: what the mind says or what the Body does?

So continue to be curious about the Body; it deserves your attention.

Ask it questions like "Should I marry this man?" and "Is this the right career for me?" Be the Body and answer the questions. It gives great advice, because it helps you tap into what you really feel. You can trust what you find there to be 100 percent truth.

And here is where it gets exquisite. What you feel is who and what you are right now. Who and what you are is "cold right now." Or sad: "I'm sad right now." Next, "afraid." Now "in love." Now "not in love." And on and on. It's all you, and it's all true. When you are attuned to the Body, you can simply feel what you're feeling in every moment and, every time you ask the question, trust the answer to be truth. Since the Body exists in the moment, it doesn't distort reality, and therefore it never lies.

Making the journey from the voices of your Mind to those of your Heart and Body is what you're meant to do with your time here on earth.

Switching from "I think" to "I feel" can be the longest, weirdest, most tumultuous journey of your life, but it's also the most important.

Or it can be an easy, simple journey, starting with a simple shift.

FEAR

That thing you won't deal with? The discomfort you keep pushing down? That feeling is the key to your freedom. Because we usually won't deal with Fear, I'm particularly interested when the body says, "I feel afraid."

Try that on right now as the Body: *I feel afraid.*

Do you feel it? It's uncomfortable, much like a toothache or a rock under the mattress.

As the voice of the Body, notice where you feel Fear now. Is it in your chest? Your lower back? Feel that Anxiety. Feel that discomfort. This is why you don't have to relive past Fear. The *why* doesn't matter. There may be an old arrow sticking out of your chest—but just be aware of the pain as it exists today. It hurts, doesn't it?

Keep asking questions. Notice any Resistance to it.

Now, what would you do if this were a toothache? Would you go see a gynecologist? A shaman? No, you'd go see a dentist. It's important to find the right intelligence to fix a problem. In this case, the problem being the discomfort, the right intelligence to deal with the discomfort of Fear is the voice of Fear itself.

Again, if you're going to get anywhere, this needs to be a physical experience. You want to ride a bike? Reading ten books on how to ride a bike isn't enough, and talking with a therapist about riding a bike won't help, either. You have to physically ride the bike to get the experience you want.

The same goes if you're hungry. Taking a photograph of a steak won't satisfy your hunger. Reading the menu with great lust won't do it. You must eat, digest, and experience these sensations. This is our practice. Until our body has a chance to do and feel something, it isn't really learned, and it will be completely unsatisfying. Consciously, then, decide to make this practice a fully embodied practice, or it will be nothing at all.

CHAPTER 8

THE VOICE OF FEAR

NOW WE GO ALL THE WAY

We're almost there. We're almost at the point of having a first-person, embodied experience with Fear, an embodied recognition of what it's like for this employee. We're about to set it—and therefore you—free from cement.

If you're not already there, go back to the voice of the Body. Feel what it feels. Your Mind will be the one to ask the questions and translate this information, but your heart, muscles, lungs, arms, legs, and everything else are also now in this practice.

ME: Who am I speaking to?
YOU: I am the Body.
ME: Notice whatever sensations you're aware of, in particular where you're uncomfortable. Notice where and how the sensation of the discomfort of Fear is present. It will be there. Maybe in your chest. In your shoulders. In your jaw.
We need to know where you feel the discomfort of Fear because I want to have a conversation with that discomfort next. I am curious about what it has to say. What is the message to be found there?

Allow me, then, please, to speak to the voice of Fear.

THE VOICE OF FEAR

ME: Who am I speaking to?

FEAR: I'm Fear. Hello.

ME: Nice to finally meet you. What's your job in this corporation?

FEAR: My job is to be afraid.

ME: What are you afraid of?

FEAR: Today? I'm afraid the Self will waste her whole day procrastinating. It's snowing outside, and the steps aren't shoveled, so I'm also
afraid of injury. I'm afraid the cat will pee on the rug. And that's just
the little stuff. There's no end in sight of things I'm afraid of.

ME: What's life like for you?

FEAR: It's been rough. Not only is my job to be afraid, which is one
of the most uncomfortable, important jobs in the corporation, but
she doesn't like me. No one likes me, actually. I've lived most of my
life in the basement—since she was very young. It's cramped, dark,
and cold down here. I feel desperate most of the time. I scream and
yell a lot. Mostly I'm afraid that she won't let me speak, won't listen.

ME: How does it feel physically to be you, living in the basement?

FEAR: I feel stressed out. Anxious. Constricted. Frustrated. Like I
want to scream. Because of all this, I get quite tired, and thus so does
the self. I'm sad, too. Pained. Unloved. And really angry. I'm even
afraid of myself, which is just weird. How could she do this to me?

ME: Are you really so bad?

FEAR: No, I feel very misunderstood. Really, I'm here to help, not
hurt.

ME: Do you have her best interests in mind?

FEAR: Certainly. But she doesn't trust me. No one does. I know I'm
uncomfortable to have around, and I've had to be a real jerk from
down here, given the circumstances. If I were treated better, though,
I wouldn't have to act so weird, nor would I feel so bad. I wish the
self could see that. I would like to be of service, like I'm supposed to
be. I really do have so much to offer.

ME: What do you want or need in order to thrive?

FEAR: I would like to be a welcomed, honored part of her life. That would make me feel much better. Calm. Less anxious. If we got along, we could be so magnificent together.

SHADOW WORK

How do you make a sword? It's not easy. You stick the steel in intense heat and then pound on it with a hammer. Then stick it in intense cold and pound on it some more. Over and over you do this. It's violent and severe, yet the beauty of who and what you are becomes more revealed each round.

Further and beyond, keep pounding it out, and you become more beautiful with each round.

Being willing to feel and even embody something you would normally avoid is the holy grail of life's practice. It's "shadow work"—a term familiar to most self-awareness practitioners. I call it owning your crap.

Own your crap and suddenly your life is no longer just a hobby. Owning your crap is about waking up and really being you—not just in your glory and comfort but also in your horror and discomfort, all the way. This is where your life becomes your practice.

Here is where you ask Fear, "What are you afraid of, and what do you see that I don't, that I'm not dealing with?" This is the key to freedom. Whatever you won't look at is always the key to freedom.

Owning your crap starts with finally looking at these voices and allowing these parts of you to exist. Simply ask what's really going on with Fear or any "bad" voice, get to know your pattern with it, and then over time learn to incorporate that voice into your life with caring and consideration.

By doing this work, you'll quickly see that these voices aren't dark at all. Shadow work is shining the light on them. Shadow work is like living in a dark room your whole life, but each moment you own your crap, a light comes on. You have a brief glimpse of a new paradigm and view, and you're like a blind man who can now see. If only for that moment, everything changes. But do it again and again. The more you're willing to be curious about the darkness, the greater your light will ultimately be, and darkness will become less common.

I make a living helping people get unstuck from patterns that don't work for them anymore and live amazing lives. Every time, it all comes down to shadow work. I look for whatever voice they refuse to acknowledge—all the crap they refuse to own that they've thrown in the basement. That's where you are stuck, always. Any bad behavior or problem you have comes from that refusal.

A shadow is the dark spot you cast as a result of your unlived life and truth. A shadow is a lie about who and what you are. If you don't do shadow work—if you avoid these parts that make up half of yourself—you are rendered weak.

My version of shadow work is when you own, feel, and even become these voices, and you are rendered powerful.

Do this and, make no mistake: The darkness never goes away entirely, because you will always be in some sort of delusion. You will always cast a shadow. What we're going for is not freedom from delusion, discomfort, or shadow, then, but rather what I call divine delusion and discomfort. Where charm is found in the dark forest.

And of course, at the heart of all shadow work lies Fear. Fear is the deepest part of the truth about who and what you are. This is why forging a Fear practice is so important. The quality of your life is actually determined by the quality of your relationship with it, and that relationship is entirely up to you.

So shine the light on it, wake up, and become aware of how you treat it, what it needs from you, and what's possible with it at your side as a trusted asset and ally. Be willing to start this work and you will create the greatest opportunity you'll ever have in life to grow up and become your most complete, powerful, and brilliant self.

"Face your Fear," people say. It's good advice, but what does it even mean? We know it doesn't (or should not) mean "Face it and then push it down and step on its face."

How about "Face it and kiss it." A little peck to start. That's a nice way to be.

For me, it started with a kiss. But it was such a delicious, slick kiss that what I did next was I get real intimate. I went all the way with it. Then I became obsessed with it.

I couldn't see it, of course. I was young, and all I felt was the passion, the focus, the "I want *more*." It felt like what I wanted more of was skiing—dangerous skiing—but what I really wanted was more Fear.

It wasn't until a hitchhiking incident in Alaska that I became brutally, horrifyingly conscious of my problem.

The weather had been overcast for nine days. No heli-skiing, like I'd planned, and nothing to do in town but wait, eat grocery store food, and read cheesy paperbacks. Exasperated, knowing the weather was not going to get better, I finally changed my airline ticket to fly home the next morning.

Before leaving, wanting to get a refund for my heli time, I walked to the edge of town and stuck my thumb out, looking to hitch a ride on the rural road to and from the heli office, thirty miles each way.

Within minutes, a thirtysomething guy in a van pulled up. It's such a cliché, isn't it? He seemed nice, though; it was a hippie van, after all. Who doesn't trust hippies? I got in, and as he drove, we started chatting. He was a local who worked at a house for mentally handicapped adults, and it was his day off. He would gladly drive me to the heli office and back, because it was a pretty drive. Such luck!

We had a pleasant conversation on the drive out, which took just under an hour. I got out and did my heli business, then got back in his van for the ride home. As soon as we started driving back to town, everything changed.

"You know," he started, "I just got out of three years in prison." Feeling comfortable with him by this point, I asked innocently, "Oh, what were you in for?" Selling drugs, he replied. Heroin. Then I asked what turned out to be the wrong question: "What was prison like?" And he detonated.

"What was it like? What was it *like*? I'll tell you what it was like!" he started screaming.

Ten minutes of high-pitched details came at me like snarls out of a lion. Until he finally yelled, "It taught me how to scam people. And that's what this is about. You think I'm some nice guy, but I saw you on the side of the road and thought, *Now, there's a piece of ass. Or money.* And you obviously don't have any money! So you're nothing but a piece of ass to me. You know there's nothing to prevent me from [raping] and [sodomizing] you, then slitting your throat! There's nothing out here—nobody! Then I could throw your dead body on the side of the road, and *nobody would ever find your [expletive] body. Nobody!*"

Sitting there, driving along as a passenger in this psychopath's van in the middle of Nowhere, Alaska, being screamed at, that was where my insight came. For in that moment, all I felt was relief. Relief! My mind said, *"Finally!"* After nine days of no fix, *"Something interesting is happening to me."*

I simply loved it. I was thrilled.

And that's not right.

For whatever reason, rapists and murderers look for a power trip, so luckily I wasn't the right girl for Van Guy. I just sat there, genuinely perplexed, thrilled as he continued to scream, and I kept asking him questions and commenting about his story as if we were having a fascinating chat. There were times when he slowed down to five miles an hour and I thought about jumping out of the van, but then I'd have a couple of broken legs and he'd just stop and come back to get me. Not a good idea.

Other times, down steep hills, he'd gun it to eighty, as if to emphasize what he was saying with excessive speed and the shuddering of an old van on bad tires.

After an hour of this, we were back in town. He abruptly stopped screaming and dropped me off. As I stepped out of his van, I paused, looked back at him, and said, "You know, you really scared me back there."

He scoffed. "It's nice to know I can still scare people."

The next day, I called and set up an appointment with a shrink. I didn't know what else to do. But at least I started a consciousness practice. Finally.

SEEING THE TRUTH ABOUT YOUR RELATIONSHIP WITH FEAR

Hank was trying to get down an Alaskan mountain that was too steep for his skiing abilities. Because he was only an average skier, Fear showed up, so he put his head down and became lost inside himself, side-slipping a foot at a time for more than 2,000 vertical feet.

A half hour into it, I skied by and said, "Hank! Hank! You're at the bottom." It was only then that he looked up and realized Fear had stopped talking a while ago. Some other part of him was stuck in robot mode. He was still side-slipping on almost flat terrain.

What I've done is given you more than a map. I've given you a helicopter. Using this helicopter, simply touch down in the Body, ask "What do I feel?", allow Fear or whatever other voice to show up, and spend a bit of time there. Like touching down in Paris, it will always be different. Each time you land, you'll have a better sense of the place than before.

While you're there, it's up to you to be fully present and get to know all of its parts. Become familiar with your patterns regarding Fear. Your patterns are your doorways to solving your problem with Fear. The patterns are not meant to be changed, just noticed. The noticing is what's important.

This is your practice.

Do this, and each time will shift your perspective. There's no need for a big shift. Any shift works. Just a .01-degree shift in consciousness will, surprisingly, often unstick any wheel.

As you do this, there are questions that the voice of Curious can ask. In the following section, I have separated them into questions to ask your Self while having this experience, and questions to ask when "you" no longer exist and are instead the voices of the Body or Fear or whatever shows up. Because I'm not there to facilitate you, I recommend either having a friend or another professional facilitate you or doing this while meditating, journaling, or engaged in any simple, solo activity, like hiking.

QUESTIONS TO GET YOU STARTED

Asking yourself questions allows you to be both subject and object at the same time. Especially fold into this practice the ultimate question: Who is the curious "I" that is even asking these questions? Take your time, ask them one by one, ask them again on different days, in different order, and over time the depths of who and what you are will become more revealed.

QUESTIONS TO ASK YOURSELF

How do you relate to the Thinking Mind? To the Ego dynamic?

What is your current reaction to Fear?

Are you aware when Fear shows up? If so, how?

Does it show up in a mature or immature way?

If it's immature, what is your contribution to that problem?

Are you stuck in one habitual pattern or voice?

What prevents you from starting down another path?

If yes, what voice is it? Is it Skepticism, Unwillingness, Habit, or maybe Belief?

What prevents you from being the Body? Or Fear?

Is your vision clouded by the voices of Intention, Goals, Confusion, or Distraction?

How long can you remain the Body feeling Fear, before you revert back?

How long can you remain the voice of Fear (if at all)?

Why do you think that is?

Do you have an attachment to a specific way of dealing with Fear?

What are your defense mechanisms that seek to reinforce old beliefs?

Who's in charge of Fear? Is it the Thinking Mind or the Controller? Or is Fear in charge of Fear?

Whose job is it to be afraid? Yours? The Mind's? Or Fear's?

QUESTIONS TO ASK THE BODY AND FEAR

Once you drop the Self and become instead a state of pure awareness, otherwise known as the Body, or the emotion of Fear, here are a few questions to ask either voice. When you answer, remember to respond in the first person, saying either "I," "me" or "my" in your answer.

What is your job in this corporation?

How do you feel?

Do you feel made of stone or made of water?

Do you have thoughts, beliefs, or stories, and if not, how does your intelligence make itself known?

What is reality to you?

Do you exist in the future? Do you exist in the past? What about the present moment?

What role do you play in the Self's life?

What have you helped the Self achieve?

How does the Self treat you?

What is your relationship with the Thinking Mind? With the Controller? The Will?

Do you judge yourself? Or does the Self judge you?

Is your wisdom considered, or is it ignored?

What do you have to say about the Self's goals?

What could you offer the Self if you were allowed to speak more often?

What kind of relationship would you like to have with the Self?

What do you see when you look at the Self? Where is he or she stuck?

What advice do you have to give the Self?

ADDITIONAL QUESTIONS FOR FEAR ONLY

What is your greatest fear?

How do you make yourself known?

Why do you express yourself that way?

Do you build alliances with other voices?

How would you feel physically if you were out of the basement?

Is the Self willing to let you out? Why or why not?

If allowed to express yourself in an honored way, how would you feel and how would you act?

If you were welcomed into the boardroom, how would that change things for this corporation?

YOUR NEW FEAR PRACTICE

You may observe that what's showing up is: You're completely unwilling to do this practice, and you just can't shake that holdback. That's fine. That's just the voice of Resistance. The noticing is all that's important. Just by doing that, you may see that you're committed to your problems, which is a huge realization. You have to be where you are first, before being anything else.

Or, if you're not sure what's going on, there's something called the wisdom of Uncertainty. Or Confusion. You can learn plenty from these voices, too, simply by remaining curious. They are a form of Resistance. Maybe that is your practice for now.

Until you're ready for something else, that is. One common theme among all humans is that we're all constantly changing. You've heard this; you know it; but really witness it now. Every time you are curious, asking new questions, feeling confused or feeling an emotion, you'll notice: Aren't things different each moment? Imagine you went to Delhi a year ago and you returned again to Delhi today. Even if you go to the same hotel and see the same people, it will have changed a lot. Will it be the same experience? Never. Every moment is different. Just like you. Just like Fear.

This is how, even if nothing happened yesterday, because today is not the same as yesterday and every moment is a new moment, it's possible yet again to be set free. Always there is this possibility. Einstein didn't think he was smarter than everyone else. He just had a high degree of curiosity. He wondered about relativity for twenty years. Surely at some point you will wonder again about Fear , the Body, or even Confusion, if it shows up, for five minutes.

Treat those five minutes like a ritual. Ritual is great, because many memories are too often bad memories, but with ritual come good memories, and a container for them, which is how this practice can become a faithful memory over time. One ritual you can use to take it deeper is this: Stand up, close your eyes, and just witness what it is you're feeling, thinking, or experiencing. Don't identify with it. Only observe. It is not you, and you are not it. It's an employee trying to get your attention.

Don't try to get anything from the wonder. Don't try to get rid of any voice. It's not only futile but also rude to that voice. Don't try to fix your problems. Just see them and be curious to learn more. Like when you notice waves coming and going. No realizations, no destinations, no looking to solidify reality. Just have an experience witnessing the voices of Confusion or Fear or whatever else shows up.

This is how, when ready, you can next allow yourself to *feel* any voice. That's the key to unlocking the door. Feel Uncertainty. Feel Confusion. Or feel Fear, Jealousy, Insanity. Feel whatever it is you're feeling. Start by stepping through that door. This works for one simple reason: Any voice even somewhat embodied, no matter which one it is, means you're now in the present moment, speaking truth. It means you're in a state of awareness itself, rather than self-awareness, and thus a bigger Self.

Anytime you do that, anytime you're free from being your Self, or the Thinking Mind, you're having a spiritual experience. For a spiritual experience is merely an experience of something other than your Thinking Mind or Ego dynamic.

This being a Fear practice, here's how you identify Fear. If what you feel is Discomfort, Stress, Anxiety, or Nervousness, know that these are just other names for Fear. If you feel Resistance, look underneath it and you'll also find Fear. If it's any of the unwelcome shadow voices, underneath you'll find Fear. If it's "a" fear "of something," such as giving a speech, or closed spaces, that's Fear—the sensation in your body, plus a story or thought. Simply notice the feeling, and observe the thought, and now, to complete the ritual, move your body accordingly. Take a big breath as that place, and when you breathe out, also make a noise that matches your feeling.

Or, if you prefer to stay seated, try this breathing exercise, which is the exact opposite of anything you've ever been taught. Breathe *in* the voice, like Fear, or Uncertainty, and now breathe *out* the hope of ever getting rid of that Fear, or that Uncertainty. Breathing is the bridge between the unconscious and the conscious, because it takes you into the Body, where truth resides.

Either way, do this, and if you're not already there, become the voice. Notice the difference between "I am feeling afraid" and "I am afraid." Notice the difference between "I feel Resistance" and "I am Resistance." Be there now.

Here's when a facilitator can be useful. You are no longer your Habitual Self; now you are this employee, this voice. Keep engaging your curiosity as you ask the voice questions.

As questions are asked, there should be no need to search for answers. If you find the questions difficult, just notice that you've shifted into the voice of the One Trying to Figure It Out, or the voice of Confusion, neither of which will be able to answer the questions. Merely shift back and start again. If Fear is still there and wants to speak, just be Fear, and let it speak for itself. Move how it moves. It will find its own answers.

And finally, whatever it is for you—one shift, one encounter, or many shifts, many encounters—my only request is that you be there fully. This is how every moment of this practice leads to awareness and a chance for realization.

The mother, holding her son's hand, approached Gandhi in the square and said, "Please help my son. He eats too many sweets. Will you talk to him about this?" Gandhi thought for a moment, then said, "Find me in three weeks. Then I will talk to him."

The woman agreed and left.

Three weeks later, she approached Gandhi again and asked him to talk to her son about his eating too many sweets. As promised, Gandhi looked at the boy and said, "Stop eating so many sweets."

"Okay," the woman said, "thank you." But, perplexed, she had to ask, "Why didn't you just tell him that three weeks ago?"

Gandhi replied, "Because three weeks ago, I myself was eating too many sweets."

It took me a while to become worthy of writing this book.

The therapist didn't help with my wild and unique problem with Fear, but the effort was one step out of many that led to meeting and studying with the Zen master, and eventually seeing my patterns with Fear.

Over the years, I learned that my darkest shadow was Fear. Anger wasn't my shadow. By fully owning Anger, I was a great activist for change, in my case changing the way women viewed what was possible for them as extreme athletes. It didn't come out in a dark way.

But Fear was another story. On the one hand, I fully owned Fear, and thus was a motivated and great athlete. But on the other hand, I had two unhealthy patterns with Fear, both of which were problematic to an extreme.

The first pattern, as you know, was that I was severely addicted to Fear. Anything that becomes an addiction is never okay. The second was that I also severely repressed it. These two actions seem contradictory. I guess that's what can happen when your whole life becomes about one thing.

The question is, though: Could I have become the athlete I was if I hadn't had these two "problems"?

The answer is no, at least not without the first problem. I couldn't have done this very dangerous sport at a world-class level without my addiction. There has to be some sort of pathology behind a choice like that. It's just important to have an exit plan when this happens; otherwise, like any addiction, it will eventually cripple or kill you—as it did many of my friends.

But I could have done it without the repression. In fact, if I'd had this book in my hot little hands back then, I could have avoided a whole lot of trauma, and I could have been ten times the athlete I was. If only I had known there was another way.

TAKE YOUR TIME

In the human world, we see lots of right angles. In all of nature, there is no such thing as right angles. Things grow only in gradual transformation. Remember that. So stop looking for a right angle; we're going for gradual. It's the way you're designed to grow. Plus, don't forget, you will always grow toward the light.

Plant this seed, then, and watch it grow. Get to know yourself without ever having to work, process, or try to understand. Just be these voices as they show up; the rest takes care of itself.

One thing that may occur is that you'll start to observe and be curious about Fear in others as well. Not only does witnessing discomfort and allowing it to speak within your own Self wake you up, but so does witnessing it in others.

And finally, savor this practice, like a baseball game. Watching highlights is great, but most people find it less enjoyable than watching the whole game. When nothing happens between plays, that makes exciting times more meaningful. When there's peaks, valleys, lulls, bursts, disappointments, thrills, the game becomes more worth watching. Even when things seem boring, you'll find they're not once you really start paying attention. Even the voice of bored can become fascinating.

Over time, this is how your life becomes practice. This is how you learn to be authentically you, all the time. What we're going for is this: When you're uncertain, just be uncertain. When you're confused, just be confused. When you're eating a strawberry, just eat the strawberry. When you're afraid, just be afraid.

This is a you that includes an honest experience with Fear, and clarity about the many ways in which it or any voice shows up in your life.

Here's how I currently deal with Fear:

1. I wake up and feel however I'm feeling. Let's say today I feel Anxiety, Stress, and discomfort. Call it by any other name, but this is Fear.

2. I ask my Self a few questions then, before starting my day: Why do I feel Fear? (Looming deadline, embarrassed about my latest Facebook rant.) Where do I feel it? (In my throat.) Am I resisting it? (Usually yes, dammit.)

3. If I am resisting it, I first spend one or two minutes fully embracing and embodying that Resistance. I might say out loud, "I don't want this" or "Ugh, not now," so the Resistance has a chance to speak. That's often enough for it to run its course so I can go on to step 4.

4. I might make hot chocolate and sip it with a cat on my lap, and just feel the discomfort. Or I may talk about it with my husband or, if he's not around, a friend over the phone. There's little to no story, just "I'm feeling afraid right now" or "I'm afraid." They know not to say, "There's nothing to be afraid of" or I will smack them. Or maybe I just start my workday, feeling the discomfort, yet remain curious about it. ("It just switched to my chest; isn't that interesting?") I may get to work on that deadline, or Facebook-post a cute kitten video to dilute my previous behavior, and the Fear dissipates because I'm doing something proactive toward alleviating the situation that warrants Fear.

5. Chances are, at some point the Stress and Anxiety (Fear) will dissipate, and all I did was feel my feelings and live my truth that showed up that morning. If it doesn't run its course quickly, I continue to remain curious until I notice that (hey, look at that) Fear is done talking, then remain curious about any new feeling that has shown up.

SPEND SOME TIME HERE

Step by step. . . . I can't see any other way of accomplishing anything.

—MICHAEL JORDAN

Now, if your coach shows you a new golf swing, it's not your new golf swing yet, is it? Of course not. You have to practice it. Integrate it. Here is how you can do that:

> Sit with any new questions—ones from this book or your own— for at least a month. Let's not skip that important step. Work on them one at a time, meditating or journaling if it helps. Or just notice the Fear and patterns swirling around when you're trying to sleep, when you're working, when you're interacting or having experiences. Remain only curious, not looking for a solution, and see what happens.

In short, just go about your life.

There's a story about a cat that thought aliveness could be found by capturing her tail. She kept trying, over and over, to get it, but all she could do was run around in circles. Exhausted and frustrated, she eventually gave up. Then she discovered that if she just went about her life, it would follow her wherever she went.

> As often as you can, shift into the open, empty, upright cup. If it ever feels full, dump it out and become Beginner's Mind again, so that there will always be room for more learning. This is how, again and again, you stay as neutral as possible about what you're feeling. Have no opinion about Fear; just see what that is like.

Always come back to this: Let it be.

I know, this can be hard. You have a powerful grasping reflex. And because we're never fully awake, your mind will wander back into the habitual pattern of judging and projecting. Notice how hard it is to just let something be.

The mind wants to force, re-create, or judge. Maybe a new judgment will even form, that "Fear is good." Your job is merely to notice this as well. If this happens, shift and be the voice of the Judge for a spell. But as much as possible, just let the whole process be—all of it. Find a way to have an ordinary experience with Fear—not an extraordinary one. The more profound realizations come from how ordinary you are. Less profound realizations come from trying to be extraordinary.

> Notice that when you want to get rid of Anxiety and Suffering, you want to do it *today*, right? Instead, say to yourself, "Today it's not going to happen. I am not going to get rid of Anxiety today," and you're there.

> Keep trusting the Body. Like everything, the Body is constantly changing (at fifty, this is very obvious), so make sure that as it evolves, these new experiences can be an integrated part of its experience, and it can carry the wisdom with it.

Do all this, then, oddly, like magic, the school of nothing—receiving nothing, getting nothing, nowhere to be—will provide for you a freedom that over time will become like deep, still water.

Keep it up, and every day is a new possibility to be free. How do you free yourself from Fear? That's easy. You become one with it. How do you free yourself from thoughts? You become one with them.

The more you allow Fear to speak, the less it will have to say, and the less of a hold it will have on you. It's that simple.

KISS OR DRIVE: FOCUS ON YOUR PRACTICE

A friend told me she was recently kissing and driving at the same time. I was horrified. That is so dangerous.

She wasn't giving the kissing the attention it deserved.

Look, we're all in the habit of doing ten things at once. That won't work here. If you're serious about accessing your emotions, you must do one thing at a time, and do it 100 percent, all the way. Kiss or drive, not both.

You can't live awareness 24/7. That's impossible. And why would you want to? What I'm asking for instead is simply that you pay attention one minute a day, or five minutes a day. And just for those minutes, go for a very active, very focused practice of observing, then feeling, then becoming whatever it is that shows up. Basically, admit that you're afraid, then feel afraid, then be afraid.

Do it, or this book will come and go and be nothing at all.

PART IV

HONORING FEAR

CHAPTER 9

KISSING THE DRAGON

||||||||||||||||||||||||||||||||||||||||||||||||||||||||||||||||||||||||||||||||||||||||||||||||||||||||||||||||||||||||||||||||||||||

I started mind-set-only ski camps—no technical tips—and hired the Zen master to teach the evening sessions. It worked great until he declared that I should become a teacher. Oh, Lordy.

I told him, "No way." It seemed too difficult, too foreign.

And goofy. I wasn't spiritual at all. Certainly not religious. (Were they the same?) I was drawn only to the mental side of sports, dealing with my hatred of skiing and sorting out what I'd learned as an athlete (besides the gratification of my massive Ego), and that was it.

Yet he insisted, over and over. "No," I said each time. *Hell no.*

He told me to meditate in the voice of Doubt. So that's what I did. I started a Doubt practice. I doubted it all. Doubted I could learn anything, much less teach. Doubted there was any meaning to life. Doubted I would be good at it. Doubted there was any merit to what I was learning. It lasted about a month, with me sitting in Doubt, before it ran its course and had nothing left to say.

So I became a teacher.

||||||||||||||||||||||||||||||||||||||||||||||||||||||||||||||||||||||||||||||||||||||||||||||||||||||||||||||||||||||||||||||||||||||

TO SEE IT IS TO STOP IT

Ever hear the words "The only way out is through"? What does that even mean?

It means this: Instead of circumnavigating Fear, as you normally would, if you spend a little time exploring your patterns around it, feeling when it arises, even allowing yourself to become that emotion, this is you going right into the heart of Fear. You enter the inside of it.

Then just listen and consider what it has to say—*which is all Fear really wants*. Allow it to speak freely—not trying to rush anything. Not searching for a solution to any problem. No effort required. What you'll find next is: Fear, or any voice, for that matter, actually runs its course and lets go of you.

This is how, without much effort, you find yourself through to the other side of any problem associated with it. Go into any voice and spend time there, letting it be, and you will always organically come out the other side to a place of freedom.

You will also come to a place of Clarity, Liberation, Wisdom, and Power. When Fear is fully owned, it transcends itself and becomes, at the very least, these four states.

Here's a small example of this. I'll get to bigger examples later. Let's say you're a husband who has been blaming his wife for all his problems. You have but a tiny shift in awareness, even just a .01 shift, such that you recognize the delusion, the shadow that you've disowned—for example, Fear and Unworthiness. And with that tiny shift, you've already arrived somewhere completely new. You're already unstuck.

What happens next is akin to chaos theory: Imagine looking at a huge chalkboard with an enormous mathematical equation on it. This represents your personal makeup. In the lower right-hand corner is the final sign, equaling you. This mathematical equation is being carried out in your Unconscious Mind.

Now, let's say you become .01 percent aware of even a single pattern. Somewhere in the equation, then, a number changes from 0 to .01. Or perhaps you started seeing Fear as a positive instead of a negative. That means that, somewhere in the equation, a minus sign changes to a plus sign. You don't have to be good at math to recognize how these little changes radically affect the outcome—which is you.

No need for grandiose effort, then. Little shifts are all it takes.

With that shift, owning that delusion, what happens next brings such complete clarity that you may say the words "I've been so afraid" to your wife. Those few words can be the most liberating words you'll ever speak. Can you see the wisdom here? A moment like this sets in motion a completely different future for you and your wife.

This is why owning your Fear can be the first step toward your becoming powerful. To avoid is weakness, but to own is powerful, for the moment you own a voice (Unworthiness, the Fear beneath the Unworthiness), you're no longer a victim to it. You have taken charge of that relationship. Empowerment comes not from denying these "bad voices," but from owning them.

Add in the apology next: "I'm so sorry for projecting this on you." Then let your wife speak—she may in that moment recognize her own delusion and apologize for her shadow, too. Listen with full presence, without interruption or an agenda, and almost immediately that relationship will start to heal. Just as, once you start to feel your Fear, that relationship will also start to heal.

Then, over time, the more you own your shadow—for a month, for a year—the more you'll start to see things. You don't even have to know what it means or where it's going. The murky water that is your life will become more and more clear. Suddenly everything will start to make sense.

This is how you'll see clearly that this voice called Fear isn't negative after all. Or Jealousy or Unworthiness—none of the voices are. When you experience Fear unconsciously, especially from the basement, it tends to be perceived as negative. But once you see it and engage with it, your experience with Fear will become more about curiosity and wonder. "What will I learn about myself today that, while hard, is also liberating?"

Stay in the wonder, and next time Fear comes back, keep at it. You'll watch it come and go each time of its own accord, without having to do anything, and ride that experience through to the other side, into your new Clarity, Liberation, Wisdom, and Power.

The same goes for all shadow voices. Sometimes seeing your Resistance to your voice of the Villain, Jealousy, or Shame is all it takes to stop it. Just by realizing your delusion, you're released of it. Then, because you've let these voices be a part of your life, too, the ultimate result will be more Clarity, Liberation, Wisdom, and Power.

This is how, with minimal effort, you will gradually, organically solve any problem you recognized in chapter 3.

This is how, through "seeing it," time will pass, things will change, until you find you've arrived at a completely different and much more powerful place than where you were originally headed. You may even put this book down now, as this can be enough.

But if you wonder, *What else?* or if you want to accelerate the process, there's more you can do. There's a whole other level, actually.

WHAT NEXT?

A hiking trail in Hawaii ends with a sign that reads, END OF TRAIL. Most people at that point have had their experience, and they're done.

But the locals know that if you keep going past the sign, traipsing through the underbrush, eventually they'll come to a beautiful waterfall.

The next journey starts with revisiting our equation:

$$\text{SUFFERING} = \text{DISCOMFORT} \times \text{RESISTANCE}$$

We all suffer. That's normal. You're not going to not suffer. Look closely at someone you admire and you'll see that they suffer, too.

It's the same with discomfort. That's also normal. We all feel a lot of Fear, Pain, and therefore discomfort. You can't be a human being without feeling discomfort.

But when the discomfort and suffering get to be excessive, and persistent, it's time to do something about it.

For example, when your guts are churning, that's not normal, so you take Pepto-Bismol and your guts stop churning. The best medicine for churning Fear is having a conversation with it; think of Shift as your emotional Pepto-Bismol.

But what if you have a chronic condition that comes back again and again? (And if you have a longtime habitual pattern of repressing Fear, it will.) You will become unconscious and repeat your patterns again, and your delusion will come back. It's simply what we do: Again and again we go into unconscious, habitual robot mode. So again and again the suffering will return.

It's time, then, for preventive medicine. It's time to aggressively address the one part of our equation that has the most wiggle room: the Resistance.

Now, as we've learned, there *is* a voice of Resistance, and it's a normal part of life. When it shows up, it deserves to be seen and contemplated as well. Do this and it will run its course just like any voice, which is important, because it's the part of us that exacerbates our suffering. Never forget: Fear is not the problem; Resistance to Fear is the problem. So please, if it shows up, don't resist the Resistance; become Resistance, for as long as it takes. Only as much as you're willing to do this can it run its course, and make room for its opposite to enter. Which is what we're going for next; Embracing or, as I prefer to call it, Honoring.

You're going to honor the Fear next, which is how you'll be able to prevent your old illness from coming back. You may not even have to take Pepto-Bismol again.

Let me tell you how to do this.

HONORING FEAR

We are in danger. There is time only to work slowly. There is no time not to love.

—JOANNA MACY

What does that mean, "honoring Fear"?

Very simple: It's up to you to come up with your own path. Start by asking yourself: How would a good mother parent? A good father? How would a Zen master parent? What's the best way to treat your pet dog? Whatever that answer is, that is how you will honor Fear.

Ask yourself, "What must I have in any relationship for it to be a good one—be it with a child, a parent, a teacher, a spouse, a pet, a neighbor, a friend, or myself?" This is what you attempt to have with Fear.

A way to start is to treat it the way you'd like to be treated. For example, if you expect yourself to be caring and compassionate toward others and yourself, honoring means being caring and compassionate toward Fear. If you want to stop being so critical of yourself, then honoring means being less critical of Fear. If you want to be listened to, listen to Fear. If you crave respect and the freedom to just be yourself, then give Fear the same respect and freedom.

You won't get it right every time. You're not perfect; no parent is perfect. A Zen master can be as lost as a fish sunbathing under a tree. Just start by recognizing that Fear, Anger, and Sadness are often not going to show up in a way you like. Start with that simple consideration.

Then, like any good parent or Zen master, simply remain curious about the experience Fear is having, and what Fear is here to teach you. We should always remain students to one another. Nurturing can come next. Then, dancing? Then . . . ? Step by step, just do your best.

Or . . . don't?

YOU DECIDE

The most terrifying thing is to accept oneself completely.

—CARL JUNG

You always have a choice, of course, whether to do this or not. And I understand that this will be unlike anything you've ever done before, because Fear is not all puppies and rainbows. It's Fear. Goddamn Fear.

I'm asking you to honor discomfort. That is quite the odd choice. It will take effort.

I'm not asking you to *accept* Fear or discomfort—that's absolutely not what this is about. This is also not about making Fear or discomfort okay. For you cannot make discomfort comfortable.

I'm asking you to honor an individual that makes you very uncomfortable, and live in a state of recognition that you will never be free from its discomfort.

Let's say you're stuck living with a roommate you hate. Accepting that he's not going to move out, saying, "It is what it is"—that is not honoring him. Anytime you say, "It is what it is" about anything, that's totally passive and a cop-out.

Honoring the roommate means being willing to hang out with him without trying to change him, and finding a way to appreciate him even though he makes you feel very uncomfortable. Let him offer you contrast and perspective. It means going right into the discomfort, recognizing that he's the best he will ever be without hope of his ever being any other way, and finding a way to enjoy him and learn something from him in the process. That's what honoring really means; this is what I'm asking for.

So if your mantra has been "I'm okay; the roommate is not okay," that was pre–chapter 6 and wildly delusional. "I'm not okay; the roommate is not okay" is a greater truth.

Now we're going for "I'm not okay; the roommate is not okay; we both totally suck. But that's okay"—and you're there.

If this is hard for you, I understand. But here's your choice: You can keep dealing with Fear and your roommate the hard way, you can refuse to own your crap or to be around his, you can fight him every step of the way and live a rough and stressful life—or you can choose the path I'm suggesting.

I promise you, if you choose it, not only will Fear suffer less, but so will you. Eventually you two may even become best friends.

You decide.

LESS EFFORT, BEST RESULT

The less effort, the faster and more powerful you will be.

—BRUCE LEE

Look at it another way. If you witnessed a crazy man on a bridge grabbing passersby and throwing them into the river, what would you do?

You might run away and just let him keep doing his thing. Or you might tackle him and try to hold him down.

But may I remind you that you're considering a new paradigm? What would a good parent do? What would a Zen master do? Become these voices and see what happens.

Here's what they'd do: They'd gently ask the crazy man what's wrong and offer an interested and curious ear, looking to address the underlying problem that is making him crazy. They'd show him the respect and consideration that they themselves would appreciate in that moment.

Now, that's not to say that tackling him isn't a fair option. But the crazy man is Fear—he can't be held down. The question, then, is what option gives you the result you desire—with the least effort?

What is the result you really desire in your life? Is it Lightness? Calm? Ease? Flow? Power? And you want it with the least amount of effort, right?

Consider then: What would Bruce Lee do? We know that in martial arts, fighting is supposed to be a last resort. We also know that merging with your opponent's energy is what creates the best martial artists—and the most powerful.

Fear is certainly energy. Let's also look at what animals would do. They don't see this energy as irrational versus reasonable, nor do they see it as bad. Animals, just like Bruce Lee, are good at merging with the energy of Fear and using it as an opportunity for success. Animals use Fear to run faster and avoid a charging predator. What do we do? We stop breathing when it's around. Animals use Fear to make them sharper and more focused. We instead go numb. Do you see the difference? They merge with the energy; you run from or fight it. Who winds up more powerful as a result?

Of course, we may not know kung fu, and we're not animals. So, then, fill a backpack with the burden of resisting or fighting Fear, and take a step. How heavy does it feel? Now fill it with the challenge of honoring Fear, and take a step. Which feels lighter?

Which feels calmer: parachuting while resisting gravity, or embracing gravity?

Which is easier: swimming upstream, or flowing with the river?

Both resisting and embracing require effort. But again I ask: Which requires less effort to get a better result? This is what you should be considering.

Which leads you to a choice: Resist Fear and have it run your life, either obviously or covertly, and deal with all that goes along with it—the Insomnia, Anxiety, Burnout, Blame, Denial, Ignorance, or Monkey Mind . . . or honor the Fear by merging with it and also have it run your life, but instead it will expand your whole mind, potential creativity, and flow. On this end it becomes your adviser, friend, playmate, and partner in adventure—a chance to be faster and more powerful than you ever imagined. A chance to be lighter and more calm.

Most people get this in an instant. They know that resisting or fighting the roommate or the crazy man is, at best, a short-term solution, that it is not the right effort because they have to work twice as hard for a problematic result.

For others, it takes a long time. They may never get it. But once you have a consciousness practice, make no mistake, it is a choice.

Suffering is not a choice. Discomfort is not a choice. But Resistance is. Resist or honor: It's up to you.

My paradox was becoming more and more obvious, and confusing. I both had a love affair with Fear, and hated it, repressing it to the extreme.

Which was it? Can you love and hate something at the same time? Can you?

This led to so many questions. Was I surfing one wave that included both love and hate, or was I surfing two different waves, riding hate and then love separately?

It sure seemed like the latter. Whenever I made the decision to take a risk—that felt like a love wave. I honored it as my motivation push, and as my aliveness pull. Out there, I loved the place it took me: into the moment, a higher state. Afterwards was the best, drunk with the resulting adrenaline, at the bottom of the mountain, back in the hotel. All these moments were a conscious love affair with Fear.

There also came a seemingly separate, unconscious experience: The moments when Fear was so uncomfortable that, under my radar, I had to strangle it down to a tolerable level.

It was as though, in all of these moments, I was laughing with Fear on the outside, yet horrified on the inside. But I see now, it wasn't one or the other. Oddly, both felt true and authentic at the same time.

Therefore, I think that the answer is that both love and hate happen simultaneously. And I went all the way with both extremes, living a whole reality of light and dark with Fear. I was really good at surfing that one, big ol', wild wave.

This gave me two different experiences. First, there was a magnificent one of embracing Fear to an extreme, which led to a love affair with life, with myself, living in the present moment with whichever of the 10,000 voices were coming through the hose and fully embracing my shadow: Anger, False Self, Insecurity, Failure, Mistrust of Others, all as fuel for radical self-expression. That made me a very bright light for a long time.

And in that wave there was a simultaneous pathology of avoidance, also to an extreme, which slowly extinguished my light, until I was in darkness, wondering what the hell had happened.

IT'S YOUR RESPONSIBILITY TO DO THIS

In December 1814, a treaty was imminent between the British and the Americans to end the War of 1812. Before this was made public, the Battle of New Orleans happened, where 285 British soldiers were slaughtered in battle, fighting a war they hadn't realized was days from being over.

Read the memo. The war is over.

Blame it on your ex-wife, parents, society, friends, coaches, therapists, or advisers all you want. Those parents now live elsewhere or are deceased. That therapist has moved on to another client. The ex has long since remarried.

And ultimately, it was you who declared the war in the first place, by putting Fear in the basement. Now it's also your responsibility to take it out and end the war. If you once had the power to resist it, you now also have the power to embrace it. So what are you going to do?

Get your sheep together—that's what—and start over.

The voice of Fear has only matured to the age at which you first started resisting it. So go back to when you were a kid, or whenever you thought it was not okay to be afraid, say "I'm sorry for mistreating you," and begin to heal the relationship. Then let it speak, and you will be amazed at how fast the relationship will heal, and how fast Fear will grow up and come around.

Your life, on your terms, starts now.

WHAT WOULD IT FEEL LIKE TO BE OUT OF THE BASEMENT?

The earthworm pokes its head out of the dirt and sees another earthworm staring right at him, and immediately falls in love.

"Marry me!" he exclaims. To which the other earthworm replies, "I can't, silly. I'm the other side of you."

Let's have another conversation with Fear:

ME: The Self is reading this book. That's a big deal for you. What's going on?

FEAR: The Self sees me and now considers honoring me. I'm scared he/she will stop, but I feel excited about the possibilities. I hope it's time to heal our relationship.

ME: How would you feel if the Self loved and treated you with respect?

FEAR: I would feel great. Calm. Peaceful. I'd no longer feel so frantic or panicked. What a relief! Whatever I feel, he/she also feels. So we all win.

ME: If you were allowed out of the basement and welcomed as an honored part of this corporation, of this family, how would that change you?

FEAR: I would have less to be afraid of, less to say, less Anxiety, and what I did say, I'd speak rationally. It would mean a lot to know that my message would be received as wisdom.

ME: You wouldn't bite the head off every hope and dream the Self ever had?

FEAR: Oh, no. That's never been my intention. I harbor no resentment for past treatment, either. I only want to get to work and do the most mature, best job I can. I want to help him/her live an amazing life. That's what I'm here for: to see to it that the Self thrives.

It's now so obvious. I'm watching Lisa climb the ladder at trapeze class for the first time, to get to the top platform. She's eight feet up, with fifteen to go, but she's frozen in place, saying, "I can't do this" over and over. Her heart is racing. She's feeling "overwhelmed by Fear" and can't go on.

"I'm coming back down," she says, in a tight, high-pitched voice. Slowly, she climbs down the ladder.

Safely back on the ground, she's clearly embarrassed. She chatters to anyone who will listen: "I've had a fear of heights since I was a kid. I know it's crazy, but it's just so overwhelming." She seems really embarrassed.

Next on the ladder comes Wendy, who also has never tried flying trapeze. Up she goes to the top. (The ladder is the hardest part.) Following the instructor's directions, at the appropriate time Wendy steps off the platform and shrieks like a little girl. Flying through the air, she has her O face on. After a two-hour class of this and eight more swings, including making the hand-to-hand catch from a knee hang at the end, she goes home saying that the class was one of the best experiences of her life.

What's the difference between these two women?

For Lisa, the fear was extreme, and her internal dialogue likely was "Oh, no, there's Fear. No, no, no. What is wrong with me? This is so irrational. I'm wearing a safety harness, for crying out loud. It's supposed to be fun. Nobody else has this problem. I just saw a four-year-old go up. Heck, a seventy-year-old just went up. I hate this. Why me? Go away, Fear, go away. I can't handle this." (The Fear, not the situation.) "I have to go down."

For Wendy, whose Fear was equally extreme (it is flying trapeze, after all), her dialogue was more like "I feel afraid." Then she climbed the ladder and set about enjoying her Fear.

It's that simple.

KISS THE DRAGON

The sun never says to the earth, "You owe me." And look what happens with a love like that. It lights up the whole sky.

—HAFIZ

Wendy, during her trapeze class, is honoring Fear. Now, I've mentioned already that accepting Fear is *not* the same as honoring it. It's crucial that you understand the difference, because it's huge. Accepting Fear is "I don't like this, but *it is what it is*, so I'll just have to accept it." Like my niece, who at age fourteen was already five feet ten inches tall. Accepting that she's tall is passive, and a cop-out. And it reeks of *I'd rather not be, but there's nothing I can do about it*. Honoring her tallness is proactive, and involves seeing it as a great thing. There's awe and celebration of it, and excitement to thrive *because* of it, not in spite of it. Honoring it means taking up basketball, becoming a model, pulling your shoulders back, and having a swagger as you walk down the hallway.

Can you see Wendy recognizing and encouraging Fear to be what it is and do what it does in its most magnificent form? Nowhere in there is mere acceptance. (In fact, you don't even have to accept Fear—everything is negotiable. But that's quite far down the road from where we stand now.)

With that distinction in mind, I'd like you to take this next step in a big, all-the-way way. This is what taking Fear out of the basement and honoring it looks like:

Start by committing to it, the way you commit to a new puppy or a marriage. All great possibilities start with a commitment.

Then find a way to like it. Or could you go a step further and find a way to love it? Or do you even dare to have unconditional, ridiculous, embarrassing love for the feeling of Fear? Ask yourself if that's possible.

If the answer is no, consider love without conditions. What does it mean? Have you ever experienced it with yourself—unconditionally loving yourself? Do you want this? If yes, if you want to be all about love, if you want love for all things, then that needs to include love for Fear, too. Yes?

So, as best you can, fall in love with yourself, every part of you. Everything in you that exists. If you do this—even if it means loving the voice of Self-Loathing—unconditionally loving yourself will be the final result of this practice. And isn't that what you want?

YOUR LOVE AFFAIR

Next, have a love affair with it. Which is different from falling in love with yourself. A love affair with another human is when you keep your heart open through the Fear. A love affair with Fear is the same.

It's a high and great art to be a great lover. The best lover is not only able to give love but also receive it, often at the same time. What I'm asking, then, is for you to engage in a radically intimate—even erotic—dance of giving and receiving of love. Look to great flamenco or salsa dancers for inspiration. Watch them move together. See how they interact.

As the receiver, how do you love? How do you dance? You taste the food slowly, you sit and listen, you bury your face in the soft belly of a cat, and you're moved by the emotion that's hurting you right now. As the giver, how do you love? How do you dance? You also taste the food slowly, you sit and listen, you bury your face in the soft belly of a cat, and you're moved by the emotion that's hurting you right now.

Now kiss it. Often. Because in Zen there's a cool saying:

Kiss a dragon, it becomes a maiden.
Kiss a tiger, it becomes the Buddha.
Kiss a demon, it becomes love.

Kiss Fear. Kiss this demon. See what it turns into.

Or, if you have a Gratitude practice, have one for Fear. Ask yourself whether you can really go all the way with Gratitude until you also have Gratitude and Appreciation shine their light on Fear.

See it as a miracle. Einstein said, "There are only two ways to live your life. One is as though nothing is a miracle. The other is as though everything is a miracle." Usually it takes a near-death experience or even the end of your life to see everything as a miracle. But why wait? If you knew tomorrow were your last day on earth, would you wish you'd had more Fear in your life, or less? What advice would you give yourself today, based on that answer?

Do rituals. As I've mentioned before, they're great. Create them! They turn any practice from a cognitive experience into a physical one, offering a shift in your body and thus deeper integration. Engage in rituals like naming an apple or a snowball "Fear," then taking a bite. Chew and swallow your bite, ingesting it. This can be very symbolic. You can also name a glass of water "Fear," then drink deeply. What do you find in there for your sustenance?

Another ritual is bowing. Whenever Fear or any emotion shows up, just bow. As you would to a teacher or a person you respect. It says, "The badass in me recognizes the badass in you, and together we are one." Or create an altar to Fear. Never, ever burn it, though—it's meant to be celebrated. Offer it flowers, incense, bubble gum.

Or find your own kind of worship. You could spend an hour worshiping a campfire, a sport—heck, a pizza—so why not Fear? Worship your emotion. "Worshiping" is another word for "surrendering to." How deeply can you surrender to Fear? All surrender leads to aliveness, and ultimately to Joy.

If you meditate, meditate either as the One Willing to Feel Fear or as the voice of Fear itself. Never the One Trying to Meditate as Fear (Yoda says: "Do. Or do not. There is no 'try.'"), or the One Thinking About Fear. If you're paying attention, you'll know the difference. How you do this is you shift into the voice of Honored Fear, and notice whatever you notice. Perhaps breathe into the different parts of your body that feel the discomfort. How does Fear feel in the solar plexus, in the heart? Keep doing this, one location at a time, and notice how long it takes before that body part stops feeling uncomfortable.

Whenever you feel stuck, come back to: in through the nose, each time breathing in something different you're afraid of . . . out through the mouth, breathing out the hope of ever getting rid of that Fear. Keep doing this until it let's go of you and you feel free and purged.

And finally, take risks. The more you do this, the easier it gets. Take that trapeze class and become a swinger with Fear (yep, cheesy). Put yourself in a position you would normally avoid. Fall in love. Can you enjoy the Fear? The discomfort? Is it invigorating? Experiment with different risks until you find one that suits you. No need to expose yourself to snakes, or heights, but if you do, just bow when the Fear shows up.

Get creative and forge your own ritual that honors Fear: 7.5 billion people, 7.5 billion options, no two relationships ever the same . . .

HOW TO ENLIST HELP

When you meet someone new (like Fear) whom you appreciate and love, you tend to acknowledge it publicly—you go out on the town together, or even have a marriage ceremony. You're saying in your own unique way, "Hey, everyone, this is my thing." The same applies here. Let your friends know you're in a new relationship with Fear and you'd like their consideration or help to celebrate that choice. Educate them, too, and require them to be kind. When you say, "I feel afraid," they should be told that the only appropriate response is either to ask a clarifying question or offer a simple, genuine "That's great."

Regardless, if someone tries to talk you out of feeling your emotions, which they will, your response should be one of the following:

"Please don't try to talk me out of feeling my Fear (Sadness or Anger). Let me enjoy it."

"Please don't try to rush me through my emotions. They're here for a reason."

"Please stop asking me to repress my emotions to make you feel more comfortable. Let me have my experience."

And remember, the second you blame an emotion on the other person or the situation, you're out of integrity. They may have inspired the emotion, but nobody and nothing is to blame for your emotions or how they're showing up, ever. That is 100 percent your responsibility.

HOW TO ASSIST YOUR FAMILY AND FRIENDS

Do we all agree that your job is not to make your child, friend, or family— or Fear—happy, but to set the stage for them to have the best chance to thrive?

Take time to consider what to say to people in your life, then, so you can best feel and express your emotions, and if they're interested, they can too. Let's get you and everyone on the same page so that Fear can be acknowledged as a gift instead of a hindrance.

When they say, "I feel afraid," no more Fear shaming! Your response should be one of the following:

"Good."
"Tell me more."
"What does it feel like to be afraid?"
"Okay. Your job is to be afraid right now."
"Do you need anything from me?"
"Okay, let me know when it passes."

LANGUAGE CHANGER

IF YOU'RE USED TO SAYING:	CHANGE TO:
DON'T BE AFRAID.	WHAT DOES IT FEEL LIKE TO BE AFRAID?
THERE'S NOTHING TO BE AFRAID OF.	THIS WORLD IS A SCARY PLACE, ISN'T IT?
DON'T LET FEAR CONTROL YOUR LIFE.	DON'T LET THE AVOIDANCE OF FEAR CONTROL YOUR LIFE.
DROP YOUR FEAR.	EMBRACE YOUR FEAR.
LEAVE YOUR FEARS BEHIND.	BRING YOUR FEARS WITH YOU AND THEY WILL BE HELPFUL.
PUSH THROUGH YOUR FEAR.	MERGE WITH YOUR FEAR.
DON'T FEED YOUR FEAR.	DON'T RESIST YOUR FEAR.

If you really want to go all the way, you must also change your language when you talk about Fear, because words are important.

For example, say out loud, "I want to be with Fear." Now say, "I don't want to be with Fear." Which feels better?

Here are some more common phrases that get spoken about Fear, and better choices to replace them.

IF YOU'RE USED TO SAYING:	CHANGE TO:
I DON'T WANT TO FEEL AFRAID.	I DO WANT TO FEEL AFRAID.

I OVERCAME FEAR.	I OVERCAME THE SITUATION.
LET IT GO.	LET IT BE.
I WON'T LET FEAR HOLD ME BACK.	I WON'T HOLD MYSELF BACK BY BEING UNWILLING TO FEEL FEAR.
DO IT DESPITE THE FEAR.	DO IT BECAUSE OF THE FEAR.
FEEL THE FEAR AND DO IT ANYWAY.	FEEL THE FEAR AND DO IT. ("ANYWAY" IS DISRESPECTFUL.)
I'M NOT AFRAID.	I AM AFRAID, BUT AM PRETENDING NOT TO BE.
IT IS WHAT IT IS.	I'M SCARED, AND I FEEL POWERLESS TO CHANGE ANYTHING.
NEGATIVE VS. POSITIVE FEAR	THERE'S NO SUCH THING; THERE'S ONLY FEAR.
NO FEAR	YES FEAR
THERE IS NOTHING TO FEAR.	THERE IS MUCH TO FEAR.
FEAR IS A HINDRANCE.	FEAR IS AN ASSET AND ALLY.
FEAR MUST BE CONQUERED.	FEAR MUST BE SAVORED.
FAITH OVER FEAR.	FAITH AND FEAR ARE EQUAL.
FEAR IS A PRISON.	FEAR IS IN PRISON.
FEAR IS A LIAR.	I AM A LIAR; I'M NOT LIVING MY TRUTH.
FEAR SHRINKS US.	FEAR EXPANDS US.
FEAR LIMITS US.	EMBRACE FEAR, YOU BECOME LIMITLESS.
FALSE EVIDENCE APPEARING REAL	FABULOUS EFFECTIVE ADVICE REVEALED
ADRENALINE ADDICT	FEAR ADDICT

And finally, learn to speak its language. When the answer to "What do I feel?" is that you feel afraid, your job is then to be afraid. So just say it: "I'm afraid." This is your new mantra.

‖‖‖

Kiteboarding gear stacked in the car, I was driving to the lake on the deserted road when I was passed by an ambulance and a cop car traveling at full speed, sirens screeching. *Oh, no,* I thought, gripping the steering wheel. It had to be one of my friends.

Twenty minutes later, I was the first to learn that Mitch had died. The police asked me to help locate his wife so they could tell her. It was a kiteboarding accident.

Later that night, after a wrenching day, dealing with the familiar feeling of having lost yet another friend to a dangerous sport, I stared at the TV in resistance, not wanting to feel anything, certainly not sadness.

I slept or sat in front of the TV in my bathrobe for days, until the third afternoon, when I stood up and went outside to get the mail. It was a windy day.

The wind was what killed Mitch. A ninety-mile-per-hour gust had picked him up, thrown him down, then trundled him through scrub oak. It was windy again today, and as it whipped the bathrobe around me, suddenly I felt fully, shockingly, everything.

I unleashed and cried and cried, standing in that wind. I just stood and felt my feelings. In contemplating his death, I've never felt more awake and alive. That's what the death of a friend can offer those still living, in a perfect world.

HONORED AS MUCH AS POSSIBLE

Another conversation with Fear, now owned and honored, out in the fresh air and sunshine:

ME: Welcome to the family. How does it feel to be out of the basement?
FEAR: I feel light, and free. I can breathe now and see clearly, for miles. I feel crisp and sharp. I'm ready for anything. I feel excited and adventurous.

And now so are you . . .

Ask yourself, though: "How much have I really let Fear out of the basement?" Is it 1 percent? Have you only cracked the door and whispered a timid hello? Or is it 10 percent? Have you also left a tuna sandwich at the top of the stairs?

Or is it really, truly 100 percent—moving Fear into your penthouse suite complete with a masseuse and peeled grapes?

Have you really examined your relationship and seen the truth about it? Can you really, truly embrace and honor it? Do you really have the guts to feel your discomfort and not hide from it, and no longer live a lie?

All these are important questions.

Maybe all you're willing to do is just feel Fear a little. And that's fine. Or maybe all we get is "Keep your friends close and your enemies closer." Start there if you must.

If anything else is hard to fathom, maybe go back to just seeing it without wanting to change anything or have a new, better, improved relationship with yourself. This will be well worth the effort. But there's more. A lot more.

Whatever you put into it, you get out of it. As with raising any child, when you treat Fear like an honored part of the family, it will start thriving. Then when you connect to it—it becomes a part of you. Once that happens, Fear will become a precious jewel in your pocket you hadn't noticed before. Resolved problems and less suffering are nothing. Keep going and there will also be untold riches in your future.

I do know that Fear offered me so much. I shiver when I think about how in love with it I was, but it was a very unconscious and hard affair. I was a young and passionate lover, in a volatile, complicated relationship.

Fear, being so simple, was endlessly patient with me. I took and took from it, and refused to even acknowledge the relationship. Every once in a while, Fear said "Screw you" and wouldn't let my knee heal. Or it blew the other knee, my adrenal system, or four disks in my neck and lower back. Rheumatoid arthritis was triggered. "Pay attention to me!" my Body and Fear were screaming.

It affected the people in my life. My poor mom had to own Fear for me. I earned a reputation for being a man-crusher.

It all finally got to be such a problem that I couldn't ignore these messages any longer and had to take a look at the relationship, because this wasn't working.

And now, after fifteen years of mending that relationship, many of my physical problems have healed. Every time I go see the knee doctor, he takes one look at the X-rays and comically drops to the ground, bowing to me, because my knees don't hurt or hold me back even after nine surgeries. My cortisol levels are normal, which means my adrenal fatigue is cured. I no longer have back or neck pain. I don't have rheumatoid arthritis symptoms. I even got married and have a spectacular marriage. All of this I attribute to my improved relationship with Fear.

I teach others how to do this, helping them forge a great relationship with Fear. That's my way of apologizing to Fear, making amends. But I have a long way to go. I guess I still feel bad for mistreating it, and hope it will continue to forgive me for being so reckless, and callous, and just young and stupid.

I've appreciated the amazing and exciting life it offered and still offers me. I take annual trips to Alaska for heli-skiing, I opened a flying trapeze school, I bring massive, flame-throwing art cars to Burning Man, and I will continue to nurture my love affair with Fear until the day I die. But it doesn't have its unhealthy hold on me like it used to. My still addicted friends don't know why I don't want to climb and ski at a high level with them anymore. It doesn't even occur to me to take the risks I used to. My friends who still do continue to die regularly.

I think it feels honored now, and seen and understood, which is the least I can do for all it has offered me: a daring and fabulous life.

It has been one of my lifelong friends and one of the best parts of my life. And for that I'm grateful.

THE FOUR INTELLIGENCES

You have a mind, and you have a body, and that's a lot. But that's not all you have. Look at how infinite the universe is—can you see how much more there is?

Consider just how much more. You have access to four basic types of intelligence: mental, physical, spiritual, and emotional. That's a lot of intelligence, all ready to be developed. All ready to help you become as creative and powerful as the universe. When you function from all forms of intelligence, you are operating at your highest level. When you function from only one, you remain limited, and you will only become as creative and powerful as your limited view.

MENTAL. All four intelligences become conscious to you from your mind, so this one comes first for good reason. In particular, I'm talking about your capacity for judgment, analysis, reason, understanding, and being rational.

In the Western world, when we say someone is smart, we're referring to this form of intelligence—the intellect. The ability to focus and cognitively understand things is what we've been building a secular shrine to and worshiping for a long time. For good reason: It's the reason we will visit Mars, we invented computers, we've found solutions for cancer, and we're creating new energy resources. If we can do all this, we reason, we can do anything. As a result, we live much of our lives immersed in thinking only, and look to this intelligence to solve all problems. It's gotten to the point that we even say sports are "all mental." Which is ridiculous.

Mental intelligence does not offer the solution to everything. Nor is it the only access to awareness we possess.

So while indeed your intellect is a staggering tool, and without it we couldn't function, if worshiped alone, it can become your greatest weakness. You lose touch with what else is available.

VOICES: Knowledge. Opinions. Beliefs. Perseverance. Reasoning. Will. Determination. Judgment. Understanding. Concentration. Consciousness. Self-Awareness. Mindfulness. It's all about me. "I can do this." "I think, therefore I am." Discriminating Wisdom.

IGNITED AND ALIVE IN: CEOs, secretaries, accountants, scientists, teachers, engineers, mechanics, doctors, lawyers, computer techs, talk therapists, most sports coaches.

PHYSICAL: The second intelligence is the wisdom of your Body. Often seen as a life support system for the mind, physical intelligence is a widely overlooked and underutilized resource. It's also become a junkyard for repressed emotions.

The senses reside here: touch, smell, taste, hearing, and sight. As does the sixth sense, our intuition and instinct. When you're in a state of awareness of what you're sensing, you're experiencing physical intelligence. This intelligence exists without past or future and is aware only of what's true right now. Which is why it never lies, doesn't distort or argue with reality like the Mind does—because it is reality. It offers you gut feelings, impulses, and access to what lies underneath apparent reality.

This intelligence exists without thought. Digestion happens without thought. Breathing happens without thought. The Body also has memory; you no longer must think to walk; it just happens. Developing physical intelligence is usually a better path for athletics—for a lot of things—than the mind.

VOICES: Feeling. Touch. Vision. Hearing. Smell. Feelings. Intuition. Instinct. Awareness. Truth. Heart. Gut. Passion. Celebration. Awareness. Self-Expression. Love.

IGNITED AND ALIVE IN: soldiers, servers, construction workers, carpenters, firefighters, assembly line workers, housecleaners, dancers, energy workers, physical therapists, musicians, athletes.

SPIRITUAL: Spiritual intelligence isn't found in morality, or scriptures. It's not found in the institution that grows around it, or the guy dressed in robes, holding court at the front of a room. In today's world, "spiritual" no longer means "religious." That's not to say spiritual inspiration can't come from religion, just that it can also come from a million other sources. Like music. Or painting. Or gardening. Or sports. By entering the inside of these experiences. It's the intimate connection you have with the other—be it nature, people, a song, or an activity.

This type of intelligence tugs at you, invites you to surrender to it. But it is not a natural experience, so it won't happen on its own very often. It is something you must pursue and ignite.

You do this by waking up the question "What is this experience that is trying to get my attention, that is bigger than my own personal view of the world and my individual Thinking Mind?" This intelligence can then be nurtured and grown by constantly asking that question "What else is there besides me?" Only once this is asked can a teacher, tradition, song, or sport awaken you to this intelligence.

The answer to this question is something you then yield or deeply surrender to. The answer will be ungraspable. It will never be something you can understand. It is only something you can become. It's where you step aside drop off your self—Body and Mind—and allow the answer a chance to speak. It's making the shift from Mindfulness to Mindlessness. It's making the shift from Form (Body) to Formlessness. Basically, lose your Mind, or any sense of you being you, then lose your Body, and you're there. Now something bigger has a chance to express itself.

VOICES: Non-Thinking Mind. Emptiness. The Tao. Christ Consciousness. Buddha Nature. The Divine. The Now. Enlightenment. Collective Consciousness. Connected Mind. The Infinite. The Zone. The Silence between the Om. Universal Power. The River. The Wind. Big Mind.

IGNITED AND ALIVE IN: spiritual guides, parents, Einstein, social workers, police, mind-set sports coaches (*wink*), professional athletes, artists, chefs. "Psyche" means "soul," so psychiatrists and psychologists originally taught from this place. Some still do.

EMOTIONAL: The wisdom of your emotions.

Much like there are three primary colors from which the entire color spectrum is created, there are five primary emotions from which your entire human experience is created. They are: Fear, Anger, Sadness, Joy, and the Erotic.

Emotional intelligence has long been supported as your ability to identify and understand—and/or manage and control—your emotions as a way to keep your feelings from ruling your life. But I assure you, this is as far off-track as wanting to become a robot. Using your intellect to talk and think about, evaluate, and control your emotions is not "emotional intelligence."

Emotions being a huge part of what makes us human, emotional intelligence is, rather, your ability to identify, feel, and express your emotions in a useful, creative, and mature way.

We are not trained or rewarded for this like we're trained and rewarded for focus and intellect . . . yet. But this book and others hopefully will change that.

> **VOICES:** Excitement, Alertness, Readiness (all from Fear). Aggression, Passion, Fire (all from Anger). Compassion, Caring, Concern (from Sadness). Happiness, Playfulness, Beauty, or, as the bro-brahs like to say, Stoked (Joy). Sexuality, Intimacy, Ecstasy (the Erotic).
>
> **IGNITED AND ALIVE IN:** nurses, artists, singers, musicians, dancers, hairdressers, actors, empaths, caretakers, massage therapists, great bartenders, nurses, the best professional athletes.

THEY'RE ALL CONNECTED

Can you see how interconnected these four are? Emotions are felt physically, so those two intelligences are often the same thing. The intellect judges the emotions as good or bad. It also tries to understand the spiritual (which it can't). The physical is often in rebellion against the mental. Round and round we go.

We all excel differently, and these are all very different gifts. The guy we call "Meathead" maybe doesn't excel mentally but most certainty excels in another way, maybe the physical—so he becomes a football player. The high-IQ girl is brilliant at mental but scoffs at or struggles with the spiritual.

You can make do without nurturing any of them, but, knowing what you know, why would you want to deny yourself? All of them can be developed, even those you weren't innately gifted with. All can be carried to the top of whatever mountain presents itself. There's even global support for this: More and more people are looking toward developing all four, as well as a new intelligence called systems intelligence, which could be interpreted as your ability to see how they all fit and work together.

Now ask yourself this: While all may be connected, are you connected to them all? Are there any you've avoided or overlooked? Are you denying yourself these experiences? Are you interested in exploring the ones you've never considered before? If yes, you are set to maximize your capacity to be brilliant, and to go all the way with your life.

It takes a lifetime to develop them all, but the good news is, that's exactly the time frame you have to work with.

WHAT TO DEVELOP NEXT?

If you had four large baskets and wanted to take them to the top of a mountain, how would you do it? You can't carry them all at once. But you can take them one at a time, or maybe two at a time. So you carry one or two, then come back later for the others.

Which basket are you going to carry next?

Modern education systems seek to help you carry up your mental intellect, so likely that's taken care of. Maybe physical has been nurtured a bit as well. If you're not sure what to take up next, then, I recommend emotional intelligence. If you're not having a mature, lovely, honest relationship with your emotions, go get that basket and start climbing. If for no other reason than all forms of intelligence, and especially the mental and physical forms you've carried up there already, are desperate for fuel so that they can function.

Sadness is fuel. Being in touch with Sadness gets you in touch with your deepest human connection: compassion. Your physical and spiritual self will love that.

Anger is fuel. Being in touch with Anger gets you in touch with your deepest fire and passion. Your intellect and physical self will love that.

Joy is fuel. It's necessary for life celebration.

The Erotic is fuel. It's where you lose yourself in something or someone.

Then there's Fear. Sweet Fear. You want to talk fuel? Fear is the most underutilized resource we have. It's where everything I'm about to outline gets ignited. Once you learn how to *identify, feel, and express Fear,* you'll have available a powerful fuel source through which anything becomes possible. And I mean anything.

When I first became a facilitator, I assumed my clients would be athletes. I had lived the bull's-eye of "It's all mental" my whole life, and my competition—sports psychologists—had only clinical training, not real-world experience. Plus every coach or instructor out there seemed to teach only the physical or mental side of sports, merely hoping the rest would appear like magic. It seemed a slam dunk.

I learned, however, that mental coaching, for whatever reason (I think it's just way before its time), was not an easy sell.

When my phone did ring, though, what was easy was seeing and transforming where an athlete was stuck.

Everyone who called, their underperforming was the result of repressed emotions—in particular, Fear. It was as predictable as the sun rising in the East.

One athlete who hired me four days before the Olympics was no exception. She'd won an Olympic gold medal four years prior but had floundered since—injuries, crashes, poor finishes. She was terrified now of being on a global stage again, having her struggles witnessed by the entire world.

Of course she was terrified. But well-meaning friends and family insisted, "There's nothing to be afraid of—you're great at what you do!" So she repressed Fear.

She was angry with the way team coaches and executives treated her. The people in her life again responded, "Everyone's just doing their best to help you win. You should be grateful." So she repressed Anger.

Repressing Fear and Anger is very taxing, so she also started to burn out and subsequently hate her sport. This made her so sad.

"Don't be sad," they chimed in. "Look at the magical life you live! Anyone would be thrilled to be you." So she repressed Sadness.

I spent three hours with her, facilitating the voices of Fear, Anger, and Sadness. Her willingness to remain curious and her desire to listen to them healed those relationships. Feeling honored, they set her free.

With the three wars being played out in her unconscious world now over, she left for the Olympics energized. Not only that, but she took her three new honored friends—Fear, Anger, and Sadness—along for the experience, as a fuel source for power and creativity during her events.

And won two silver medals.

THE BENEFITS OF HONORING FEAR

"Is nature flawed?" contemplated a man sitting underneath a walnut tree. Before him was a watermelon patch. The watermelon vines were small, yet grew such huge fruit. The walnut tree was huge, yet grew such small fruit. Perhaps nature got it backwards?

Then a walnut fell from the tree and hit him on his head. Oh.

Even though life doesn't always make sense, if you contemplate the walnut tree, it is exactly as it should be. Fear is exactly as it should be.

Welcome to a new kind of life, where things start to really make sense.

If we started our practice just seeing Fear—the relationship you have with it and how it affects your life—then we moved into a place of honoring and allowing Fear its rightful place in your life with respect and consideration, this chapter is about how seeing and honoring Fear isn't just a way to radically shrink your problems, but also a way to radically expand the best parts of your life.

You're about to hear the truth about Fear—that it possesses more ancient, all-knowing wisdom than any other voice in your corporation. Isn't it time to let it help you instead of hold you back?

This priceless jewel, the one that's been in your pocket all this time, is about to be revealed.

Honoring Fear . . . Makes You Strong

Have a love affair with Fear and you are powerful. Avoid it and you are weak.

This seems counterintuitive. Repressing Fear feels more powerful. But it's a false sense of power. Like the power Batman might feel if he beat the crap out of Robin. Does that really gain him the power he wants? Or does it ultimately take away his power?

Real power comes from partnering with Fear. Come together with it and you can harness the true power of that connection, versus the false power of denying it. Next thing you know, you'll have a great sidekick helping you take care of business, a trusted adviser reminding you that you're responsible for who you are, for your actions, and for the effect you have on other people by the choices you make. This is why owning Fear can be very empowering. You would be a pretty lame superhero without Fear.

Fear also makes you stronger by giving you something to push against. Put your arms up and push through the air. Pretty unsatisfying, right? There's nothing to push against. Now push against something weighted, like Fear or Self-Doubt. Notice which builds your strength? Which develops your mental, physical, spiritual, and emotional muscles? Even though it's difficult, the second helps you become a healthier, more powerful being.

Great athletes know this. Animals know this. The question is: Do you know this?

. . . Makes You Wise

Nature does have it right.

Imagine an animal living without Fear. Imagine watching that animal interact with the world—how long would it survive? How would it get along with other animals? You'd probably wonder what the heck is wrong with that poor creature.

Same with you. Don't be a poor creature. If you have a healthy relationship with Fear, you come alive with wisdom. You become like the shaman, sage, or magician who is wise with Fear. Listening to it becomes the same as listening to your psyche, intuition, and instinct.

But if you don't have a healthy relationship with Fear, you are rendered stupid.

. . . Keeps You Safe

Bambi is eating grass in a field. Suddenly Fear jolts his system awake with a startle. There's a rustling in the bushes—what's that?!

Looking around, thanks to Fear, his hearing is sharper, his vision more clear. Alert, focused, completely in the present moment, he scans the bushes in this heightened state. There! A wolf!

Off he leaps, running faster than he ever has in his life. He runs and runs and manages to evade his predator.

Five minutes later, he's back eating grass in a field again. There's no PTSD, no need for therapy, no feeling sorry for himself. It's as if nothing ever happened.

There's also no residual paranoia, because he knows that Fear will alert him of danger again when the need arises, and help him survive. It's Fear's job to be afraid, not his. With it on the job, this is how Bambi is free and able again to just be Bambi.

This one is so obvious, do I need to even mention it? Fear is the key to your survival. If it weren't for Fear, the human race wouldn't even exist. Nothing would have survived past that first single-cell amoeba. That alone should make you bow in respect.

Of course, today's world is very different from the prehistoric world. And while some people like to argue that Fear is no longer so necessary for survival, I call BS. We rely on Fear every time we walk across the street, every time we decide whether to eat a doughnut or not. It's designed to be uncomfortable, prompting you to take whatever action is needed to make yourself safer. It does this for you all day, every day.

Yet we don't acknowledge this incredible, unconscious role it plays in our lives. With often devastating results. Remember spiritual teacher James Arthur Ray, who coached his clients to mind-over-matter Fear away and stay in an Arizona sweat lodge even though the heat was preposterous? Three people died.

Or take self-help guru Tony Robbins, who facilitated people in Texas to "overcome what you're afraid of" by walking over hot coals on their bare feet. How the coal-walking "trick" is supposed to work is that Fear makes your feet sweat, and the sweat protects you. Telling people to overcome their Fear doesn't help them—it's actually what hurts them. More than thirty people were treated for burns.

With the Thinking Mind taking over everything—including your emotions—can you see how it's making you less safe? Fear is supposed to create action without thought. It's supposed to be "There's a tiger—run away!" Not "There's a tiger—now, hmm, let me think about this. Is Fear really necessary here, or . . . ?" *Dead.*

If we keep on this path, things will only get more confusing, you'll become less intuitive and less wise to your own limitations, and action will take longer to occur.

If you embrace Fear, you will recognize your limitations until they are no longer limitations at all, but choices. Wise choices. Like "Get me the hell out of this sweat lodge."

. . . Helps You See Clearly

I get it. We'd all rather look at the stars than at the gutter to find our truth. You may be quick to dismiss Fear-based decision-making, arguing that Love and Joy are better sources of clarity. But that's as shortsighted as dismissing one of your two eyes or ears. If Bambi chose only Love to help him see clearly when scanning the bushes, that would be kind of ridiculous. Without Fear, you have no depth perception. In fact, you can even be rendered blind and deaf.

No good decision is ever made without Fear. It may not seem like Fear—it may seem more like a decision made out of Anger, Shame, or Guilt—but, as we've explored, underneath lies Fear. Almost all decisions are Fear-based. Not 100 percent, but it's pretty much always there somewhere.

Consider a friend who wants to leave her abusive husband. Fear is not only a realistic and honest adviser; it's also a clear way to access your yeses and nos and inspire quick, smart action.

If she leaves, her fears may include the fear of being alone; not being sure what she'll do about money; her husband possibly chasing her in a rage; and the fear of giving up the fantasy of who her husband could be. Today these fears may be far bigger than the fear of staying, so she stays. Whatever you're more afraid of wins. This is how, when Fear is honored, you can see contrast and make clear decisions.

If Fear isn't honored, she subsequently never feels clear about what she feels at all, much less about the choices she is making and why, and she stays stuck in confusion about what to do, often forever. The universe is always there, tickling you with its wisdom, but if you're unaware of your feelings or avoid them, you are without eyes to see and ears to hear its message.

If, instead, she has a Fear practice, she'll notice that as she constantly changes, so do her fears. Fear is a brilliant tool for getting in touch with what's true for you, moment to moment. She will always be in a state of awareness, making a conscious choice. *I choose to stay because my fear of leaving is greater than my fear of staying.* She can also finally hear and acknowledge fears coming from friends and family. Only by seeing and understanding your own Fear can you have compassion and consideration for theirs.

The culmination of all this is: One day she's yet again guided by the greater fear of the day, which is the fear of still sitting there, ten years later, ten years older, embarrassed as hell, and nothing's changed. Only then does she decide it's time to leave.

Fear, which once made her stay, now makes her go.

I look down at the pee strip, stunned and terrified. My God, I'm pregnant. By accident. Not two weeks after Tom asked me to marry him.

At thirty-eight, I'm going to have a baby and be a mom? Wow. I sit on the bathroom floor and think about this for a long, long time.

Then I call Tom. I'm in Mexico kiteboarding, and he's home working. I know he's not going to like this, but I wasn't prepared for just how little that would be.

No no no no is Tom's response. I fly home upset. *No no no no* remains his ongoing message, for weeks. It's alarming. Clearly I'm on my own. I also realize I absolutely do not want to marry this man.

Over the next few weeks, fears show up in waves: Fear of having and raising a child by myself . . . Fear of being tethered to Tom for life . . . Fear of never getting to pursue the work I desire because I have only so much energy . . . Fear that I won't like being a mom.

On the other hand: fear of never having the experience of being a mom . . . fear of having regrets.

As I feel them all, I heed the advice they give, which is surging in my unconscious mind. The question being played out down there is: Which Fears are greater? Which whisper the loudest? Those are my bigger wisdom. A month later I get an abortion.

And a door shuts. Fear had answered an important question. Being a mom was not my path in life. I was not meant to have a child, and certainly not with this person.

I'm sad to have gone through an abortion, but I'm glad I knew how to listen.

HOW WILL FEAR MAKE YOU A BETTER PARENT?

Your child has a headache—oh, no, it must be a brain tumor! Your child falls down the stairs—you're a terrible mother! Your kid smokes pot once—he's a future homeless crackhead! Once you have a child, Fear is more at the core of your life than ever. You feel 100 percent responsible for whether they survive or perish on the freeway, whether they thrive or become serial killers.

Now add in Guilt ("Hey, they didn't ask to be born—this was your choice, so don't mess it up") and Worry (the Siamese twin to Love—however much you love is so often tied to how much you also worry). These "icky" three—Fear, Guilt, and Worry (and, mind you, there are many more)—can either become your and your child's greatest companions or your greatest enemies.

Repress any of them and they'll run your parenting style in a covert, immature way. Guilt will speak as blame. Worry will come out as excessive control. Fear will come out as Anger. They all can come out as overprotection or, conversely, you shutting down, all putting Stress on your child. The list goes on and on. Basically, the child has to deal with whatever it is you won't see or acknowledge.

But if you do see and acknowledge Fear, Guilt, and Worry, they will instead come out in mature ways. Guilt will show up as Empathy, Presence, and Involvement. Worry will come out as Consideration, Caretaking, and Love. Fear will come out as Concern, Alertness, and Protection.

All making you a great parent—but only if they're owned and honored. Otherwise their immature versions are available only to you.

Look at it this way: You should feel guilty if you don't spend time with your kids. You should worry about your kids; it's inevitable because you care. Fear will prompt you to attend more soccer games, help with their homework, or make sure Junior sees a dentist. It will also make you talk to them about the pot, versus just blowing it off or, worse, screaming at them.

The key is to let these voices be, and to find a way to enjoy them as part of the natural process of being a parent. Embrace the Fear,

Guilt, and Worry and they'll become divine advisers helping you be the best parent you can be. Plus you'll be modeling for your children what it looks like to have a healthy relationship with the dark side of life. Life is not all kittens and awards ceremonies, now, is it?

And, finally, the Controller will have a break, so you'll be living in freedom and flow, which helps anyone access more often, in a bigger way, other gorgeous voices like Love, Connection, and Laughter.

. . . PUTS YOU IN HIGHER STATES OF AWARENESS

Let's go back to the woman leaving her abusive husband. As she leaves, she may still be afraid that he will follow and terrorize her. But not to worry: Fear is there to make her more intelligent on all levels.

This phenomenon is one of my favorite things about Fear, and I'll cover this in greater depth in chapter 12, but for now: With Fear at your side, like Bambi you become more alert and aware of your surroundings. Fear takes you into the present moment, where past and future melt away, time and space cease to exist. You melt into a heightened state of intuition and impulse and become all about smart choices and, if needed, reaction.

This is especially evident in sports, where blasts of action can occur in milliseconds without the brain interfering. I ran with the bulls in Pamplona, Spain, and wound up in the bullring with a large black bull, horns down, bearing down on me at full speed. I'll be damned if I didn't run and execute a front handspring off flat dirt and over a five-foot wall. When I was a gymnast, I couldn't even do a front handspring off a springboard over a four-foot vault. Fear is the tool that helps you run faster than you ever have, jump higher, drive your race car, and see open spaces that otherwise wouldn't be obvious. This is how you can lift a two-ton bus off a man's legs. Together with Fear, you are unstoppable.

In fact, step a wee bit out of your comfort zone, which adds a little (not too much) Fear to anything you do and you'll have more energy, become more powerful, be more aggressive, and reach an optimal state for higher levels of achievement, whether it's boxing, math, love, dancing, cooking—anything. I say add 4 percent (not 2, not 6) of Fear to everything you do; it'll be like 4 percent more butter in any recipe, and who doesn't like butter?

. . . Gives You More Energy

By embracing Fear, you'll have a lot more energy, for two reasons.

First, the energy you usually spend avoiding Fear can now be used for a million other things. It's like fixing a huge energy leak in your house. Or like paying off a loan. If half your budget goes toward paying interest, there's not much left over to live on. But if the loan no longer exists, *party time*.

Second, because emotions are energy in motion, Fear becomes excellent fuel in your engine and will take you onto a highway and drive you anywhere you desire. Maybe you're a Ferrari, maybe a Honda; everyone is different. But no matter: No fuel, the car goes nowhere. Tainted fuel, the car runs poorly. You must seek to do your very best by Fear, then, so your fuel is of the best quality possible. This way, you could be a Pinto or an Edsel, but you'll still win any race. Go anywhere. Do anything.

CHAPTER 10

THE ULTIMATE MOTIVATOR

FEAR IS GREAT MOTIVATION

Love gets too much credit. Passion is wildly misunderstood. It's Pain, Fear, Anger, Dissatisfaction, etc., that are your best motivators, hands down. Especially when you're younger, your childhood demons, insecurities, and fears (Fear + story) can be your greatest gifts. Your wounded personality has a *lot* to do with how good at anything you become.

In athletics, this is pretty obvious. Having a pleasant character during intermission or while giving interviews is important, but I laugh when people say, "Oh, he's so humble." Yeah, right—maybe during dinner, but don't be fooled about what's happening on the court. He's not playing from a humble place. He's playing from a competitive place birthed from some deep wound he can't see.

Ask pro athletes—preferably after their careers are over and they have no more illusions about themselves or their hype—what made them great. They'll eventually admit that it was the perfect storm of many things, but mostly the right childhood demons and fears. Perhaps a need to prove something to someone. Or Fear—of (as with me) not being special, of being invisible, of not being loved, or of failure and rejection. This is what makes for a great athlete, and anyone who tells you different is either in denial or lying.

Genetics are important, too, of course. If you have a bubble butt, maybe swimming is out. Opportunity also matters, as in "Hey, Bubble Butt, here's a soccer ball instead." But the rest of the equation is: Best chance is to get hit over the head with a frying pan by your mother a few times, then wait twenty years; you might just be pissed off enough to run a marathon in under 2.2 hours.

Anger is good, clean fuel, especially with Fear beneath it. Anger has both passion and vigor behind it, which is the perfect power combination. Anger translates into immediate and fiery action. We know it can cripple you by showing up as finger pointing and put a shadow over your greatness, but, when harnessed right, it can be a lion's roar, an unwavering fanatic, or an impenetrable defenseman. Some coaches who know this will even abuse their athletes and call them useless, as a tool to help them access the power and brilliance that can come from Fear and Anger, but that isn't for everyone.

Ask yourself, then, what your motivation is, not just in sports but for doing anything magnificent. If you answer, "To be the best I can be," know that it's an insincere answer. Likely a borrowed one, too. If you're 100 percent honest with yourself, you'll find the real answer after pondering, "*Why* do I need to be the best I can be?"

Is it to gain acceptance? To get chicks? To spite that kid on the playground who called you Fancy Pants? That's where the truth lies. You're here to express your truth, and the truth is found in realizing that behind your greatness always lies Fear.

It all made sense now. Fear was behind every decision and every ski experience I had, in ways I couldn't see. My entire fearless past was, in fact, all about Fear. And Anger.

Anger came from Dad, who was dismissive of anything I deemed important. Fear came from Amanda next door, then Beth down the road, both of whom rejected my eager-beaver friendship. These were the best things that ever happened to my skiing.

Once on the mountain, the people and stories long forgotten, all I knew was the residual intense fire and passion to express myself in a radical way.

In my unconscious mind, Anger at my father translated into Anger at men in general, wanting to show them that I was better than them. This was bad for relationships, sure, but fantastic for skiing, which is a male-dominated world. Subsequently I couldn't care less about other women skiers or what they were doing. My standards were what the men were doing. I wanted to kick their butts, which is why I got so good.

Fear of being rejected made me jump off that first cliff in front of the cameramen and overnight become known as the best woman extreme skier in the world.

Fear of being invisible propelled me to ski twenty miles an hour faster to impress Rob. I became a world-class athlete in one run because of Fear.

Fear of looking like an idiot made me bring my A game to nearly everything I did.

Fear of failure made me work so hard as to never fail.

Without Fear, few of us humans, actually, would have ever amounted to anything.

DOES FEAR MOTIVATE OR CRIPPLE YOU?

It's in our nature to be screwed up. You, me, all of us humans—we're all screwed up. Screwed up meaning having issues that need attention—5,000 of them, actually, all rotating and showing up alongside Fear and, depending on how you treat them, operating either covertly or obviously in their own unique way.

If you're a parent, then, recognize that you will screw up your kids, because you already have, just by giving them life. The key is to screw them up in just the right way that they're motivated by their fears, instead of crippled by them. This is the key to success.

How to do that, though? How can you become motivated by Fear rather than crippled by it?

Hopefully, by now it's obvious: The only difference is the way you approach your "issues." Embrace Dissatisfaction, Anger, Shame, Doubt, Fear, etc., and you'll do great. Love these voices, eat them, digest them all, use them as fuel, and with Fear as their ringleader they won't be issues at all, they'll transform into motivational energy to help you achieve your goals. This works not only for the reason I showed in my personal story but also because, being so uncomfortable, you'll never want to get stuck in them, so they'll keep you moving. Basically, the best formula for success is this: the right pathology, a hearty steak, throw in a dose of FOMO (Fear of Missing Out), and you'll be off the couch in no time.

On the other hand, resist them and you'll be crippled by them. Avoidance will leave you stuck on the couch, unmoving, wallowing in them. They will poison you.

It's unconscious, of course. Certainly, before having a consciousness practice, no one has a clue that this is happening. If you love Fear, you will thrive on it, be pushed by it, and it won't feel like Stress or Discomfort, either, only like drive, passion, and excitement. If you hate Fear and try to get rid of it, you won't thrive on it—and you'll feel stressed out and afraid all the time. Could it be that simple? Yep. Sit and ponder and you'll find the connection. I promise.

People who accomplish great things, then—make no mistake—don't do them despite the Fear; they do them *because* of the Fear.

HOW TO MAXIMIZE FEAR AS MOTIVATION

Don't ever forget that Fear is uncomfortable and stressful. The discomfort is what drives you. The tension is the gift. Comfort doesn't offer you the shove you need. Only discomfort does.

Consider birds' nests. Mama bird builds her nest with scratchy sticks, thorns, even. Then she places feathers on top to make it soft for the chicks. As the chicks grow, they disrupt the feathers until the thorns and sticks become exposed and uncomfortable, prodding them to take flight. Fear is the universe prodding you with its own thorns, to take flight. Your job is to heed the message of this discomfort and get moving.

Don't wait too long, though, or you could get stuck in the Stress or damaged by the sticks and thorns. As the Buddha said, "A good horse runs even at the shadow of the whip."

Even with a shadow of Fear, then, it's time to move. Don't miss this opportunity. Move this energy like fuel through your system. If you're into sports, don't think about it; just go running whenever you feel Fear. You'll know you're harnessing emotional intelligence if there's no story behind it and all you feel is the energy. Or ski in the voice of Anger. Allow it to lead to aggression, competitiveness, showing off, being a badass, or any other form of self-expression.

Not into sports? Then feel the energy of the emotions in your body. Spend time noticing what that's like, then express it in whatever way works for you—poetry, painting, singing, sex, acting, caretaking, cooking, all from your emotional state. Overexaggerate the emotion when you paint. Actors, give it a funny name and see who you become. Don't try to understand the emotion. Just feel it, be it, then experiment with it by expressing it in your own unique way.

Look for ways Fear motivates you to be more you. Look for ways it makes your day brighter, more interesting, more creative and expressive. Fear is the reason why a person you admire has done incredible things. Get on this ride, too, do it now, or be left at the station forever.

WHAT TO WATCH FOR ON YOUR JOURNEY

Quickly I learn it's best to work for only a few hours with any pro athlete, helping them embrace their issues, because any more and those issues may run their course so fast—sometimes in a day instead of a decade—that it would end careers.

Fear will always motivate you. That's what it's designed for. But the energy of Fear is meant to burn hot and fast. When fully expressed, each specific moment of Fear should push you to the next level, but at some point you'll hope it extinguishes and lets go of you.

That's not to say that some motivators derived from Fear, like Competitiveness and fears—such as the fear of losing—can't push you for a lifetime. But as you get older, most if not all of your usual underlying fears should stop being primary sources of motivation. If they're allowed expression, they run their course and something else comes in to take their place.

It may be a new fear pushing you to the next level, like the fear of living your whole life stuck in fear of losing. But one thing you'll notice, as each level incorporates and transcends the last, is that your new fears will always show up in higher and holier ways. Until eventually, as you near the top of the mountain, one day your motivations have nothing to do with Fear anymore.

At least that's what's supposed to happen.

If instead you find yourself still motivated by the same fears at age thirty that motivated you at twenty—or, at seventy—that's a sign that something has gone wrong. I see this all the time with skiers, guys in their fifties who are still trying to prove something. This is why aging athletes trying to keep the dream alive or make a comeback appear so stuck. For when you repress Fear, you loop the same motivations your whole life.

Look at it this way: You're climbing a mountain. That's your job in this lifetime. If you repress Fear, you get stuck camping too long in one place, playing out the unfulfilled loop of that one fear of something, and there's never a chance for you to move up the mountain to where new motivations lie.

To make it to the top of your potential, you must keep moving.

How you keep moving is by seizing the opportunities when things seem off. The times you feel pathetic or unhappy, or when you wonder, "Is this really who I am?"—that's a sign that it's time to be curious about why you're stuck, to ask, "What fears have been motivating me, and what new motivations lie beyond this stuck place that are trying to get my attention?" Address these questions and you'll be moving on in no time.

My worst near-death experience happened in Chamonix, France, on the side of a seventy-degree face of ice. Skiing the north face of the Aiguille du Midi requires mandatory rappels. It was during one of these that I found myself standing head to toe in a line with three friends, each of us balancing on one-inch chips of ice in our ski boots, skis held to our chests. That was a bad situation in itself, but far worse was the three hours we'd had to periodically hold our breath while avalanches—up to seven stories tall and rushing down at up to 100 miles an hour—pounded down our backs.

Our trauma wasn't so simple as the fear of dying; it was more that we just couldn't comprehend how it was possible we were still alive. To watch walls of snow and ice roaring at us at full velocity and having nowhere to run felt like being tied to a chair with your eyes held open while a man came toward you with a pair of pliers.

The best I could figure was that the slope above us was so steep that the tiny chunk of rock above deflected the avalanches a bit, keeping us from being swept away.

Eventually, a helicopter showed up and hovered nearby. Our rescuers assumed they were coming to retrieve four dead bodies in the debris pile below. They flew back to town for a winch system, returned, and lowered a 165-foot-long steel cable the width of a shoelace. One by one, already wearing harnesses, we clipped in. We were pulled off the face like droopy kitties in Mama's mouth and deposited unharmed to the glacier below.

This was a horrifying day, and to summarize it in a few paragraphs seems almost disrespectful. It deeply affected all of our lives, but the bigger story that matters here is what happened next.

Twenty-four hours later, while attempting to get "back on the horse," I almost died again, on another death-defying face in Chamonix. I fell and started accelerating down the top of a 3,000-foot wall of ice and cliffs, but managed to dive, tuck, and roll back onto my feet in less than one second. After this, it was crystal clear that the universe was screaming at me, through Fear. "Quit this nonsense, learn this lesson now, or be crippled or die, you stupid, stupid girl. Are you even listening?"

It felt like my last chance. No way was I not going to listen this time.

WHY FEAR CHANGES YOU

Notice when something "bad" happens to someone—which always involves considerable Fear—people say, "He'll never be the same again." Well, that's the whole point. If Fear comes in and you stay the same, something has gone wrong. Fear is here to change you, always for the better. It provides an opportunity to break you free from who you've been and seeks to help you grow into who you'll become next.

You actually can't learn anything new unless there's Fear involved. If you stay within your comfort zone, where there exists less Fear, you stagnate. You must embrace or pursue challenge, which will involve conflict, crisis, and considerable Fear, in order to change. These are the things that support your evolution and will always prove to be your greatest teachers.

To understand how this works, consider the name Lucifer. It comes from Latin, meaning "morning star"—the bringer of light.

For ages, all things "Lucifer" have been known to help you see clearly and ignite change. This is because, when bad things happen, subsequent Fear brings up your dark shadow, while little else does. It dredges the bottom of your Unconscious Mind and brings to the surface dark voices like Disgust, Guilt, Shame, and Humiliation. It attaches to the worst doubt and trauma from your history and amplifies it. It does this so you can use these experiences to your advantage.

With it comes a small, essential truth that, if you're willing to look at it, can become the source of decoding your deepest confusions, issues, and problems. If you're willing to feel Fear, what lies deep in your unconscious ocean is finally accessible on the surface, where you can deal with it rather than have it remain eternally buried and inaccessible.

This is how the abused woman not only leaves her husband when she's ready but also comes to clarity about why she was there in the first place— and begins to unravel the wounds that caused her to choose such a life. This is how I was able to quit, and therefore survive, my ski career, and even learn a few things about myself along the way.

By honoring Fear, then, you can finally see the light and come through the other side with perspective and healing. But this happens only with a Fear practice. Without it, you never "bounce back" with more clarity and wisdom than before. You only stay stuck with your dark secrets buried forever.

HOW TO MAXIMIZE THIS OPPORTUNITY

Most Fear involves someone else instilling it—through abuse, neglect, criticism, etc. But look at it this way: If someone is instilling Fear in you, know that they're not doing it *to* you, they're doing it *for* you. As best you can, be grateful. For the Fear they have provoked is actually the universe challenging you to align yourself at a higher level. This is why these moments can become your greatest therapeutic resources, your greatest advisers, and your greatest opportunities.

Consider a tree that gets pruned. It always grows back thicker and fuller. This is what you're going for. The breakdown that occurs—the contraction and the pain—are meant to support your growth and evolution.

Go through the Fear and discomfort, then; let it contract you. The contraction will inspire your new favorite: questions. Questions are a sign that you want something more out of your life.

The main question being: This isn't working, so what do you want instead?

Sometimes it's easier to start with what you don't want: What's intolerable? Maybe this person or thing that's causing you such Fear? Now focus the lens some more. This problem exists to push you to the next level. What level is that? What's ripe?

Usually, whatever is ripe requires risk-taking. It requires you to do things that involve potential failure or humiliation. Which doesn't just make Fear your "push" (*Get the hell out of this relationship!*)—it can also become your "pull" (*California is calling*). Step by step, Fear will motivate you out of your stuck place and also pull you into the next level of your potential.

One always precedes the other. First the Fear, then the growth. Then more Fear, then more growth. This is how the people who overcome the most terrifying hurdles grow to become the most inspirational leaders in our society. Maybe you're meant to be one of them?

To maximize this process, don't wait for others to do bad things to you, even though they will. Seek out an appropriate environment in which to feel Fear. Go ahead and put yourself into tough situations. Do it. Do it now, whenever you want to build upon your genius. Don't forget this. You can reach the top of your potential without pain, trauma, or drama. You can support the universe, which seeks to align you with your greatest potential, by simply going out and doing something that scares you anytime you're ready to grow.

EVERYTHING YOU EVER WANTED

As we forge on, I must ask: What's the difference between most people and Einstein?

Here's what: Most people, when asked to find a needle in a haystack, scoff, "Yeah, right," and go watch TV. If you're curious, though, you'll look and probably find a needle. What you find may be the solution for a problem found in chapter 3. The needle may be that this practice calms Insomnia, Depression, or excessive Anxiety by addressing the underlying cause. The needle may be the end of overeating, alcoholism, or drug addiction by seeing what you've been dodging and that it's not that big a deal after all. It may alleviate mental or physical illness, ending the intense tension and denial created by Resistance. And on and on.

But if Einstein were asked to read this book, he would look until he found that needle, then keep looking until he found a second needle, a third, a fourth, and so on. I want you to be like Einstein. For solving these problems is just the beginning. Making friends with Fear can also expand and grow you from here to infinite proportions.

As we forge on, then, keep looking for all the ways in which Fear offers you riches.

I've found a few needles, which I'm sharing with you, but keep looking and you will find even more on your own. Be Einstein. Keep using your imagination to see what else is possible.

Aliveness

Life is either a daring adventure or nothing at all.

—HELEN KELLER

If you remember, I asked many people, "If given the choice, would you rather feel happy or alive?" and 99.8 percent said "alive." I suspect you feel the same.

Many argue that aliveness comes when Fear stops. I say it's the exact opposite: Aliveness actually comes, and is most poignant, when there's an element of Fear. I know this from the center of my being. And you can, too, if you give yourself that chance to feel the percolation.

It's the primary ingredient behind excitement (Fear + Breathing = Excitement). It is the most important part of adventure. I mean: Is it really an adventure if there's no Fear? Reinhold Messner, one of the greatest climbers of all times, even went so far as to say, "Without the possibility of death, adventure is not possible."

Consider this question: What was the most important moment of your life? It's almost certainly going to be a scary time: giving birth, when you were robbed or attacked, when you almost died, when you had to spend the night alone in grief and despair. Discomfort holds your attention much more than comfort.

Have you ever noticed that the family that gets mugged in Paris comes home talking only about that—not about the Eiffel Tower, not about the Louvre. No one wants to hear about those things, either, because even being around someone else's Fear makes you feel more alive. "You got *mugged*?" "Yes, we got *mugged*!" Wow!

We go to scary movies to feel alive. We handle snakes to feel alive. What's more memorable: sitting at home in front of the television or leaping out of a plane? How about the day you asked for a raise versus another day you sat silently at your desk? I imagine that most everything on your bucket list involves Fear.

Now, this is not for every day. And you must have your own approach—you don't have to jump out of a plane to feel alive. Maybe it's just saying something you've never said before. You don't have to wrestle alligators—maybe just be around others who do. But consider adding a drop of Fear to your life in some way, whether it's by falling in love, singing in front of a group, or dancing freely.

A loving relationship with Fear and the inevitable vulnerability that goes along with it will actually make you want to do things that are scary, because you know they will make you feel alive. And they will make your life *worth it*. Fear can be the greatest reward you give yourself, even if it's only on the weekends, for all your hard work.

The Meaning of Life

If it's not already clear: You're here to feel. You're here not to feel good or feel bad, but *just to feel*. Period. So can we please scrape off those No Fear bumper stickers now?

People ask me all the time to help them limit Fear while skiing. They believe their skiing experience will be better. I laugh and say, "Why would you want to do that?" The main reason people spend thousands of dollars to ski is to feel Fear. That's the reward. It's why people find such meaning in the mountains—for mountains are dangerous. People are even desperate to find a way to take whatever they feel home with them into their everyday lives. Which makes me wonder, could I bottle Fear and sell it on eBay? Billions—we're talking billions!

Without Fear, even Love wouldn't be very interesting, because there would be no associated vulnerability. It might even become annoying. Few would do it. Without Fear, entire industries would die. The experience we have on earth would have no oomph.

A mandala is an artistic geometric rendering that symbolizes how the universe shows up in a person, a city, a planet, etc. Consider that in the center lies primal Vulnerability, which is one of your most lovely employees. Vulnerability is the center of your being. It's the center of all humanity's being, in fact, not just yours. These two employees being so closely tied, if you limit Fear you limit Vulnerability, and vice versa. That means limit Fear and you limit the center of your being.

This is why, without Fear, all meaning gets lost. Without Vulnerability, your heart is dead.

But be okay with Fear and the inevitable Vulnerability that comes with it and your heart thrives. When you're at the bottom of a ski run after you've skied just a little bit too fast, or when you're tasting that drop of doubt about whether this person loves you back, the core meaning of life—which is to feel—will be shining like a 1,000-watt lightbulb from your eyes. I know you know what I mean.

Because life with Fear is raw, real, and beautiful. "I'm as human right now as it gets. *I'm afraid.*" It's the drop of blood in your shark tank. How wonderful.

Look, we're all going to die, so why not really live while you're here? Come alive with Fear. Let it open your heart to the full opportunity and meaning of what it means to feel, to be fully present, and to be fully human.

THE LONELY WATER BUCK ON THE COMPOUND IS VERY DANGEROUS, read the sign near the tourist desk. I was alone in a Ugandan game park, and I mean really alone. I was the only guest. Most of the animals had been eaten, and it's not as if Uganda has a huge tourist infrastructure. I'd slept the night before in my sleeping bag underneath a broken, oily bus, hiding from wandering hippos. There was a two-inch black spider attached to my chest when I woke and three water buffalo standing 100 feet away, looking very freaked out by my spider freak-out.

"Tell me about the waterbuck?" I asked the man at the desk, perplexed.

He explained that it was odd to find a waterbuck alone. It had been attacking people, two this week, both of whom wound up in the hospital. He thought there was something mentally wrong with it, like it had gone insane.

I grabbed my backpack, pondering the waterbuck, and set about making plans for the day. I was going to hitchhike to the nearest town, fourteen kilometers away, and I figured that with so few cars, I'd have to walk through the game reserve the whole distance.

Excited for my adventure, I stepped out of the compound. I had just started down the dirt road when, not five minutes later—you guessed it. Around the other side of a bush was that damn waterbuck. Mother@#%. It was enormous. I had no idea these animals were so big. He must have been 600 pounds. The tops of his horns were maybe eight feet high? His eyes seemed a foot apart. And he was staring right at me, frozen.

I froze, too. I hadn't seen him until I was past the bush, so that put me about fifty feet away. *What do I do?* screamed my mind. *Do I run? Do I look him in the eye? Do I make myself big and shout?* My heart pounded like a bass drum, and instinctively I cast my eyes to the dirt in submission. I stood there, unmoving, for what felt like an hour, barely breathing. I could feel his eyes locked on me. I don't know why I knew this, but I didn't want to turn my back to him. But if I kept walking down the road, I'd have to come closer first, before getting away.

Finally, like a foot-bound geisha, eyes down, I microwalked one step in front of the other, down the road in his direction, until he was twenty-five feet away. Then I kept walking past until he was a few hundred feet behind me, before I slowly turned around. He was still staring at me. I gently turned back and continued at the same pace, not looking again for another 2,000 feet. Then I collapsed into a little ball on the ground, sobbing.

It was one of the most ecstatic moments of my life.

Ecstasy

Feeling leads to pleasure. It can also lead past pleasure into, say, ecstasy.

Yes, you read that right. Not only will honoring Fear mean less suffering; it will actually lead to ecstasy.

Let me explain.

Fear, of course, produces adrenaline, which is a natural ecstatic high. That's basic, great stuff. Greater stuff, though, comes from the new connections you now have.

You know you can get to ecstasy by intimately connecting in Love with another person. But maybe you don't know you can get there when you have an intimate connection with anything. Even pain. Even discomfort.

Recognizing that you are not Fear, and Fear is not you, is not just a huge realization with enormous perspective; that realization also offers you important choices about how to react. One choice is: When it shows up, you honor it by becoming Fear. Which is a great choice. For you are now connected to that voice, like lovers, which connects you to yourself. This makes you Connected Self. Anytime you become whatever voice is showing up right now, that's you becoming your biggest, most connected Self (a.k.a. spiritual intelligence). Which is a place of pure ecstasy. Ravers, take note: You don't even need to take the pill to get there.

Learning to connect with Fear also leads to connection with all 10,000 voices. Do this and you no longer feel alone; you have 10,000 companions. You are finally able to connect to your whole and true self. Only after this happens can your whole self fully connect to other—be it a person, an animal, a river, a moment, or life itself. When this happens, even more ecstasy.

Don't believe me? Next time you have discomfort, try this: Take five minutes to really feel it, cry into it, dive headfirst into the pool of that discomfort—before taking your pain pill, going shopping, eating the doughnut, or having that drink.

You'll know exactly what I mean.

Connection

Let's talk more about Connected Self. You're born with two primary intuitive paths: the need to separate or individuate, and the need to connect or come together.

As you know from chapter 2, anytime you are separate from other, there exists Vulnerability, and thus Fear. The same goes for being separate from the 10,000 voices: With the subject being you, and the object being other—which can hurt you—comes Fear.

But once you make a connection with your 10,000 voices, things change—and they change fast. Here are but a few more tidbits of change that will appear in your life.

For starters, less Fear.

Okay, let's pause for a quick slap across the face. *Say what?*

As I explained, when you become Fear, or any of the 10,000 voices, these voices are no longer separate from you; they are you, and you are them. And what do you get whenever you have this level of intimacy, besides a great relationship? When Fear or any voice is no longer other, you're no longer vulnerable to it. It being you and you being it, there's no subject/object anymore, so Fear dissolves. There simply is nothing left to be afraid of.

If, however, you remain merely an observer to Fear, it also works for different reasons. This is a big point, so pay attention. Like I mentioned briefly with Bambi (did you catch that?), you will recognize that it's Fear's job to be afraid, *not yours*. Fear has one of the worst jobs in the corporation. Its job is to be afraid. Fear should be considered a hero, then, because if you let it do its job, that means you and all the other 9,999 voices *don't have to.*

Taking a final step: Have you heard that there are only two innate states we humans experience: Fear and Love? If that's true, then what you have now—all that's left—is Love.

This is how, if you connect with Fear, that voice will transmute itself into not just Connected Self, but also mutual Love between you and Fear—where, from this place, just as with any lovers, Fear will seem perfect and unable to do wrong. As will you; as will the people in your life.

GIVING UP ON FEARLESSNESS

It may be intoxicating to seek Fearlessness within this practice, but I warn you: Don't do it! It's a trap. We seek whatever it is we don't have or are not satisfied with.

If you seek a car, that means you don't have one. Once you get a car, though, you no longer seek it.

If you seek Fearlessness, that means you don't have it. That means you are living in Fear.

If you seek Fear, though, that means you don't have it. Which means you are living in Fearlessness.

Interesting, eh?

Conclusion: Seek Fear. Give up on being Fearless and, even though that is not the goal, you attain it.

Caring and Kindness

A book came out recently saying that one in twenty-five people are sociopaths. Sociopaths have no interest in emotions—either that or they simply can't feel them. They also have no capacity for empathy.

Can you see how these are tied together? Of course, if you can't feel anything yourself, how can you expect to feel for others?

But if you are able to feel, you will be able to feel for others.

If you are able to recognize Fear in yourself, you'll be able to recognize it in others, and as a result you'll be more sympathetic and understanding.

If you have more compassion for your own Fear, you'll have more compassion for Fear in others, and you'll be more caring and complimentary.

If you honor your own discomfort, you'll be able to honor others' discomfort, and you'll be more welcoming and considerate.

With a Fear practice, you'll have more compassion for Jealousy in yourself and in others. You'll have more caring for Guilt in yourself and in others.

The list goes on and on.

Which is why this practice leads to Kindness. When asked on his deathbed what's most important, Aldous Huxley said it was simply to "be a little kinder to each other." Can you see how the ability to sense and feel your own Fear would allow you to be kinder toward others? And isn't that what's most important?

Peace and Joy

It turns out that inner peace doesn't come from the absence of Crisis and Stress, nor even from the acceptance of Crisis and Stress, but from the *honoring* of Crisis and Stress. Are you still fighting Fear? Are you still fighting any other voice, like Sadness, Anger, or your Erotic Self? If the answer is yes, notice how honoring these voices immediately ends any war. And whenever war ends, what's that called? It's called Peace.

Not only that, but, with the resulting friendship, everyone is at Peace. You are at Peace with this primary part of who you are, and thus you are at Peace with yourself. Fear will be at Peace with you, and will become an asset and an ally rather than a perceived enemy. If you are at Peace, notice how that also affects the people in your life.

There's more. Whenever war ends, what comes next? Why, everyone celebrates. Joy, the other one our five primary emotions, will also show up. Remember, you cannot repress one emotion and not have them all be affected. However much you're willing to feel and honor Fear is in direct proportion to how much Joy will also show up in your life.

The word *caterpillar* is related to the Middle English word for "plunderer," for they eat twenty times their body weight in leaves per day. That's a lot of leaves. You can imagine, then, how much they poop and barf. Eventually that caterpillar becomes so bloated that it can't move.

Once this happens, microscopic imaginal disks show up. Each imaginal disk is coded with a part of the butterfly it's intended to build. The caterpillar's immune system will resist 100 of these disks, even 1,000, but eventually there's a tipping point where it can't resist the sheer numbers anymore, and transformation starts.

The process that occurs next is called deliquescence. The caterpillar turns to muck, then slowly, over time, transforms into a butterfly held within a cocoon. Eventually the butterfly has to struggle and eat its way out of the cocoon to gain the strength and nourishment necessary for survival.

Now, I'm not sure where we are in the transformation of humanity, but I suspect it's somewhere around the bogged-down part. The imaginal disks are folks like you and me—coded with the part of this world we're intended to build—who are doing this kind of work. They're the ones who ignite the process of turning this caterpillar into a butterfly. The more imaginal disks there are, the less plundering and the closer we are as a whole to deliquescence.

FOR EVERYONE, NOT JUST YOU

This is an exciting time indeed.

We affect each other so much. That's pretty obvious. Yawn and everyone yawns. You can't deny that your feelings affect others.

In fact, look closer and you'll see that each of us affects the whole world. One country goes bankrupt and we all have a hard time. One country's emissions affect the whole planet. In a very real sense, every individual human problem is a global problem.

When you do your part with Fear then, your practice has a profound impact on the world. As the spiral of you expands and goes higher, it mimics the spiral of life itself. If you are at peace with Fear, not only do you see the world in a different way, but you do your extraordinary part to make the world a very different place.

Imagine, then, if not just you but *all* of us had this practice. Where everyone is at peace with Fear and thus themselves. What that would mean?

Imagine if world leaders also had a more honest relationship with Fear. Can you imagine the impact?

Imagine the impact on collective Fear.

Imagine the impact on collective Anger.

Imagine the impact on collective Joy, Peace, Courage, and Compassion.

Imagine the impact on war.

And . . . the world dramatically changes.

With collective evolution being a core impulse, do you see how each imaginal disk—such as you—changes everything?

This is why your deepest obligation to the whole of humanity is for you to be exactly and uniquely who and what you are.

Creativity

Conflict is the spark that lights the fire of invention and creativity.

—KAREN VALENCIC

Consider the concert pianist about to perform to a sold-out audience. Ten minutes before she is to go onstage, her assistant receives a phone call—the woman's mother has just died. Hanging up the phone, the assistant has to decide: Do I tell her now or wait until after the show?

Most people would wait, thinking the news would ruin the pianist's performance. But those who live within a creative world know, because emotions are fuel, that she must be told now. So that's what the assistant does.

And how do you think the woman performs?

Brilliantly. Of course.

It's the best performance of her life. And no one in the audience knows her mother has just died. All they know is that they are moved to tears by her music.

This is the role emotions play in creativity. Ballet dancers know that emotions are more important than technique. In popular singing competitions, judges say that emotions are more important than pitch. The same applies to sculpture, painting. If you capture emotions in your creations, you're a brilliant artist.

But what if you're not an artist? Then emotions don't matter, right?

Now, hold on. You're not an artist? If we know nothing else about life, at the very least we know this: All of life is insanely creative. Look at your immune system, your eyes, your heart, your fingerprints. Ain't nothing more creative than that. You're a work of art.

That also makes you an artist, doing your part to help the universe creatively express itself. You cook dinner. You train dogs. You feel the sun on your face, drink a glass of water just so, or contemplate what color carpet to buy.

Let that sink in. You are an artist, and every moment of your life is a work of art.

How do you maximize this realization? Why, by accessing and expressing your emotions, of course. Just like the pianist or the painter.

Artists, painters or you, have been using Anger, Sadness, Joy, and the Erotic as inspiration for millennia. But now I have to ask: What about Fear? Doesn't it seem as though all of the emotions have been invited into the creative process except Fear?

It's time we change that. If you disassociate yourself from any emotions, including Fear, you will lack the wholeness it takes to be amazing. You will leave a lot on the table that could otherwise render you and your audience amazed.

SHIFT AND THE CREATIVE PROCESS

Fear is creativity waiting to happen. It's just asking for a place to be expressed.

Many agree that art created out of conflict and discomfort is always the best art. Music in a minor key breaks open hearts. Painting with angst stops people in their tracks. Art from the amygdala? It sure seems to sell for higher prices than hippie neocortex art. That's because it captures our essential nature, the core of who and what we are—namely, fearful creatures looking not only to stay alive but to thrive, despite the reality of self/other and our looming deaths.

Now, you can't explain what it means to be creative. It's not in the realm of thought. But you can experience creativity. That's easy.

It starts with feeling something. It doesn't start with doing something—that comes later. It starts with your new favorite question, "What do I feel?" And noticing, "Wow, I'm scared right now." Is it because Mom is watching? Is it because I'm wasting my potential? After you become that emotion, entering the inside of that feeling, now it's time to get to doing, which is expressing that feeling in whatever unique way you desire. This is how the emotional energy running through you becomes your creative power source.

On the other hand, if you don't know what you're feeling, all creativity dries up. No juices flow.

Only from the reverence toward that energy can you become fluid with it; only then can the emotions flow out, expressed through the movements of your arms and legs, or the workings of your heart and voice. You can even bring in the neocortex now, and, combined, you become a conduit of universal Fear energy. It's like a stewardship you take on, adding to it your own vision and insight that has never occurred before in the universe—until now, as you give whatever wants to happen, form.

With Fear as your muse, it becomes one of the colors in the painting that is your life. You can use it for every walk you take, any song you sing, every selfie you snap. You'll know you've got it right if you become better at your job, more talented at your hobby, or anytime you think outside the box. You'll know you got it right when just saying the words "I feel afraid" makes you fall madly, deeply in love with yourself.

Since starting a fear practice, I really like who I've become. For the first time, I have a healthy, loving relationship with a great guy. I learned flying trapeze so that I may continue to experience Fear in a creative way, without the worry of dying.

At trapeze, I also find myself more curious about others' experience with Fear: *Look at that! He's gripped. And she's not. How fascinating.*

At the same time, I have more and more clients appear. They're regular people, not just athletes. Men trying to decide whether to get a divorce or not. Women struggling with self-doubt. Kids who are depressed.

One by one, I facilitate them to having a healthier relationship with Fear, and one by one, with just a few hours of work, their problems dissolve. A man with chronic high blood pressure and excessive Anxiety, after two days working together, suddenly doesn't have high blood pressure anymore, and his family writes saying, "He's calm now—what happened?" A woman who always felt like a victim in her marriage takes ownership of her shadow with integrity and changes that relationship. A man with sleep issues—after one session, his issues are gone. Business was booming.

And me? I've started to like skiing again. Now I go skiing sometimes and find the cutest guy up there and say innocently, "Hey, let's take a run," then take him to the most ridiculous steep, narrow chute and destroy it for old times' sake. But mostly I go up there to work with clients, because that's my new passion. It's way more interesting than my own Ego trip or hedonism (well, most of the time).

Fear still motivates me. But now it's the fear of not getting this message out when I have the ability to help. That's what drives me now. That fear is my new reason for being.

CHAPTER 11

LIGHTS AND SHADOWS

YOU'RE DOING SOMETHING REMARKABLE

What is the point of being alive if you don't at least try to do something remarkable?

—JOHN GREEN

In a self-help magazine, I read that an editor wished for "the ability to try new things without fear of failure."

Now, hold on. If you took the fear of failure out of the equation, there would be no excitement. The challenge would be eradicated. The reward of completing a job well done would end. If the fear of failure didn't exist, there would be no heroes, no victories, no praise from others—or from yourself—for having beaten the odds. I shuddered a bit. Be careful what you wish for.

I say put yourself in any position or place that's new or unfamiliar—the more unfamiliar the better, because Fear is a natural response to the unfamiliar. With that comes the feeling that you might fail, which is great. Then you know it's a big enough challenge and you're on the right path toward maximizing your chances of doing great things that are beyond the impossible.

Basically, if there's Fear, it's a clear sign you're on the right path. If there's no Fear in your job, your job is not big enough for you. If there's no more Fear in your sport, you're stagnating. You'll hate your sport in no time.

No Fear means you're not living a remarkable life. The most remarkable things will always involve Fear, even if that something remarkable is leaving your husband, or being as kind as possible to a terrified rescue dog.

FREEDOM

The most important kind of freedom is to be what you really are.

—JIM MORRISON

With the 10,000 voices free to do their thing the way nature intended, whatever freedom they feel, you also feel. With all of your voices by your side, the truth of who and what you are is now available to you, and that truth will set you free. What a relief. Finally, you can get over Mom's death, your ex's abuse, gulping like a fish in front of your first audience—anything that's been holding you hostage for years.

Freedom, to be clear, is achieved by allowing yourself to be whatever is showing up right now. This has never been about freedom from suffering, which not only is unobtainable but should never be an ideal, because that will thwart your aliveness and all I outlined in the last chapter. Instead you're going for freedom to suffer—to cry, or be angry, or, when Fear shows up, to say, "I feel afraid" without apology. That is freedom. You are now free from the small, limited cage you've been living in. The bars dissolve. A big, wide world appears for you and Fear to explore. You and Fear now have fresh air, sunshine in all directions, and room to expand and become anything at all. Go anywhere you like.

I was recently asked to give a seventy-five-minute speech in front of 3,000 people. *Oof.* I give a lot of speeches these days, but it never gets easier. It's like being asked each time, "Are you willing to do a bunch of work and endure the giant pressure of Fear on your chest, in exchange for money, maybe affecting people's lives, and possibly a sense of accomplishment afterward?"

I responded yes, because, I mean, Fear's my thing, right?

The moment I said yes, Fear of course showed up. I had three months before the talk to marinate in it. Is it worth it?

Well, sure. You can't ever feel like you've accomplished anything if you don't actually do anything. There's that. And however scary it is beforehand is in direct proportion to how good you'll feel after. Like skiing the Grand Teton, which had a Fear rating of 10. My feeling of accomplishment afterwards was also a 10. An audience of 3,000 people had all the makings of a spectacular feeling afterward, something you can't get with five people.

Now, there was also a chance I could crash and burn up there. Done that before. Which is why Fear needed to get to work prompting me to prepare, so it wouldn't be an AFGO (Another F–ing Growth Opportunity). Fear increased the possibility of that amazing feeling afterwards by reminding me, "Put the remote control down, you slacker, or you'll regret it."

On the day of a speech, I also like to be a little underprepared so that drop of lingering Fear makes me more present and focused when I speak.

The moment I step onstage, my emotional hose kink-free, there's space available so that I can shift into whatever state I choose—for me a connected place. Even a half second of this place is worth the three months of preparation, and I'd give the speech for free if this were all it meant. I shift into connecting with these people—whom I can't see because of the lights—and a desire to have this intimate shared experience. Fear guided me all the way here.

Fear, Fear, everywhere—anything worth doing involves Fear. Then it's over and it feels so good too, that the pressure is finally gone. And, yes, it does have to be that hard. Otherwise what will you have accomplished?

ACCOMPLISHMENT

In hospice, it's said that the people who are the most accepting of death are the ones who have risked the most. Notice I didn't say anything about who have succeeded the most. It makes no difference whether they succeeded or not—all that matters is the willingness to feel Fear. The guy in hospice who started his own business but failed had no regrets. But the guy who never started his own business had regrets. He felt he had never accomplished anything.

At the end of your life, imagine thinking back and admitting the truth to yourself. You'll relive what you did and didn't do: *My God, I did that speech. I got to experience Fear.* And it was a huge success. Or it wasn't . . . but the humiliation afterwards was one of the best growth opportunities of my life.

The only regret you may have in that moment is wishing you'd known sooner the true nature of Fear and what it offers.

THE ORIGIN OF CONFIDENCE

Ever since you were a little kid, you've been taking risks.

Now, how do you suppose confidence is born? Why, by taking risks.

You took a risk when you went to kindergarten, and that worked out. Kindergarten led to the confidence to attend elementary school. Which led to high school. To college. To work. To that time you wore a thong on Halloween. Each level transcends and includes the last.

Even if today you feel you have no confidence, that's not true. Maybe you ride the bus, work a job or go to school, have friends. All of these involve Fear. All of these require courage, which is a willingness to do something scary (like, say, feel Fear), which is tied intimately to confidence.

Let's look back at my four-month trip to Asia, which strengthened my self-esteem and led overnight to my ski career. It illustrates how your willingness to put yourself in fearful situations is directly tied to the growth of your confidence.

We humans are drawn to testing ourselves. We love the challenge of survival. Look at TV shows for evidence of this: *Survivor, Alone, Fear Factor*, pretty much anything with Bear Grylls . . . and that's just a short list of reality TV. Break into scripted stories and just about everything, from *The Walking Dead* to *Game of Thrones* to *House of Cards*, centers around survival somehow. We love participating in—and witnessing—the experience of being alive taken to the next level of intensity. For one reason only: This kind of action is tied directly to confidence.

You want to be more confident? Do something that scares you. You don't even have to be confident that you'll succeed—we get that wrong. The only requirement is your willingness to try something unfamiliar, and you'll get there.

This has to be within reason, of course. Not "I think I'll climb the Empire State Building using a couple of suction cups." More like "I think I'll apply for this position for which I'm slightly underqualified." Okay?

And you may fail. You go to the job interview and get denied. You get denied at the next one and the next one, too. So what do you do? Stop going to risky job interviews to avoid Fear? No. If this saps your confidence, you don't trust the process. That's just a sign that you don't have a Fear practice. Go back and read the section called "Why Fear Changes You" (page 242) and get to work learning the lessons from rejection. Let Fear inspire you to create better skills so you can function at a higher level and get that job.

Trust the Fear. Trust the rejection. And confidence is yours.

WHAT ABOUT SHADOW VOICES?

With Fear now being your ally, any shadow voice influenced by Fear will operate differently. This is resonance theory: If one family member is 1 percent calmer, the rest of the family will also become calmer. If one muscle is looser, all other muscles are affected.

This is why the other shadow voices will adapt and reorganize in response to even a small change in your relationship with Fear. With Fear acting less neurotic, the shadow voice will become less confused and thus less confusing, more autonomous, distinct, and clear. With the ice called Fear mostly or entirely gone, Anger, Struggle, and Anxiety—all tied to Fear—also melt away. You'll experience less Jealousy, Insanity, Guilt, Shame, etc. Only the flavor of these voices will remain.

Then, if you forge a similar practice with these shadow voices as well, expect even further transformation. Keep in mind that it can be hard at first to recognize these voices as gifts. Arrogance, Dissatisfaction, Revenge—gifts? But if you spend time exploring them through Shift, you'll learn to see and honor them as much as you did with Fear, and you'll find that there's actually nothing inside of you that can hurt you—all are here to help.

Allow them into your life, be willing to ride their peaks and valleys. They, too, will become your greatest motivators rather than sources of darkness, flowing you toward excellence and clarity. Be them, become intimate with them, and you will experience freedom, quicker resolutions, completeness, connectedness, peace, stillness, contentment, pleasure, compassion, integrity, and more—even in the face of inevitable suffering.

PERSPECTIVE SHIFT ON ANGER

Anger is a great example of shadow, as it's one of the most hated voices in your corporation. Having a Fear practice calms it down. But having an Anger practice on top of that also changes everything.

Part of being human is being angry. It's such important energy. Without it, you are weak and pathetic. A wimp. With it, you take charge. And even though it comes from the same place as Fear, you're never afraid with Anger. You cut right through Fear and wake up to your power. You're strong, clear, and intent upon righting a wrong.

You're not depressed when you're angry. Or sleepy. Or bored. Anger is the employee that revitalizes unawakened energy, like frustration, and uses it as a clear, sharp knife toward transformation.

It's also intoxicating. Even just to be around Anger is exciting. You can never be empty and angry at the same time. Therefore, you must be careful, because from a place full of Anger, you feel righteous, free of doubt, and you will not take no for an answer.

You must express it. Otherwise it's like trying to hold back a cough—

eventually it will take over your whole body and wreck it. It's adrenaline looking to release. With no release, it rages.

That's why Anger is often described as fiery. Like a blazing forest fire, it has the power to clear out the debris at the bottom of the trees and, if channeled properly, is brilliant at getting rid of the crap in your way and turning it to fertilizer.

Usually, however, that's not what happens. Without a Fear or Anger practice, it can get away from you in milliseconds. Immature, dangerous, and unleashed, it can instead destroy everything in its path.

HOW TO KNOW IF YOU'RE HONORING ANGER

A samurai has the man who killed his master cornered. He has his sword out and ready to cut off the man's head when suddenly the man spits in the samurai's face.

In shock, spit dripping off his nose, the samurai pauses, then puts his sword away. The spit made it personal. There's no integrity in that. Turning to leave, he'll have to kill him another day.

Throw some golf clubs and then you can finally *think*, right? Driving on the highway, when you scream at the guy who just cut you off, it's such a relief. Anger that shows up without integrity is poisonous Anger, and a clear sign that Fear and Anger have been repressed.

With a Fear and Anger practice, though, things change. You change. Anger changes. It instead becomes sacred. What's sacred Anger?

Zen masters, athletes, even Gandhi—they all let their Anger rip. But that doesn't mean they attack strangers or smash their windshields (some do, but that's not what I'm trying to capture here). They turn that Anger into competition, certainty, intensity, aliveness, and creativity. They probably have no idea they do this, or awareness of the Anger beneath it. It just comes out as the activist who won't allow abuse of moon bears. The runner who wipes out in the middle of her race, is passed by everyone, then jumps up and speeds past the others to win anyway. That's how owned and honored Anger comes out in a sacred way.

In movies, we see sacred Anger all the time. A man's daughter is killed, and it sparks a crusade of revenge. Only you don't hear sinister music in the background; you hear inspirational music. Anger burns throughout the movie with all the properties of a fire—it is very combustible, but when it's sacred, it's a slow burn. It doesn't rage; rather, it's a steady, deliberate quest to right a wrong.

Once the movie reaches its conclusion, so, too, does the Anger. There's resolution. With sacred Anger, you don't feel it again and again. There's no recycling.

That's how Anger drives the hero. Now look at the way it drives the villain. Can you see the difference?

When Anger is owned, there's also no blame. No one is ever the reason for your Anger. When you talk about it, you don't ever say, "You are making me angry." Instead, your sentences start with "I": "I feel angry," said with integrity, without drama. That's saying, "I own this energy. It's mine. It comes from me. I am not a victim to it, but instead made powerful because of it." This is how it turns you into a master.

A masterful use of Anger can help the boxer win the boxing match, and keep it from being personal. In fact, it's so impersonal, it doesn't even need a reason to exist. Anger can just course through your body as fire and passion and not have a story in your head, looping behind it.

If you're only angry at yourself, that's also a sign that you've honored Anger. You say things like "I'm angry for having made the decisions that led to this bad relationship." You take responsibility for your life, and complete responsibility for your emotions. This is how you are never powerless over them, but instead made powerful.

Choices also come easy. You don't snap at the guy who just cut you off on the freeway, for you have cut people off numerous times, too. Instead you pause and use it as an opportunity to inspire realizations—usually about how delusional you've been.

And finally, if, after your pause, you're still going to use this sword of Anger, you don't use it selfishly. The samurai does not seek to harm anyone, even when avenging his master's death. There's no looping story of justification beneath his actions. Anger is just the energy that rights a wrong.

It doesn't represent angst. There is no seething blame. The death of his master was not something someone did to him and thus he now has to get even; it's about his duty to make sure his master is taken care of. He is compassionate toward his target, and walks the earth looking for him with a quiet calm beneath which lies a sparkle of energy. Leading him toward his destiny of making the world a better place.

FEAR AND ANGER AND SHADOW VOICES: GETTING IT RIGHT

You may be wondering, while honoring Fear, Anger, and all the shadow voices, whether you are doing this right. My answer is: probably not. At least not yet.

Here's how you'll know you've gotten this practice right:

Fear or Anger doesn't overtake you all the way.
They don't hijack your mind or get the Ego involved.
There are no stories behind the emotions—it's Fear instead of "fears."
No one else is to blame for them.
You also take responsibility for your life, and the choices you make.
They motivate you to take care of yourself and your environment.
They motivate you to set boundaries and influence change.
You understand what you're now doing, with clarity.
You understand that how you act has a huge impact on other people.
You have compassion and tolerance for others and their own emotions.
You have clarity for other people's struggles.
When someone is being a jerk, you see the Fear beneath it.
You know you, too, can be a jerk, and are curious about that realization.
You may still feel judgmental, frustrated, angry, revengeful, even
     hateful, and own that, too.
But these voices don't make you aggressive.
You feel mostly perplexed. Curious about it all.
Until everything they're trying to teach you becomes clear.

You then express them in a sacred way, with integrity.

Until they run their course and run out of things to say.

Until a new emotion arises, where you use that, too, as another step in your climb.

Each step you take, like when trying to learn anything, you get better and better. Stronger and stronger. More and more living in integrity, over time.

BALANCE

Everything in this chapter leads to this moment, so pay attention. Whenever talking about mental, physical, spiritual, and emotional health, we say we want to be *balanced*. Or *centered*. Choose your word; they're all similar. *Whole. Complete. In harmony.* But what do they even mean?

I'll tell you what they *don't* mean. *Balanced* is not the sweet spot between Happiness and Joy. *Whole* does not mean only Love and Comfort.

"Nice" voices are only one wing you have with which to fly. Without the opposing wing, you can't fly. Only one leg? You can't walk.

Balanced suggests the sweet spot between opposites. This is depicted in the yin-yang symbol, which can represent masculine/feminine, but also Love/Hate, Comfort/Discomfort. When someone is healthy, it means that both the good and the (perceived) bad voices are working together to help you walk or fly far in life.

Whole means saying, "I love all my children equally," and bringing all 10,000 together to make you complete.

Go for whole reality, then, the light and the dark, if you want to be healthy.

Light needs the contrast of dark in order to even exist. The Infinite makes "sense" only because of the Finite. Day without night wouldn't be nearly the rich experience it is. Loneliness makes Love more poignant. Exposure to death is what makes you feel most alive.

It's this balance that you want. Besides, it's all that exists. Life wouldn't even make sense without it.

And with a love affair with Fear, balance is what you finally get.

THE APEX

Beyond balance, what we're going for is transcendence. To transcend, mind you, does not mean to get rid of or let go of something. It means to take the wisdom of a voice like Fear and bring it along, then combine it with its opposite—in this case let's call it Peace—for your highest flight. You embrace both, then use them as a way to go beyond what each is capable of on its own. Like a married couple who are stronger together than apart.

Live your life at the apex of opposites if you want to be the Master. If you meditate, sit in lotus position with Fear and Peace like dials on both knees. From this place, the play of opposites is not running you anymore; you're running it. Only now, after embracing it all, you get to turn these dials in whatever direction you want your life to take.

Sometimes you want Fear. So turn up the knob. Say yes to the speech. Fall in love.

Sometimes you want Peace. Say no to the speech. Stay single.

Explore one, then the other. Or bring them together and explore both at the same time. (Hint: Fearlessness is not the absence of Fear—it's found by experiencing Peace *with* Fear.)

The goal, then, is not to be happy, or to be satisfied. Or fearless. Or at peace. That's a trap—it's fleeting, and causes you to cling, to disown voices and become delusional.

The goal is to be living your life on a see-saw in between, exploring how deep is your capacity for Peace and how deep is your capacity for Fear. If you have only one and not the other, you are incomplete. With both, you're complete. Plus it's the only authentic, sustainable, and realistic option you have.

WHAT'S BEYOND THE APEX?

In your dark room, perhaps the light has come on. *Oh, my God,* you think. *Everything I thought I knew about Fear has been wrong—how wonderful!*

This can be a big moment or a little moment, but it is indeed a moment. Even a tiny glimpse of this can change everything. What do you see? At the very least, can you see that Fear is one of the most magnificent experiences you'll ever have, up there with Love and Joy?

Can you see that if you develop the virtues of Fear instead of trying to correct the faults, the faults get smaller and smaller, and the virtues become unmistakable?

In the tantric world, this is called "transmutation of energy"—in this case, turning perceived negative energy into positive energy. It's like manure: Put in the right place, it helps wheat grow, from which you can make bread, from which you can make toast. (Yum.)

It turns out Fear and Anger are not deficits at all. With the right perspective, in the right place, they're assets that double your value and help you grow. They're not flaws, but perfect, irreplaceable gifts from the universe.

So please, hold this light on Fear as long as possible before it turns off again. The more it stays on, the more you'll see to enjoy. And yes, there's more to see—much, much more. You won't even believe where we're going next. Now that you've gotten the basics down—reframing the way you see and interact with Fear—you're about to use this new awareness as the wave you ride, to go all the way with your life.

CHAPTER 12

GOING ALL THE WAY

When cheese makers created Swiss cheese, they thought, "All these holes? Nobody will want to eat it—it looks terrible." So they tried and tried to replicate the taste without the holes, with no success. Finally, they put the cheese on the market and hoped for the best.

Little did they realize that the perceived flaws—the holes—were the very thing that would come to represent their delicious cheese.

That's what we're going for here, where a perceived negative—Fear—will become viewed not as a flaw, but rather as a sign that something delicious is about to happen.

Learning to ride a bike is a simple process, but if you want to go all the way and win the Tour de France? That's a much longer process, filled with ups, downs, plateaus, victories, and crashes. Going all the way is the theme of this chapter. We'll talk about everything that's involved in getting you to your greatest potential, and the role that Fear plays along the way.

I'm using elite athletes as our example because they go all the way. They say crazy things like "I'm going to win the gold," then often do it, even though the sensation of Fear is there all along—plus fears of failure, rejection, injury, or humiliation. Many of us wonder, "Where's the struggle? What magic do they know that we don't?"

I'm going to tell you what the magic is. I'll also tell you what I wish I'd known back when I first started my journey, so that I could have excelled in all areas, not just some, and without such consequences. For you *Star Wars* fans, here's where to find the Force, and how to jump in.

Over the years, what have we argued is the key to great athletics? First, we emphasized Will and Determination, which are great resources, but limited on their own. Then we fussed about the Zone. Everyone wanted to find this elusive Zone, where, twelve miles into a run, time stands still and you become the wind, the pavement, your own breathing.

Now we're all talking about Flow. Just say that word and everyone in sports nods their head in agreement. It's not just in athletics, either, but in all of life—we all want to be in Flow. This is what elite athletes have tapped into, right?

But what is Flow? The athletes know it when they feel it, yet they can't explain it. The coaches can't explain it. I have yet to see a clear explanation of what Flow even is. But we're gonna need one—because it's the wave you'll ride to go all the way.

FLOW

Remember our hose? I promised we'd get back to this. The 10,000 voices flow like water through your hose (otherwise known as you). If you're connected with what you are feeling, and allow all 10,000 states to move through the hose, then you are in Flow. It's that simple.

What Flow is not is the absence or avoidance of any voice—like Ego, Anger, or Fear. And it's most certainly not clinging or trying to force any voice, like Joy, Gratitude, or Forgiveness. Flow is when *any and all voices*—good, bad, spiritual, not spiritual—are allowed to flow into, through, and out of your life like water. As you constantly change, from moment to moment, simply allow room for it all—and I mean *all*—including Jealousy, Unworthiness, Guilt, Resistance, dukkha, Ignorance, Blame, and more—to come into, through, then organically out of your life.

Then you are in the dynamic called Flow.

THE JOURNEY OF FLOW

Enlightenment is intimacy with all things.

—DOGEN ZENJI

Flow is not a passive experience. It's an active, dynamic one. It's not a voice, or a place you arrive. It's the moving dance of asking questions: "What am I feeling? How about now?" and then seeing, feeling, being, and expressing that truth. To stay in Flow, just keep dancing from state to state by always asking the question and remaining curious about the answer.

Right now I feel Fear, which is uncomfortable. Now I'm Thinking Mind, which seeks to understand reality through dualistic judgments. Now I'm firmly in the dynamic of my Ego, which argues with reality. You are up to 10,000 things a day. Which is why you can never pigeonhole yourself or another person as being "smart" or "rude." They may be one of those things in the moment, but in the next moment they're another thing entirely.

If you deny any of them—for example, "I'm not being judgmental" or "I'm not afraid"—you will be kinked, and the voice you repress will become all you know. But when you are in Flow, each voice moves into, through, and out of you, often in mere seconds. This way, you're never stuck. *Flow includes all voices but is not limited by any of them.*

While you're reading this book, for example, you may see Agreement, Understanding, Truth, Hope, or Insight showing up in your hose. Or you may see Confusion, Doubt, Skepticism, Mistrust, or Frustration.

Simply stay aware of what's flowing into and through your hose. Stay in touch with who and what you are, moment to moment. Which is a constantly changing human being.

Do this and something gorgeous happens: That curiosity gives meaning and purpose to your life. Like the singer whose meaning and purpose are found in her singing, your meaning and purpose will be found in your everyday life.

It will answer your ongoing question: Who and what am I? For when you're in Flow, you always have an answer. Who and what you are is your unique expression of whatever state is coming through the hose. Constantly changing. Never the same.

Right now, I am afraid. Now I am sad.

It will provide a clear sense of reality. This awareness of what you feel will never argue with reality, because it *is* reality. You can trust it completely to be your truth.

To go all the way with maximizing Flow—as we've explored since the introduction, where I first introduced Shift—remember that you don't just want to witness these voices. Nike almost got it right. "Just do it" is a great slogan, but so much better is "Just be it." You want to become them.

What that looks like is: If the voice of Bliss shows up, don't just witness or listen to it—*be it*. Fear shows up? Be the voice of Fear. Whatever comes through the hose—Curiosity? Confusion?—be it all the way. Embody it until you become it, and it becomes you. Because you already *are* it, whether you realize it or not.

What you're going for is that dance of intimacy. Let's look further into what that means: "intimacy." If you're intimate with a person, you're connected to them, you feel them. It doesn't have to be sexual, but it is erotic. To be intimate with Fear is simply: You feel it. And you feel it feeling you back.

Try to intellectually understand what this means and you'll go insane. You can't intellectually understand the voices of Intimacy, Love, Connection, or any voice, and why would you try? That's a way to avoid it. When making love, do you stop and say, "I'm just taking a moment to think about what we're doing here." Of course not, because that'd just be weird. Same thing with being your voices. You want to surrender to each one, and let that immersive dance take you wherever it wants. In this way, each new moment becomes an opportunity to fully embody who and what you are, and live your truth.

Now, as lovely as that sounds, I'm sure it's not a stretch to learn that Flow is not all Bliss and Happiness. If anyone says, "Follow this path and you will become peaceful," that's deceptive advice. If you're in this practice with the goal to create more peace, it won't happen, and it will take you away from Flow, not toward it. Stop trying to bend the river to take you somewhere nice. That's not what this is about.

Instead, merge with it. When you're peaceful, great—be peaceful. But when you're restless, great—just be restless. Find peace in your restlessness. If you're in a bad mood, just be that bad mood. Honor your bad mood. One time during a bad mood, I decided to go skiing. On the mountain, I remained in a bad mood, but now I was really enjoying it, feeling snarky and condescending toward other people and life. Also learning from it. Until it ended a few hours later, as it always does.

Fear will end. When seen and understood, it will run out of things to say. Peace will end. Don't cling to anything, or try to push anything out before its time. Just wait until it lets go of you and something else enters.

If you're in Flow, there will always be room for something else to enter.

Which is important. You'll want room for something else to enter, because in the space that now becomes available, in the pauses that exist between thoughts, in the emptiness between each moment, bigger forms of intelligence than your limited personal view of the world or your Ego have space to enter. Through Flow, you will organically arrive there.

Welcome to spiritual intelligence. In sports we call it the Zone.

WHAT IS THE ZONE?

One cup of water contains the whole spring.

—STEPHANIE RUSSELL

Some argue that Flow and the Zone are the same thing. They're not. Flow is merely the dynamic that takes you there. Flow is the river that takes you—as rivers tend to do—to the ocean.

The ocean is the original truth of who and what you are: you are not an individual drop of water, but rather a representative of something much bigger. Whenever your hose isn't kinked, and a vacancy opens up in your

Unconscious Mind, this fundamental reality will move right in. The bigger the space, the more room it has to enter.

With the flowing river all around you, ready to be tapped, your whole life, including Fear, is designed to help you come home to this truth, to recognize that you are something much, much bigger than your limited personal view—that, in fact, you're connected to everything and everybody in ways you can't normally see.

It's ridiculously important to have this experience at some point. You lose your connection to all that exists starting at age two, and it's up to you to find it again in your lifetime. In fact, I base the quality of my life on how much I'm able to tap into this truth—of coming home to my original nature. It's why I loved skiing so much. The skiing didn't matter; the place it took me was what mattered. Most athletes would probably agree.

If you're athletic, chances are at some point you'll access this innate spiritual intelligence. By calling it the Zone, we have avoided calling it by other woo-woo names such as the Tao, Nirvana, the Infinite, Buddha Nature, and so on, but make no mistake: That's what it is. It's possible, then, that sports, or movement in general—not church, not even meditation— are the most common way for humans to access a spiritual awakening. Yet it is the least understood and discussed path for waking up.

Which inspires this question: Why do sports take us to this bigger place, this connected mind, and little else does?

Because of Fear, of course. If you're willing to feel your emotions, those become the raindrops that become the river that takes you to the ocean.

LET'S START WITH EMOTIONAL INTELLIGENCE

Enlightenment isn't found with a full stomach, or on a soft pillow.

—CONRAD ANKER

When athletes who are stuck call me, why do I always solve their problem by getting them in Flow with Fear?

Easy. Because if you're nurturing emotional intelligence and thus in Flow with Fear, you quite simply, organically arrive at a Big Mind, Infinite perspective. You don't even need to train for decades or run a marathon to get there.

It works like this:

You are not a separate self (human) out there on the mountain, court, or road, looking to have a connected experience (what I'll now call "being"). We get this backwards. You are a being looking to have a human experience. Thus, you have to first go all the way with being human, which is one side of the coin, before you can come home to or even recognize the other side of the coin.

In fact, however much you're willing to be human, and the separation that entails, is exactly how much you can access being. You can't have one without the other, and you can't go all the way with one if you don't go all the way with the other.

Now, what does it take for you to be fully human? Mental intelligence. Great. Let's get that in Flow. Let the mind do what it's designed to do. When it chatters while you're trying to sleep, be sure to ask what it wants to say instead of tricking it away. There's also Ego, which is the full metal jacket of your humanness. As we'll explore soon, please don't drink the Kool-Aid and think that annihilating your Ego is a way to access spiritual intelligence. That will take you further from it—just like the denial of being a fool isn't going to make you wise.

And we have emotions. They also make you human. And while all paths take you closer to your truth, and all lead to spiritual intelligence, this one is key because it's the one we've gotten most confused about—in particular, the emotion called Fear.

Not only because Fear is the biggie that most people need to work on to achieve a state of Flow—few people kink their hose around Joy, for example—but also because it's primary, old, and designed to get your attention. Fear is a call to action. It wakes you up to your humanness like a punch in the stomach, requires immediate attention, gives you more oxygen, and increases your breathing (unless you're trying to repress it, in which case you stop breathing).

Don't get me wrong. Joy can also be a call to action. Joy will inspire you to spend Christmas feeding the homeless or excitedly smack your wife's butt. But with sports as our example, notice that Joy, which is newer than Fear, doesn't help with your performance. Consider the Olympian on the balance beam performing in the voice of Joy. If she falls, does she care? No. And no football player ever said in a pregame interview that he wants to play from a place of Joy. He would also never admit he's scared—but that Fear is still there. Always. Especially before any big game.

Fear is by no means soft and cuddly. It's very aggressive. It doesn't cajole or invite, but rather demands action: "Wake up, dammit, and *feel me*." Fear calls on you to pay close attention to what you're feeling. And where are feelings located?

In your Body. If you're willing to feel it, even a little bit, you ride those raindrops—that emotional awareness—into the river called your Body.

Turns out emotional and physical intelligence, if you look closer, are interchangeable. Those raindrops and the river are pretty much the same thing.

RIDE THAT WAVE INTO PHYSICAL INTELLIGENCE

Feel it, then be it—this is called embodying Fear. You are now in your Body.

Anytime you're in your Body, congratulations, for a magical thing has happened. Anytime you're feeling Fear—anytime you're feeling anything, for that matter—you're not in your head anymore. You're no longer the Thinking Mind. Not your Ego. Not in the cage anymore. The chalkboard is wiped clean. The wild horse is out to pasture. Hallelujah.

Now, magic happens.

There are other ways to arrive here without Fear. Three deep breaths or any kind of focus on your breathing is a way to trick yourself into getting out of your head and into your body. Just moving your body can also take you there, but it doesn't always work. I know lots of people who start moving but stay in their heads. Maybe they focus on technique, or try to control their thoughts as a way to get there—and that just keeps you in your head. Remember, you feel Fear in your Body, not in your head.

How do you tell the difference? Ask yourself: Do you feel afraid, or do you feel energy? If you feel afraid—or, more commonly, have fears (of something) that involve a story, belief, and thought—you're in your head. If you feel energy and excitement, you are in your Body. The Body that exists in the present moment, with no past or future, no story, belief, or thought, is a state of pure, unjudging awareness, truth, and energy. That is all you'll sense.

Now in the Body, a great place from which to perform, you could stay here and it's quite the ride, but the next experience is, at some point it too will run its course and also let go of you. And with the mind dropped off, the Body also dropped off, there's a whole lot of room in the hose for something else to enter. Enough room, in fact, for the Infinite.

Welcome to the ocean.

RIDE THAT WAVE INTO SPIRITUAL INTELLIGENCE

When accessing spiritual intelligence—which to this point we've been calling the Zone—you transcend being human and all that entails. You, as you, cease to exist. Which is why this place is ungraspable. There's no you anymore that can even attempt to understand.

So go with the melody instead of the words. Feel the music of this section and see where it takes you.

It goes something like this:

When you're in a state of spiritual intelligence, you transcend the mind. It's a place of No Mind. You also transcend the Body. You are dropped off Body and dropped off Mind. No longer about Thinking, Striving, and Doing (valued in society, understood), you are now Non-Thinking, Non-Effort, and Non-Doing (undervalued, not understood). Now you are just Being.

You've heard the phrase "Time stands still"? That's because time is merely a concept, a human creation. When you're in the Zone, when you become the Infinite, you transcend being human. You cease to exist. Which means time also ceases to exist.

The greatest moments of your life will always be when time stands still, because you're living free of the past and future. Free of Ego. Free from being "Kristen." Free from being "the guy who was adopted." Free from being "the woman who was abused by her boyfriend." Free from all the superficial details of your cage bars. Space also ceases to exist. You are form-less. You are empty. Unmolded clay. You have nothing to say; there simply is no one to say it.

And from here, because no self remains to feel it, there exists no Fear.

Standing at the top of an icy fifty-degree you-fall-you-die ski slope in Chamonix, France, seems more like standing atop a cliff. I can't see below the first thirty feet, because it's too steep.

Unbeknownst to me, because I'm willing to feel it, Fear right now is my greatest teacher, my mother, my father, my lover, my friend, and my enemy. I feel complete rapture with this moment. I didn't run twelve miles to get here. I didn't take drugs. I didn't even get a good night's sleep. Just by traversing from the tram and stepping out of my comfort zone, here I am, and this turn I'm about to make just is.

The wind blows gently in my face. Not Kristen anymore. I am only desire to express my unique self and feel the snow underneath my feet.

I point my skis downhill and accept a little bit of speed. Not too much. Then take a single certain turn and stop. When skiing you-fall-you-die faces, you do it one turn at a time.

The snow is grippy—it's a yes—so I take another turn.

Except now it's icy. Fear shouts an alarm. Slower. Cautious. Then my skis shoot out from under me. Whoa! Grip. Pause. Indecisive. Side-slip to steadier snow.

Then yes—another turn.

So it goes, all the way to the bottom. Caution. Yes. The Erotic.

Emptiness. Dissatisfaction. No. Caution again. It's all there. All states moving and expressing themselves physically, through me. I am the athlete—the factory using 10,000 intelligences, motivations, and energies to create a product, which is this performance. I am the tool by which the 10,000 states become conscious of themselves, and get to ski. Now, I am the Infinite, and I stand five feet seven inches tall.

At the bottom, then, comes the adrenaline. The cortisol. I'm gooey with it all night.

NO FEAR

If you don't know the nature of fear, then you can never be fearless.

—PEMA CHODRON

Wait . . . what? Giving up the hope that you'll ever attain freedom from Fear is how you attain it? If you stop trying to control things you can't control anyway, and honor your moods, foibles, and discomforts, then yes, that's right: Exactly what you want—complete freedom from thoughts and Ego—occurs.

Include the suffering of Fear and Anger—remain willing to not always feel good—and be fully human, and only then will you be free from this madness that is your human side.

Do professional athletes know this is what happens out there? Actually, no. They rarely have any awareness of Fear transcending itself and taking them to the expanded states they achieve. All they're aware of is that from this place, as they push off down the mountain or enter the basketball court, a switch flips and they feel no Fear.

All that's left is reaction and deep original intelligence on the beam, the football field, while having sex, singing, or writing poetry.

It's something you must experience, though. I've done my best to explain how this happens, but it's only my interpretation, based on fifteen years as a pro extreme athlete, fifteen years as a facilitator, and my attempts to know something that is ungraspable. It's been like trying to explain why chocolate tastes so good.

If you really want to get it, I recommend eating the chocolate, then decide for yourself.

FEAR AS SPIRITUAL PRACTICE

When you truly possess all that you have been and done... you are fierce with reality.

—FLORIDA SCOTT-MAXWELL

Here's where I'll switch away from athletes, but first let me explain. If you're an athlete, you have a better chance of accessing spiritual intelligence for one simple reason: You're slightly more willing to feel Fear than most. Otherwise you wouldn't have chosen the sports lifestyle. (Note: This is especially true for those participating in extreme sports such as big-wave surfing or base jumping—which are notorious for taking people into higher states. Specifically because there's so much fear involved and the athlete so obviously loves feeling it.)

I say "slightly" because most athletes are severely emotionally repressed. Ignoring Fear is, sadly, the more common way to arrive at (a mostly false sense of) Fearlessness than what I've outlined. But if there's at least a tiny crack in the basement door where you're willing to let Fear come out to play, that changes everything.

That crack—even if it's just 1 percent—combined with decades of technical and physical training, is the most common formula for invoking this connected, expanded state. And while 1 percent Fear only allows room for 1 percent access, it's still life-changing. Even being 1 percent connected to the intelligence of the whole universe feels amazing. *This* is why you train so hard. *This* is why your sport is so intoxicating and addicting. One percent awesome is enough to win an Olympic gold medal.

Then that higher state is gone and you wish it would come back. So you get back to training, hoping it shows up again. It's the reason you do your sport. Not the lifestyle, not the medals—they're just sprinkles on this ice cream. The higher state is the real treat.

But if the door allowing Fear to enter is suddenly slammed shut? It doesn't matter how much training you do; with war now draining all your resources, Flow is kinked, and you'll have no access to this higher place anymore.

What about the opposite, though? What if the door is cracked 2 percent, or 10 percent? Or, shudder at the thought, 100 percent? Can you see what's possible?

Everything would change. You could get really good really fast, without so much training, like I did after Asia. Being in 100 percent Flow with Fear and your life, you could access this intelligence on *the very first day* of your first ski lesson. I've facilitated perhaps 500 skiers to take a single run in the voice of the One Dancing with Fear. That experience, on its own, turns otherwise average skiers into solid athletes.

They felt limitless. Capable of anything. They were able to "get out of their own way." Yet so far, this is only an ideal, hopeful future. I'm also keenly aware that, if we head in this direction, in the words of my friend Andy Walshe, who runs the Red Bull athletic performance lab, "we haven't even scratched the surface yet, athletically, of what's possible."

Now, most people are not athletes. So what about the rest of us? How do you turn Fear practice into spiritual practice? While it's awkward for many folks to explore spiritual intelligence, and safer to avoid it, do you feel the Infinite tugging at you? It's the "something missing" in your life. The connection you seek. The home you crave—that doesn't get satisfied by marriage or by purchasing the three-bed/two-bath of your dreams.

You want to wake up to your true nature, too, but you don't do sports?

You're in luck. No need to train twenty years, run marathons, or surf Mavericks to get there. Because life is naturally scary and begging for your attention, you can get there by sitting on a park bench. The day I realized this—that I can feel this deeply connected to my truth at any time—was the day I quit risking my life in the mountains.

Simply your willingness to be human and feel what you're feeling can lead you to access Being. Just by taking a giant step with one leg, feeling something you would normally avoid, or the flap of one wing—enjoying the pain of a disappointment—you will be in flow with your humanness and can finally connect with the other leg or wing, that missing part you're always searching for.

A good facilitator who hasn't built a shrine to your Thinking Mind can help. A spiritual therapist, intuition guide, or emotional teacher who isn't hung up on the words "overcome" or "let go of" is a good resource. There are people out there to assist you. It can be as simple as my asking you to become that Connected Self with a simple shift, and you enter that room in an instant.

Or you can do it on your own while meditating, by asking your favorite new question, "What do I feel?" In your willingness to then feel it, whatever it is—Joy, Anger, or Fear—and then *be* it, without trying to understand what that means, you're there. If you feel inspired, also get up and express it in any kind of mature, creative way that strikes you.

This is how just cooking spaghetti and meatballs can be your spiritual practice.

CONGRATULATIONS

Let's say you do this. You get to know key employees in your corporation. You've let the Thinking Mind do its thing. You've opened a new dialogue with Fear. You've gotten in touch with the Body. Fantastic! What a ride. Flow will take you wherever you want.

With a simple perspective shift on Fear, you're now in Flow and nurturing greater emotional intelligence.

Through Flow, you also get to explore the wisdom not just of your Mind but of your Body. You are nurturing greater physical intelligence.

You can also ride Flow to a much bigger place—a connected place—to the moon and beyond, into the infinite nature of the Universe. Bravo.

Which is why I hate to tell you . . . This is not the end.

You haven't arrived yet. As lovely as this experience has been, we're only in the middle. Flow will take you into and through yourself and connect you to the universe. Then, because it all changes so quickly, Flow will also be the wave taking you back down to earth—and into Separate Self again, which is what you're meant to experience so long as you're alive. Back to your delusions, judgments, and inability to figure out who or what you are, stuck yet again.

Here's where you stop going up, up, up. There's a higher state than Infinite Wisdom, higher than freedom from the cage and the resulting Fearlessness. But to get there, it's down, down, down, back into the chasm.

I'm sorry, but learning is like that. States of consciousness being free, but—just as in the Tour de France—stages must be earned.

YOUR CRASH

Many spiritual teachers argue that you can move to Marin County or an ashram in India, meditate ten hours a day, or sign up for a course to achieve a permanent state of Being, Connected Self, or "Enlightenment," and thus live without Fear forever. Neocortex junkies not only suggest that this is possible but insist that they themselves are doing it.

Beautiful effort, but it won't work. Perhaps you've heard the koan "If you meet the Buddha on the road, kill him." While I don't recommend killing anyone (even if you're a samurai), certainly run from anyone who claims to be Enlightened, as fast as you can. For while you can have multiple glimpses of spiritual intelligence, and it can be pursued, found, and enriched—especially by embracing Fear—it will never be permanently sustained, because your Ego will always find a way to attach to any kind of achievement. And we're back.

Don't believe me? Ask yourself: Who is doing all this cool stuff—seeing, honoring, expressing, or transcending Fear? Who is this Being, formless and free from Ego and Fear? Ask and you'll see how quickly, in the answer, you're still *you*, living in your mind as always, being human and all that it entails.

You must and will go back to it all—to Ego, the cage bars, Judgment, Delusion, a kinked hose, thinking, and your primary intuitive need for separation between self and other.

Which, of course, is where Fear lies. You start in Fear, and after all of this, you end in Fear, for remember: You are here to have a separate human experience, where always there is Fear.

It turns out that spiritual intelligence is a trap. Connection to the universe will always be lost. The Zone is only meant to be temporary. You can't stay in the Infinite for an entire two-hour basketball game, even if you're Michael Jordan—let alone the rest of your life. And you will go unconscious again. Always, you will come back to being separate and stuck, living in Fear. It's in your nature. And if you've ever believed otherwise, you're being unrealistic.

Remember, the Buddha says, "Enlightenment is delusion." The enlightened man on the road who claims to have arrived somewhere significant is having a huge Ego trip about not having an Ego, and is completely unconscious about it. He *is* the Buddha, make no mistake—we all are—but if he doesn't also see his delusion that goes along with being human, he's a stone Buddha, blindly stuck yet again in preference and judgment. And so are you.

A quarryman, seeing a rich man who could buy anything he wanted, grew unhappy with his life. He wished things were different. He wanted to be rich. Only then could he be happy.

Poof! A genie appeared and granted his wish! He was now a rich man! And he was happy! Until he saw a king, who had power. He wanted to be him instead. Only with power could he be happy.

Poof! The genie made him a king. And he was happy, until he noticed that the sun was far more powerful than a mere king. If only he could be the sun.

Poof! He was turned into the sun. And he was happy, until he noticed that the clouds could block his rays. If only he could be a cloud.

Poof! He was turned into a cloud, and he was happy. Until he noticed that he had a profound and immediate effect on all things except rocks. They were so strong. If only he could be a rock.

Poof! He was turned into a rock, and was happy. Until a quarryman came along . . .

BACK IN THE CAGE

I've mentioned several times and ways that having a Fear practice takes you out of the cage and can become the river you ride to freedom from Fear. This new stage you've achieved is very appealing, so you may be upset to learn that this is not "all the way."

Let me reassure you, though, that things *are* better than they were before. For many moments, the light was on, and the whole sky was visible to you. You've swum in the Infinite ocean, and you can never undo that experience. Your cage is now more spacious. You're listening to more instruments in the orchestra. Your view is further up the mountain. You've danced intimately with the truth of who and what you are.

But, alas, where you live now is in the judgment and belief that Connected Self, spiritual intelligence, and the fearlessness found there are superior to the separate, stuck egoic self. And that realization . . . is the new mud and dirt in your cup, the new cement that encases you.

And, oddly, this new cement is even (brace yourself) . . . the belief that Fear is good. This is your new stuck place—the new thing you know for sure. And we're back, clinging, like a monkey with his hand in a new jar, to a new identity, a new revelation—that embracing and flowing with Fear is the best way to be.

What happens next (I know this one personally) is that you'll think that your cage is better than others' cages: You'll become judgmental toward anyone who represses Fear (or eats gluten), who isn't in Flow, who hasn't achieved a level of spiritual intelligence or is only interested in mental intelligence. In this you're delusional and ignorant all over again, thinking you're free when really you're stuck again, living a new delusion/belief. And everyone can see it but you.

Crazy, isn't it? What you've worked you butt off for is your new problem! All this effort to be an expanded human being—first with the radical denial of Fear, next with the radical embracing of Fear—yet here you are, back in the chasm, clinging to new beliefs, still afraid.

This is what has to happen, though, in order to get to the next level.

Stay with me.

You've seen the movies where a hero learns something new and difficult, like the guy seeking the holy grail? Nothing is in vain; each level includes and transcends the last. The music only gets more dramatic as the story progresses.

You're moving in a tighter and tighter spiral, heading upward toward your greatest potential.

Stay with the map, stay with Flow. You're always in Flow whether you realize it or not, even when you're stuck. It's your greatest asset in finding what you're looking for. Take another dive into Fear and let's see what we can find.

LOOSEN THE REINS YET AGAIN

A Master is watching a man struggle with his horse and cart stuck in the mud. The man tries everything to get unstuck—pushing the horse, pulling the horse, encouraging the horse with a carrot, pushing or rocking the cart, sticking boards underneath the wheels.

For an hour he struggles, until the Master can't stand it anymore and approaches the man and finally, gently, whispers in his ear, "Loosen the reins."

Animals and young children make great examples of this, for they don't try to manipulate the universe. They feel whatever they feel, then react. Use them as your model.

With any problem or discomfort, you're given an opportunity for a delicious moment of awareness and pause. Merely take the time to notice yet again that you've been trying to force the river, because that's what we do. Always come back to recognizing dualistic judgment, shadow, beliefs, and things you know for sure. This is your ongoing, inescapable delusion.

Use every new opportunity to jump into Flow again. Loosen the reins and let Fear and all the 10,000 voices that are back (they actually never left) do their thing. And you'll never stay stuck for long. Just come back to letting your life do its thing, and you and your cart (hell, *Ferrari*) are free to go anywhere you like, yet again.

Keep it up. Own your discomfort, delusion, and ignorance over and over. Let your mind run as free as possible, so it can seek, find, and explore other forms of intelligence. Let the 10,000 minds all play their instruments.

There is no place to arrive. There is only *this journey*.

WHAT IS THE RABBIT?

This may come as a shock to many, but, while it's an important experience, we have got to stop saying that the Connected Self, the Zone, Enlightenment, Freedom from Ego—any words we use to depict spiritual intelligence—is the highest state, or sustainable. It absolutely is not. I don't want you to become intoxicated by it and think you've found the holy grail.

Frustrating, I know, and you probably want to kill me, but there actually is a higher place than spiritual intelligence, one that includes but isn't limited by it.

To find it, let's review the word "Enlightenment." It's a cheesy word. No one says it nowadays, because it sounds ridiculous. Being free from Ego, from Fear, from time and space? Living in a state of "I am you, and you are me"? There's a reason no presidential candidate has ever run on the platform of "What we need is more Universal Consciousness and Enlightenment." They'd be laughed off the stage.

We see the delusion in that. We know truth when we see it, and this ain't it. You *are* separate. You *do* have an Ego. You will always live in Fear, and always have a shadow. All the effort of trying to breathe (and now honor) these things away hasn't worked.

People cry BS on the word "Enlightenment" because they know something is off. Here's what's off: "Enlightenment" is not the absence of Fear, Ego, Shadow, and Mind, as so many suggest. It's not even the *opposite* of Fear, Ego, Shadow, and Mind. Nor is it a place where you arrive. True Enlightenment is the *pursuit and ongoing effort* to *include* all states, reached by going back as you organically have, again and again, seeing and owning all the voices that make you human, and doing your best to flow with them.

Take Tiger Woods as an example. He was probably in a state free from Ego, time, and space (the Zone) thousands of times in his golf career, but that does not mean he was in Flow with his life, in balance, nor does it mean he is "enlightened." Which is why I say that the rabbit we now chase is to include this place, this experience of spiritual intelligence, for without it you are like a bird with only one wing—unable to fly to your furthest potential. You are missing key voices, and experiences.

But you should always recognize the other important wing, which will become more and more developed only as much as you're willing to own and embody the most basic, essential part of you, Fear. Together these two wings—that of human and that of Being—are what take you all the way with being who and what you are: a unique and fascinating Human Being.

This is what makes for a complete, whole, freely functioning you. This is the ultimate balance we seek, between all states and all opposites—including human qualities such as Fear, Ego, Shadow, and Thinking Mind, which are radically necessary for success and are what make you *you,* as well as the beingness of spiritual intelligence as the core truth of who and what you are. The pursuit of all this, combined, is the highest level of what you're supposed to experience here on earth.

And that's it. Becoming a Human-Effing-Being. Where *ordinary, everyday mind* that includes Fear is True Enlightenment. This is the rabbit you should be chasing. All the while, like the greyhound, knowing you will never catch it, feel it, eat it, savor it fully, but happy to chase it day after day, regardless.

THE HOLY GRAIL

A man was searching for the Holy Book of Truth his whole life. He trained as a great scholar, lover, and warrior, traveling the earth and using all of his acquired skills to find this holy of holies.

Each mental test was progressively more complex. Each woman more challenging. Each battle more vicious. Until one day, behold, the elusive, coveted book was at last in his hands.

With great ceremony, he prepared to open the book. This was his life's quest! The most important moment he'd ever have! Carefully, expectantly, he placed the book on his lap, opened it, and, at long last, took a look.

Inside was a mirror.

Your job in this lifetime is to become fully Human. Which means doing your best to experience and be all 10,000 voices—in particular Fear, because it will help expand you to the biggest you possible. This is great news. When in Flow, these employees could also be called the 10,000 motivators or the 10,000 energies. They're all driving you to win the Tour de France, be the best couch potato who ever lived, create a new tech business, or, yes, even win the award for "most spiritual."

Stay in Flow and they will also be called the 10,000 wisdoms. I could write a book about every single one of them, not just Fear. Because every voice makes an important contribution, and there is an art to each one of them. Owning them all, one by one, is perhaps the most empowering experience you'll ever have.

So ask yourself: "Can I do my best to radically embrace and merge with all that arrives moment to moment? Can I make my life my practice?" It means merging with your Resistance or Avoidance when you notice it. It means merging with how unconscious, ignorant, and delusional you are about Fear, about everything, over and over again.

This is the highest level of achievement you can ever attain. This is the biggest game there is.

This way, instead of spending your whole life fighting who you are, now you can get down to the epic, wild, uncomfortable, absurd, ignorant, delusional, and wonderful business of . . . just being who you are.

What is my relationship with Fear now? Still complicated.

But at least I've developed a sense of humor about it, and clearly I still enjoy it. Same with all the shadow voices. After I broke up with Tom, the Despair I felt and became for almost a year was one of the more amazing experiences of my life.

Do I still have huge issues with Fear? Yes. And I still hate and repress it. Not in a nostalgic kind of way, either, but in the blind way. It takes me weeks before I even notice—and I wrote the goddamn book about it.

I still have PTSD that needs addressing. Every dream I have involves skiing, even though I hardly ski anymore. Watching sports crash videos is out. I can feel their wipeouts violently in my body.

I'm also such a light sleeper, an ant could sneeze and I'd jerk awake with a rush of "What's that!" I travel with earplugs and noise-canceling headphones, and that's still not enough. You know I've never once spent an entire night in the same bed with my husband? I fall asleep cuddling him, get up in the middle of the night to pee, then bolt like a scared cat to another room.

Fear, Fear, everywhere, and always. So it goes.

This is my story. It's about my relationship with Fear. It's a love story, though—can you see that? And it's mine.

You have your own relationship with Fear. Maybe someday you'll write a book about it, too. Maybe you'll name your book "That Son-ofabitch" or "No Way He's Getting the House." But I really hope not. I'm hoping it will be you, dancing your own dance with Fear, and us witnessing it like a streak of light in the night sky. I can't wait to read it.

For the story of your dance with Fear is the story of your life.

ONE LAST CONVERSATION WITH FEAR

ME: Hey, Fear

FEAR: 'Sup?

ME: So what do you think of all this?

FEAR: It's about goddamn time.

ME: You're not angry with us, are you? We kind of messed this one up.

FEAR: *Nope. Not anymore.*

THE FUTURE

In the mid-sixties, President Kennedy toured the Space Center at Cape Canaveral. In a famous exchange, he asked a man in overalls who was sweeping the floor, "What do you do here?"

The man replied, "I'm doing my part to put a man on the moon."

The floor sweeper, you, the president of the United States—we're all, in no small part, fearful, Lizard Brain creatures.

But we're changing. All of us. In ancient Greece, a man actually owned his son. People were property. If he wanted to blind him, he could. This was the norm.

Until recently, slavery was also the normal order of things, and it wasn't something many people—the people in power, that is—wanted to change anytime soon.

But change, as you know, is unstoppable. What we are seeing now is a revolution in every major field of humanity. We laugh today at what people thought was okay a hundred years ago. And in a hundred years, people will laugh at what we thought, too. Now imagine a thousand years from now. Ten thousand?

If you're still doing things the same way as they were being done a hundred years ago, ten years ago—hell, even one year ago—basically you're doing it wrong. But how exciting is that? We take the best insights from the past and include today's discoveries to transcend for a better, more hopeful tomorrow.

Our efforts are not always spot-on. We get off course all the time. We've come to a place where we can walk by one another and not see how brilliant each of us is. We've come to a place where Fear is seen as a hindrance. But we're like a plane on its way to Tokyo, always in need of constant minor corrections, and that's how we finally arrive at our distant destination. With Fear, we've just been off course by a few degrees, and this is that correction.

Once we make this shift regarding Fear, once we make this correction, in 100 years the world will be a very different place. We'll have updated our human programming on Fear in such a radical way, who knows? Maybe Fear will be done with its part in our evolution, and the neocortex might even take over. And if not in 1,000, then maybe 10,000 years, maybe a million.

I mentioned in the beginning of our journey together that I have a certain arrogant side. I even said you will never be without and can never get rid of Fear, or the Ego or Thinking Mind, for that matter. But this is only what I know so far—and you know how it is when you know something for sure. It is entirely possible that folks like the Buddha, Muhammad, and Jesus transcended these voices. Maybe even Eckhart Tolle. Who am I to say?

Is it possible that in 100 years, more and more people will do that? Sure. This earth experiment isn't over yet.

But for now, we're not there yet, and we don't have a chance of getting there so long as we avoid and repress these essential parts of us. Especially Fear, which so thoroughly deserves your respect and consideration.

But I will say this: If we go all the way, I think anything is possible after that.

In a village lived a king who was rumored to be so smart that people traveled from all over the world to ask him questions.

In this same village lived a boy who fancied himself smarter than the king. To prove it, one morning he captured a butterfly and held it in his hand. His plan was to ask the king whether it was dead or alive.

If the king said "Alive," he would discreetly crush the butterfly and open his hand, proving the king wrong. If the king said "Dead," the boy would open his hand and it would fly away, also proving the king wrong.

He had to wait in line all day, until finally he had his turn in front of the King. With great aplomb, the boy extended his arm and asked his question: "I have in my hand a butterfly. Can you tell me whether it is dead or alive?"

The king paused and looked at the boy. He looked at his hand, then looked back at the boy. Finally the king said, in the gentlest way possible, "It is up to you whether this butterfly lives or dies."

It is now up to you.

I play Yahtzee by myself, often every day, for relaxation. I like to ask the dice questions, like "Should I buy that house?" or "Does so-and-so like me?" If I have a good roll, the answer is yes.

About five years ago, knowing that this book was ripe inside me but feeling so daunted by the task, I told the dice, "Okay. The day I get four of each on the top row—1 through 6—then I'll write that damn book."

For three years, nothing. Until one day—*gulp*—it happened. I finished the game and there they were, four in each column. I sat back and felt a wave of horror. And excitement. The next day I set about manifesting a book contract.

It didn't happen for another year, but during that time I started organizing notes. This book is an accumulation of personal experiences I've had while facilitating clients, listening to the wisdom of Fear speak honestly through these brave souls, and from insights I've received from a medley of teachers—in particular Zen master Genpo Roshi, who is my cherished mentor and muse. He is a genius at transmitting wisdom in a clear way, and those who study with him will see a lot of his style in this book. Megan Sillito also filled in some crucial blanks. As for the hundreds of other influencers, such as Alan Cohen or Shinzen Young—you may also see a modification of your words in this book. Thank you for your wisdom and poetry.

Thank you to my mother, Dolores, for giving birth to me and for allowing me to run free and be my controversial self instead of molding me to fit into polite society. Thank you to the ski industry for supporting my pathology. Thank you to all my clients, friends, and boyfriends for also being great teachers. Thanks to Ed—who promised to pay me $5 for every time his name is mentioned in this book. Ed, you're great, Ed. Best big brother ever, Ed.

Thank you, Adam Bellow, for being curious. Thank you, Karen Rinaldi, for giving me a book contract on an idea only. Thank you, Panio Gianopoulos and my other editors, who helped turn what was often regurgitation into sculpture.

And finally, thank you, Kirk Jellum, my badass, creative, sexy, riveting, adorable, and funny husband. You kept encouraging me to write this, but never pushed too hard. It was always just the right thump upside the head that I needed. I love you. You are the best thing that ever happened to me.

ABOUT THE AUTHOR

KRISTEN ULMER is a facilitator who offers courses and events around the world. She is known for helping individuals and groups resolve—finally, quickly, and permanently—unconscious problems that hold them hostage. Her specialty is Fear.

Having spent fifteen years being labeled fearless by the outdoor industry—named the best woman extreme skier in the world for twelve of those years and voted the most fearless woman athlete in North America—Kristen seeks to challenge existing norms regarding this deeply misunderstood emotion.

"Sometimes we humans get a little off course," she observes, "and need a gentle shift to continue our journey in the right direction. Ending the humanity-wide, unwinnable war with Fear and making friends with it instead is one of those shifts. Not only will it resolve many epidemic problems we face but it will also allow us the greatest chance to achieve our whole mind potential." For more information, visit www.kristenulmer.com.

Kristen lives in Salt Lake City with her husband, Kirk Jellum, and their two Savannah cats.